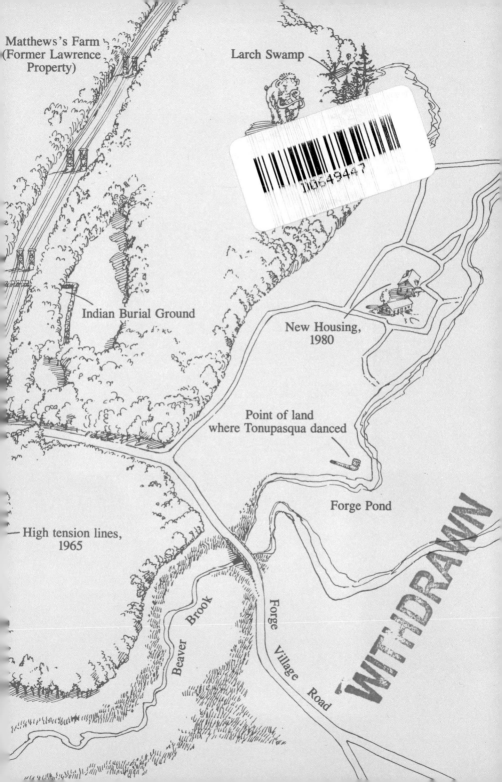

Matthews's Farm
(Former Lawrence
Property)

Larch Swamp

Indian Burial Ground

New Housing,
1980

Point of land
where Tonupasqua danced

Forge Pond

High tension lines,
1965

Beaver Brook

Forge Village Road

974.44 M681c   EV.
MITCHELL
 CEREMONIAL TIME : FIFTEEN
THOUSAND YEARS ON ONE SQUARE
MILE   15.95

CEREMONIAL TIME

CEREMONIAL TIME

Fifteen Thousand Years
on One Square Mile

John Hanson Mitchell

Drawings by Gordon Morrison

ANCHOR PRESS/DOUBLEDAY
Garden City, New York
1984

Designed by Virginia M. Soulé

Library of Congress Cataloging in Publication Data

Mitchell, John Hanson.
  Ceremonial time.

  1. Littleton (Mass.)—History. 2. Wamesit Indians—History. I. Title.
F74.L77M57 1984   974.4′4   83–24023
ISBN 0-385-19194-4

First Edition

for Lelia, fellow traveler

SCRATCH FLAT

AREA: 1 square mile.

LOCATION: Nowhere. Everywhere. 35 miles west of Boston, 30 miles north of Worcester, 12 miles south of Lowell in a region known to geologists and geographers as the Schooly Penaplain. To be more specific, Scratch Flat can be found 42 degrees, 33 minutes, 45 seconds latitude, 71 degrees, 28 minutes, 45 seconds longitude. You will see it there on the United States Department of the Interior Geological Survey map of 1966 in the Westford Quadrangle for Massachusetts—Middlesex County, 7.5 minutes series. You may also see it if you happen to drive past on Massachusetts Route 495. Look west as you pass the sign for the Littleton Common, Groton exit, and you will see there a low hill, very like a whale. That low hill lies more or less at the center of the kingdom of Scratch Flat.

TOPOGRAPHY: Flatlands, west. Marshlands, east. Woodlands, north and south. Scratch Flat is 320 feet above sea level.

POPULATION: *People:* 150, of which the majority (98 percent) are of European descent. The remaining 2 percent are of African descent. No American Indians remain.
Livestock: Cows, 200. Pigs, 14. Horses, 5. Chickens, 56. Turkeys, 8. Guinea fowl, 4. Ducks, 3. Donkeys, 1. Dogs, 70. Cats, 40.

CHIEF CROPS: Dairy products, green beans, strawberries, beets, asparagus, apples.

MINERALS: Sand and gravel, quartz.

OTHER
 RESOURCES: Firewood, freshwater fish (bullheads, pickerel, black bass), muskrat pelts.

MEAT
PRODUCTION: 40 bully calves per year.

PER CAPITA   2.1 acres.
ARABLE LAND:

NATURAL   *Plants:* Morel, reindeer lichen, British soldier lichen,
RESOURCES: turkey tail fungus jack-o-lantern, fairy ring mush-
                    room, bracken, Christmas fern, spinulose woodfern,
                    hayscented fern, cinnamon fern, yew, white pine, red
                    pine, red spruce, larch, hemlock, red cedar, broad-
                    leaved cattail, pondweed, barnyard grass, timothy,
                    reed canary grass, fescue, orchard grass, spike rush,
                    sweet flag, pickerelweed, false hellebore, clintonia,
                    weeping willow, cottonwood, sweet fern, butternut,
                    bitternut, black birch, white birch, speckled alder,
                    chestnut, white oak, red oak, black oak, American
                    elm, curled dock, knotweed, sheep sorel, pokeweed,
                    soapwort, spring beauty, spatterdock, sassafras,
                    blackberry, chokecherry, red maple, flowering dog-
                    wood, pipsissewa, blueberry, forget-me-not, black-
                    eyed Susan, aster, goldenrod, robin's plantain, and
                    yarrow.

                    Animals: Wolf spider, jumping spider, orange garden
                    spider, praying mantis, field cricket, May fly, damsel-
                    fly, dragonfly, back swimmer, European earwig,
                    ground beetle, click beetle, diving beetle, June bug,
                    Cecropia moth, black swallowtail butterfly, cabbage
                    butterfly, monarch butterfly, house mosquito, deerfly,
                    tachinid fly, white-faced hornet, polistes wasp, corn-
                    field ant, carpenter ant, carpenter bee, honey bee,
                    common sucker, pickerel, spotted salamander, com-
                    mon toad, green frog, spring peeper, gray tree frog,
                    red-bellied snake, milk snake, water snake, snapping
                    turtle, painted turtle, American bittern, little green
                    heron, Canada goose, black duck, wood duck, red-
                    tailed hawk, broad-winged hawk, ruffed grouse,
                    American woodcock, mourning dove, great horned
                    owl, screech owl, whippoorwill, yellow-shafted
                    flicker, hairy woodpecker, great crested flycatcher,
                    phoebe, tree swallow, barn swallow, blue jay, nut-
                    hatch, long-billed marsh wren, catbird, mockingbird,
                    woodthrush, cedar waxwing, warbling vireo, yellow
                    warbler, prairie warbler, yellowthroat, grackle, star-

ling, red-winged blackbird, tree sparrow, chipping sparrow, field sparrow, possum, short-tailed shrew, common mole, little brown bat, raccoon, skunk, red fox.

EMPLOYMENT: Architects, 1. Barbers, 1. Computer programmers, 8. Educators, 4. Executives, 3. Farmers, 2. Farmhands, 5 permanent, 12 seasonal. Psychologists, 1. Salesmen, 3. Secretaries, 6. Social workers, 2. Writers, 1. Retired, 7. Unemployed, 5.

TOURIST ATTRACTIONS: None. (Or too many to cite.)

FAMOUS RESIDENTS: None. (Or too many to cite.)

HISTORY: (See below.)

CAST OF CHARACTERS

(dates indicate period of action)

Pokawnau (A.D. 483): A shaman who could turn himself into a bear. May have lived as a man on Scratch Flat, c. A.D. 483.

Sir Hugh Sinclair (A.D. 1399): A Scottish adventurer and seafarer. May or may not have seen Scratch Flat in 1399.

Tom Dublet (1640–1680): A Christianized Pawtucket Indian, known to have had a fishing weir at Scratch Flat circa 1670.

Sarah Dublet (1650–1734): Tom Dublet's wife, sister, or daughter. The last Indian to inhabit Scratch Flat.

John Eliot (1650–1676): Established the Christian Indian Village of Nashoba, on or near Scratch Flat.

Proctor Family (1652–present): Constructed the earliest extant house on Scratch Flat.

Lawrence Family (1670–1900): Landholders on the west end of Scratch Flat.

Mary Louise Dudley (1700–1725): May or may not have lived as a witch on Scratch Flat.

Thankful and Virtue Pease (1725): May or may not have been bewitched by Mary Louise Dudley.

Jeremiah Caswell (1750–1780): Constructed house on Scratch Flat circa 1750.

Eve Caswell (1755–1780): Jeremiah's daughter. At age 16 betrothed to Enoch Pratt. Took him as a lover and died shortly thereafter.

Enoch Pratt (1750–present): Reported killed on the western frontier, French and Indian War. Returned to Scratch Flat in spirit form. His ghost last sighted in 1975.

Johnny Putnam (1810–1845): Witnessed the death of the last bear on Scratch Flat, 1812.

Brown Family (1810–1900): Landholders on Scratch Flat, latter half of nineteenth century.

Uncle Peter Hazzard (1830–1870): Renowned fiddler and local hero.

Peter Riley (1882–present): Self-confessed time traveler. Born County Cork, Ireland, circa 1860; died in Ayer 1922. Born again Ayer, 1927.

Barnabas Barnes (1840–1870): Purchased Caswell estate. Selectman, overseer to the poor, and pillar of community.

Hannah Barnes (1840–1870): Daughter of Barnabas. Educator and founder of the North School on Scratch Flat.

Margaret Lacey (1887–1982): Local historian. Collector of anecdotes and guide to nineteenth-century history. Resident of Scratch Flat environs.

Billy Sherman (1922–present): Truck farmer and "Cauliflower King." Forced in recent years to turn his farm into a housing development.

Henry Hodgson (1930–1960): Scratch Flat survivor.

Corky Trilling (1954–present): Scratch Flat survivor. Right-hand man for Billy Sherman. Breaker of horses.

Ted Demogenes (1927–present): Dairy farmer, chicken farmer, truck farmer. Sold the town poor farm to an industrial developer, 1975.

Jimmy-George Starkos (1930–1983): Greek immigrant and brother-in-law of Ted Demogenes. Truck farmer. Sent three children to college on the proceeds from a seasonal roadside farm stand.

Toby Beckwith (1930–present): Amateur archeologist, raconteur, dramatist, dreamer, and sometime farmer. Resident of Scratch Flat.

Charlie Lignos (1953–present): Dairy farmer, former Barnes/Caswell land. Lost two barns and one house to fire. Third barn dismantled by town officials. No longer works the land.

Matty Matthews (1952–present): Dairy farmer. Determined to continue farming in spite of economic pressures.

The Red Cowboy (1974–present): Guide to glacial history and connoisseur of edible wild food, including whistle pigs. Visitor to Scratch Flat.

Nompenekit (1978–1982): Part Micmac, part Mohawk. Active in local Indian affairs. Guide to time. Visitor to Scratch Flat.

Tonupasqua (1978–1982): Wampanoag medicine woman, guide to time, and storyteller. Occasional visitor to Scratch Flat.

Peter Sarkesian (1980–1983): Computer wizard, runner. Guide to the new age.

CONTENTS

CEREMONIAL TIME

CEREMONIAL
TIME

There is a plum grove just above the house in which I live, a tangled, unproductive group of some twelve trees that were planted sometime in the late 1920s by an old curmudgeon who lived in the house in the decades following the turn of the century. Every morning between April and November, weather permitting, I take a pot of coffee up to that grove to watch the sun come up over the lower fields and to think about things. More and more now I find myself thinking there about time, how it drifts in from the future, how it brushes past us briefly in the present, and then drifts off again to become the past, and how none of these stages, neither past, nor present, nor future, are really knowable. Presented with this dilemma, I have come in recent years to accept the primitive concept of ceremonial time, in which past, present, and future can all be perceived in a single moment, generally during some dance or sacred ritual. Ceremonial time was perceived easily by the people who lived on the land around the plum grove for most of human history. The Pawtucket Indians would summon it up regularly during certain periods of the year, and I have found that it is a convenient method of understanding the changes that have taken place on this particular patch of earth over the last fifteen thousand years.

I should say at the outset, since this is a book about time and place, that history hangs heavily in this area. Fifteen thousand years ago the last of three glacial advances smoothed the rough edges of a small patch of land about ten miles north of the Concord River. After the glacier retreated, it left behind on that particular section of land a deep bed of sand and gravel which, in subsequent centuries, was overlaid with a rich layer of topsoil. Even before the last ice of the glacier had melted from the barren, rolling hills, small bands of fur-clad hunters, known technically as Paleo-Indians, moved into the region in search of game. In due time, that is, after some five thousand years, the descendants of these Paleo people settled into semi-permanent villages, some of which were located not far from the square-mile tract of land in question. A thousand years ago these Indians, who by now had organized themselves into a tribe known as the Pawtuckets, found that by clearing off some of the existing vegetation in the area and replacing it with other plants, the production of food could be substantially increased. This revolutionary development gave birth to an agricultural economy which has survived on that little section of earth ever since.

Five or six centuries after the Pawtucket agricultural experiments began, a group of new settlers moved into the region and improved on the technique. These newcomers had white skin and brought with them from Europe new crops, exotic animals, and an attitude toward the land that, in the space of a few decades, altered the entire environment. Whereas in 1630 the area had been characterized by deep woods broken only by a few primitive garden clearings, by 1790 the land consisted, for the most part, of open, rolling fields of English hay, rough grazing meadows, orchards, and large kitchen gardens.

The white settlers who moved into the area also constructed a new kind of shelter. In contrast to the rounded wickiups of the Pawtuckets, these were squared-off, framed structures designed to keep the natural world at bay. By 1850, there were about seven of these buildings in the little patch of land that the glacier scraped off. One of these, a small farmhouse, was constructed on an east-facing slope by a farmer named Peter Farwell. About one hundred fifty years later, I moved into that house and as a result have come to know and love the square-mile tract of land that surrounds it.

My understanding of this land is circumscribed by time as we measure it here in the West. I seem almost always to be stuck in this little slice of history we call the present, but there are days, there are periods, when some obscure combination of forces seems to release an awareness of ceremonial time so I can see the history of this little stretch of land in sharpened detail. Invariably on these days I get up from my chair in the plum grove and begin to walk, and invariably I seem to cover a certain territory on these walks, not unlike a dog or a bird. It is bordered on the south by a highway, known locally as the Great Road, which runs from Concord, Massachusetts, north-north-west to the small villages of southern New Hampshire. The Great Road was originally an Indian trail which meandered through what is now known as the Nashoba Valley. In its recent history, the road carried a number of important personages and was involved in a small, obscure way, in national events. For sixty or seventy years, the brightest and the best in the American establishment traveled on this highway between Groton School and Harvard University in Cambridge. And one April morning in the late eighteenth century, a group of militant farmers marched down the Great Road to a bridge over the Concord River to start a revolution. But all that is another story.

To the east and north, the territory in question is bordered by a stream known as Beaver Brook which the glacier gouged out during its retreat. It is a pleasant little body of water, offering clear, and in places, deep waters for swimming and good courses for skating in winter. In any other part of the world, Beaver Brook might be termed a river; it is slow-flowing and deep in some sections, and in places it widens to 50 yards or more. As do most of the rivers in the region south of the Merrimack River, the brook flows northward. Its wide grassy marshes provide excellent habitat for ducks, geese, otters, muskrat, as well as a few rarer species of plants and animals. The brook curves westward at the northern end of its course and empties into a shallow lake which the early white settlers called Forge Pond. The waters of this lake are relatively clean and swimmable, and fishermen still seem to find something worth casting for there in spite of the fact that in recent years it has been surrounded with the habitations of modern-day Americans. The houses are of a type that were built originally as summer cottages and then later winterized for permanent dwellings. On a point of land, so far undeveloped, on the southeast shore of the lake, the Pawtucket Indians and their progenitors would hold festivals and, if my sources are accurate, the normal flow of time as we now measure it, would stop, run backward, or collapse altogether so that the primal shamans of who knows how many generations, the spirits of dead bears and wolves, would come alive again and dance there in the half-lit regions between the firelight and the forest wall.

The western edge of the tract of land is bordered by a deep pine forest and a brooding larch swamp. Whippoorwills nest in the pine forest, and although I rarely see them, I can often hear barred owls, great horned owls, and screech owls calling from the darkened interior. On the east side of that pine forest and about an eighth of a mile behind my house, there is a grove of very old hemlock trees. Some of the trees in the grove are hollowed and broken, some may have been standing in the years when local rabble-rousers in the community were mobilizing against the British; and the general sense of the place is gloomy and dark, as if some unspeakable acts took place there, some brutal rite whose aura has been carried forward into the twentieth century. As you will see, this may or may not be the case, but I will come to that in due time.

Just south of the pine woods there is a wide field that is usually planted in corn by Matty Matthews, a hardworking dairy farmer who is determined to continue farming in spite of the fact that economies of this region appear to be working against him. Just south of Matthews's cornfield, you will come again to the Great Road. There are five farms in this square-mile tract, four of which are located on the main highway. Next to the Matthews place there is a 120-acre spread known as Sherman's Acres which, in recent years, has sprouted a lucrative crop of suburban tract houses. East of Sherman's there is a farm run by a Greek immigrant named Jimmy-George Starkos, which is by far the most pleasant and the best-tended of the five farms in the square-mile tract. Jimmy-George's farm is made up of beet and bean fields which rise up to a wooded ridge to the east. Beyond the ridge there is another farm which, for more than eighty years, housed local paupers and transients. The house is still there, but a few years ago the farmer sold off his hayfields to developers and now there are several large, flat buildings on the land, owned for the most part by computer companies. The place was once known as Beaver Brook Farm; now it is called—without a touch of conscious irony—Beaver Brook Industrial Park.

Walk north of the industrial park along the banks of Beaver Brook and you will come full circle. There is a stretch of oak and pine woods owned by a local sportsmen's club (again, no irony in the name) and just to the north you will come to a group of fields which are more or less central to this story. For one thing, this particular farm lies at the center of the square-mile tract that I am describing, and for another, a lot of history has been played out in that 200 acres of old fields and woods. The property is owned by a man named Charlie Lignos who owns a dairy farm in the next town and who, for some obscure reason, is allowing perfectly good agricultural land to grow up to woods. The farm consists of some five fields, each separated by stone walls and hedgerows. The fields rise up from Beaver Brook in a series of terraces and are interspersed with untended apple orchards and patches of dense woods. The soil is good in the area and in all likelihood, given the location, the land has been farmed for more than five hundred years, first by the Pawtuckets, then by Christianized Indians, and then finally by white Europeans.

A man named Jeremiah Caswell was the first European to work this land; in the mid-eighteenth century he cleared most of the tract, planted orchards, and unlike his Indian predecessors, brought in livestock—oxen, dairy cows, pigs, goats, and later horses and sheep. In 1973 there were three barns and three houses associated with the original Caswell holdings; by 1979 there were only two structures left. Vandals had burned two barns and an abandoned house, and the town had torn down the third barn because, officials said, it was an attractive nuisance, an indication, in my opinion, of the economic direction that the community is taking. The main house, the old Caswell estate, has been restored and is now surrounded by extensive flower gardens. The four acres of land surrounding the other Caswell house are being farmed once more in an odd sort of way, but the house itself, although sturdy enough, is in continual need of repair; I know this for a fact, since I am the one who lives there.

During the brighter years in this town, that is, during the height of the nineteenth-century agricultural period, the square-mile section of land which I have described was called Scratch Flat. One local legend suggests that Scratch Flat was so named because in the 1860s a number of families living there suffered from a "certain cutaneous itch" for seven years. More likely the tract got its name from the fact that the flat land surrounding a low hill in the area was so thoroughly cultivated. Whereas the rest of the community was known for its apple and pear orchards, Scratch Flat was always known for its good soil and its truck farms. My friend Margaret Lacey, a ninety-five-year-old woman who had ice blue eyes and a long memory, told me that on summer nights during the 1890s the air in Scratch Flat was heavy with the smell of celery, and even up to the 1950s the area was known for its farms. Billy Sherman used to be called the Cauliflower King by the buyers in the Haymarket in Boston, and Jimmy-George Starkos sent three sons to college on the money earned from a roadside stand which was open only four months of the year.

All of them, Starkos, Sherman, Caswell, and the Pawtuckets, can thank the glacier for their success in life. The deep bed of sand and gravel, the easy slopes, the drainage patterns, and the deep layer of organic topsoil made it easy to farm in this area. It is no accident that the industrial development that swept through New England during the nineteenth century skipped over Scratch Flat and the valley in which the town is located. On the other hand, the same factors that make the land good for farming also make it good for housing and modern industrial development; and, in spite of the good soil, in spite of the fact that arable land is something of a rare commodity in New England, more and more now, computer companies and new houses are appearing on the farmlands of the town.

All this is really only one side of the history of Scratch Flat, however. It should be borne in mind that the greater number of living things that inhabit this little section of the planet are nonhuman and most of them have lived in the region in an unbroken continuum for thousands of years. There are at present approximately one hundred fifty people on Scratch Flat, most of them living along the Great Road, in Billy Sherman's housing development, and on Beaver Brook Road which cuts through the eastern section of the tract. There is also at least one family of gray foxes, one family of great horned owls, one or possibly two barred owl families, innumerable families of red foxes, skunks, raccoons, squirrels, groundhogs, rabbits, mice, voles, and bats, as well as at least one otter and several families of mink, muskrat, and short-tailed weasel. Least bitterns, sora rails, wood ducks, and other species of water birds nest in the

Beaver Brook marshes, and any number of common and, in cases, uncommon species of birds nest in the woods and old fields. I have seen eagles flying over Charlie Lignos's fields; I once saw an Eastern coyote track here; I have seen deer; and I have heard, seen, and even caught any number of species of reptiles and amphibians, one of which, the blue-spotted salamander, proved to be rare and endangered.

In spite of the abundance of wildlife, however, the human community in the area, with a few exceptions, is not aware of the animal community, so that when I tell some neighbor that there are great horned owls living in the white pines beyond Matthews's farm, they tend to doubt my word. They are interested, of course, but not so interested that they would get up from their comfortable chairs and walk out through the snowy woods to witness that chaos of hooting and yowling that takes place during the great horned owl nesting season at the end of February. Wilderness and wildlife, history, life itself, for that matter, is something that takes place somewhere else, it seems. You must travel to witness it, you must get in your car in summer and go off to look at things which some "expert," such as the National Park Service, tells you is important, or beautiful, or historic. In spite of their admitted grandeur, I find such well-documented places somewhat boring. What I prefer, and the thing that is the subject of this book, is that undiscovered country of the nearby, the secret world that lurks beyond the night windows and at the fringes of cultivated backyards.

I have gotten into the habit recently of walking through Scratch Flat at night; it offers an exotic alternative to a walk during the day. Time collapses more easily then; the world entirely alters itself and the true and almost frighteningly inhuman landscape that characterized the area for most of its history reasserts itself. On summer nights in the lower fields near Beaver Brook, I can hear the intense energy of the Carboniferous period in the calls of katydids, coneheaded grasshoppers, and snowy tree crickets. I can hear the Jurassic in the caterwauling of the great horned owls; and in winter, in the dark line of hills beyond the icy marsh, in the spare spruce-dotted bogs, I can sense something of the lifeless, barren landscape of the glacial Pleistocene. For all our frenetic work and our apparent ability to alter the biosphere, we human beings are insignificant little creatures in the perspective of geologic time.

Nevertheless, even at night, our present has a way of insinuating itself into these vast time scales. One of the things that I can hear at night, along with the timeless calls of the Carboniferous and the Jurassic, is a strange roaring hiss that sounds something like a distant rushing stream. That sound is created by Route 495, which runs on the other side of the ridge that separates Scratch Flat from the town in which the tract of land is located. In 1965 a number of local officials, most of whom owned farmland in the area, arranged to have the highway constructed through the western edge of the town, no more than half a mile from the town common. For a few years after the highway came through, nothing much changed. Traffic decreased slightly on the Great Road, a few farmhouses were torn down or moved, a good pear orchard which was split in two by the highway went out of business; but other than that, Route 495 did not seem to have much of an effect on the economy of the place. Then quite abruptly things began to change. Ted Demogenes sold off the former town poor farm and the industrial development that once skipped over the place began to work its way in. If Scratch Flat would not come to the future during the nineteenth century, if it refused to give in to current economic trends, then the future, in its inexorable way, would come to Scratch Flat.

In our time, if you ask people in the town where Scratch Flat is, no one will know. In effect, the place died sometime in the early twentieth century when transportation and communication lines improved and the quarters of the town—the West End, Hog End, and Scratch Flat—became more or less unified. And if you were to drive along the Great Road, apart from the marshes of the Beaver Brook, and perhaps the beauty of the rolling farmlands of Jimmy-George Starkos and Billy Sherman, you would not say that this place is any different from any other place in this section of New England. But that is only the superficial appearance of things. Scratch Flat is at once a real and imaginary country; it is nowhere, and it is everywhere, unique on the one hand and totally indistinguishable on the other.

I first came to Scratch Flat not because it was a region of rolling farmlands and pleasing vistas, but because there happened to be an old house for sale there and my wife and I were looking for a place to live in the general area. It seemed a pleasant enough place to settle. The dwelling was a small farmhouse built sometime in the early

1800s; the four acres of land that came with the house sloped gently up from the house to a dark stand of pines; and, although in a semiwild state, it was clear that the two or three acres of open land had been cultivated in the not too distant past. Just behind the house there was a square of short grass that served for a lawn, on a rise on the southwest side of the property there was a fallen barn, and beside the ruin, there was the tangled and overgrown remnant of a plum grove. Open meadows, a few old apple trees made up the rest of the open lands, and in this forgotten, overgrown landscape there lived leopard frogs, snakes, toads, rabbits, meadowlarks, woodchucks, yellow garden spiders, crickets, grasshoppers, butterflies, and all the other plants, mammals, birds, insects, reptiles, and amphibians that are commonly associated with an old-field ecosystem. The woods behind the meadow were made up of white pine on the southwest corner of the property and a mixture of deciduous trees on the northwest side. To the east, across the road, there were more woodlands, and north and northeast of the property the land was surrounded by terraced hayfields, old barns, and cows belonging to Charlie Lignos. Given its proximity to Boston and its western suburbs, the place was a demi-paradise if you were of a mind to enjoy that sort of thing, which I was.

Shortly after I moved to Scratch Flat I began to wander—first east to the Beaver Brook and the hayfields and orchards, then west and north through the woods to the lake and the cultivated fields of the farms over the hill behind the house. From the very beginning, I felt there was something about the lands surrounding the property, some vague and almost indefinable quality of time, or space, or history, that lingered in the area. Clearly Scratch Flat had been intensely cultivated, had been lived upon and walked over, cleared and plowed, planted and then planted again. Everywhere you looked you could see the evidence of previous habitation, in the cellar holes of ruined farmhouses, in the isolated stone-lined wells, in the carefully constructed stone walls running through the pine woods and the swamps, and in the fallen and dying barns, the numerous bottle dumps, and the rutted memory of old carriage roads. Something was alive amidst these ruins that could not be seen, there was a definite presence in the area.

At first, during my early walks, I thought this presence might be some kind of an animal, a bobcat perhaps or a coyote, or even possibly a mountain lion. Such things had been reported from time to time in the area and there was, it seemed to me, enough territory in the northwest section of the tract to hide, if not support, one of these larger predators. But the more I walked over the land, the more convinced I became that whatever was lurking at the dark edges of the woods at Scratch Flat was not an animal. It seemed to be human, and yet at the same time, definitely nonhuman. By the end of the first year, I began to believe that something had happened on Scratch Flat at some point in its history, some act, or event, or continuum of events that had managed to transcend time. At the end of the second year, after I had gotten to know a number of the old families in the area, I decided to actively search out the thing or the event, grab it by the tail, so to speak, and drag it out into the light of the present.

This was, I realize now, just one more journey, one more voyage of exploration for me. Ever since I was able to leave the confines of my own backyard, I have been fascinated by the idea of trespassing, exploring either legally or illegally the backyards of the larger estates in the town in which I grew up. As I grew older, I extended these explorations to nearby woodlands, and then later still, when I was about ten or twelve, to a long neck of woods that ran along the Palisades on the Hudson River, woods that were dotted, in those days, with the ruins of estates, overgrown gardens and escaped daffodils and periwinkles. Later still I extended these explorations even farther, developed for a while a definite wanderlust, so that sometimes I would travel simply for the sake of the trip, simply to know what this or that place was like. There is nothing unusual about all this, I suppose; it is just one more aspect of the American restlessness, all a part of the lack of a sense of place that seems to be a defining characteristic of the culture.

When I began to explore Scratch Flat, I had a sense that I was setting out on another one of these earlier journeys. I began to learn more about the history of the place, and the more I learned, the farther back in time I found I had to travel, until finally I reached into prehistory and bumped up against the great white wall of the glacier. There was no sense in going any farther. Before the glacier there were no people in the area and therefore there could be no history, no human perception of the place. And it was at this point that I realized that I was embarked on the greatest trespass of all. I was not exploring a square-mile tract of land 35 miles west of Boston; I was exploring time.

About a year after I began my research, after it had come to me that Indians had lived the better part of the history of this place, I met a man named Fred Williams who is part Pawtucket and part Micmac Indian. Williams's "real" name, he says, is Nompenekit, or Man Born Twice. The name was given to him by his grandfather and later in his life, when he became active in Indian affairs, Williams resumed the name. He is a man of about fifty or sixty with the deeply lined face of an old man, bright black eyes, and the trim body of a young man. His hair is a rich gray, the color of the cloudy winter sky, and he wears it long, sometimes in braids, sometimes held in place with a decorative headband. He has a classical American Indian face, hooked nose, reddish-brown skin, and full, chiseled lips, and, like many of the Indian people that I have come to know in recent years, he smokes a lot of cigarettes. When I first met him, he seemed diffident, almost painfully shy and polite, yet always willing to share his views. Later, after I came to know him better, I realized that this apparent diffidence was actually a state of calm fortitude which seemed to spring from a deep confidence in his worldview. He was very firm in his beliefs, very steady, as if he were operating according to certain basic truths which were unknowable to me, a white man.

Nompenekit was a fairly well known figure among the few remaining New England Indians and was known also in the white community. He would occasionally appear at lectures and similar events to give the Native American side of the history, although his views were decidedly radical, and not always appreciated even by Indians. I met Nompenekit in connection with an educational program I happened to be involved with once in the Lowell school system, and after I started my exploration of Scratch Flat, I called him to ask if he had any information on the native peoples that might have lived in the area. He directed me, as you will see, to an excellent and unique source; but more importantly, he was the one that taught me to think in Indian time.

Indian time, Nompenekit explained, does not move according to western tradition. Morning is when the first light shows. Noon is when the sun is at its highest point. Spring comes—or used to come —when the herring appear in the rivers; fall comes, Nompenekit

said, not in October or September, but in August when the migratory
birds start to collect together at the woodland edges. Indian time
stretches itself out on occasion, on occasion contracts or reverses its
apparent flow. It is not exacting, not measured by dials or digits on a
lighted screen, and at the base of this system is the concept of ceremonial time. It is then, said Nompenekit, that you can actually see
events that took place in the past. You can see people and animals
who have been dead for a thousand years; you can walk in their
place, see and touch the plants of their world. And more importantly, when ceremonial time collapses, the spirit world can be seen,
the gods, ghosts, and monsters of the Indians manifest themselves.

Nompenekit's Indian time more or less came naturally to me. I
am not one who is particularly obsessed with the measurement of
hours or days. But ceremonial time, the more interesting aspect of
this way of thinking, did not come so easily, and steeped as I am in
western tradition, it is likely that I will never be able to thoroughly
free myself from the belief that time flows linearly from past to present to future. But after I learned about ceremonial time, I began to
try to use it as a tool to explore the past. As I said, there are moments on Scratch Flat when the past seems to me to be closer to the
surface, when events that I know took place there seem to be somehow more real; this is a phenomenon that has happened to me most
of my life, and after I met Nompenekit, I began to think that this
state of mind was close to the idea of ceremonial time, and began to
consciously exploit it. I found that when the moment was right, by
concentrating on some external object, an arrowhead that was found
on Scratch Flat, for example, or the running walls or foundations of
the area, I was able to perceive something more than a simple mental
picture of what some past event was like. I not only could see the
event or the place in my mind's eye, but would also hear it, smell the
woodfires; and sometimes, for just a flash, a microsecond if you care
to measure things, I would actually be there, or so it seemed. This is
nothing like the experience with the madeleine in *Remembrance of
Things Past;* what I would sense is the reality of an event that I could
never have witnessed. Nor is it anything mystical; I don't claim to
have experienced these things in some previous existence. It was
simply a heightened awareness or perception of the way things must
have been. And yet, I learned from Nompenekit, that is all that is
necessary. "If you see those things in your mind," he told me once,

"you must believe that is what happened. That is the only thing you can know."

There are many versions of history according to Nompenekit; there is the Indian version, there is the written version of the white man, and there may be another version, something somewhere between the two. He never denied official history, he simply would say that that is the way the white man believes things happened, but they might have happened in another way.

More than anything else, I have found that this liberal attitude toward reality is the key to understanding the past in Scratch Flat. One aspect of the history of the area, the formal history of the politics, of the crops that were grown and of the people that served on the various town boards, is fairly well documented for the 260 years of the town's existence. That history does not record, however, the struggle, the sorrows, the ecstasies, the joys, and the anger of the people that actually lived and worked on Scratch Flat. Furthermore, the recorded history of the general region tells only of approximately 300 to 400 years; the rest of human history, the 15,000-year stretch between the arrival of the Paleo-Indians and the recent past, is unwritten. But I have learned from Nompenekit and his friends that this past is not entirely unknowable; it exists in the legends and the folk tales of the local Indian tribes and, to some extent, in the racial memory of the descendants of the people who lived in the region for most of its history.

It occurred to me, after I came to know Nompenekit, that if I were to thoroughly understand Scratch Flat, genuinely dig out the story of the things that happened here, I could not rely solely on the maps, town records, and other official documents; I would have to get all the sources. And so I began asking everyone I could think of who might know something about the place or its past—archeologists, historians, old farmers, local eccentrics, Indian shamans, developers, newer residents, and local farmhands. I began to take on all comers, so to speak, all views of the past, present and future, and all the official and unofficial histories. And from these various sources, all of which I set down here without prejudice, I think I have uncovered the mystery; I think I have discovered what it is that I sensed in the woods and fields on my first walk over this insignificant little patch of the planet.

2

THE KINGDOM
OF ICE

For fifty thousand years, give or take an interglacial period or two, the area known as Scratch Flat was buried under a mantle of ice one mile deep. There was a world before the onset of the glaciers; that is to say, there was dry land in the area, and there were plants and animals, life and death, trees and rocks and all the other things that make up an ecosystem. In fact, geologists have theorized that the landscape that existed in the area was far more dramatic in aspect than the landscape of today. In the valley of the Beaver Brook which runs along the eastern edge of Scratch Flat, there was a vast uplifted fault running north and south for fifty or sixty miles. Living things grew or foraged above and below these immense cliff faces. But the fact remains that everything that existed in the area before the glacier—the landscape, the soils, the living things, and for that matter the entire world—was obliterated by ice.

The last Ice Age began sixty to seventy thousand years ago. It came on slowly, to be sure, but it came on inexorably, a long winter one year, a slightly longer one the next, until finally there was nothing but winter for fifty thousand years. Snows piled on snows, compressing the bottom layers into ice packs; the ice packs moved out

from under the incredible weight of year after year of snow, crushing
the very rocks and soils beneath, so that finally, unable to withstand
the downward pressure, the whole mass moved southward like a
hideous all-encompassing plow. No living thing could endure these
timeless winters, and, as the ice moved southward, generation after
generation of plants and animals were forced into the more benign
climates of south central North America. Although there may have
been two or three interglacial periods of warming, the world at
Scratch Flat was dead, and would remain dead until history wrote it
into existence.

This interminable season of ice is the overriding reality of the
landscape of Scratch Flat, and indeed of the entire northern half of
North America. The record of the glacier, and most specifically, the
record of its departure, is inscribed on the land; you can see it in the
rounded drumlins of Scratch Flat, in the streams and ponds, and in
the boulders, the numerous stone walls, and the deep beds of gravel.
There is no escaping its presence once you are aware of it; if God had
a hand, it was the glacier.

This overbearing reality, the fifty-thousand-year reign of ice, is
lost on the general public in the Scratch Flat region. Beaver Brook,
the drumlin, the flat farmlands, might just as well have been created
by the hand of a giant as by the hand of ice. I can't say that I blame
the public for not appreciating the great timeless scales of the ice
ages. The coming and going of the glacier is an event which has
almost mystical overtones. Geologists glibly throw off statistics as if
they were comprehensible—the glacier endured for 50,000 years,
they will tell you; the sheet of ice was one mile deep, and locked up
one-quarter of the earth's water. Such statistics are beyond compre-
hension in some ways, mere figures with no apparent base in reality.
And yet over the past few years, and through a variety of methods, I
think I have come to understand something of the way in which the
piece of land I am writing about was formed.

The traditional view of the creation of Scratch Flat, its birth by
ice, comes for the most part from a friend of mine whom, for years,
my wife and I have called the Red Cowboy, simply because he comes
from Colorado and has flaming red hair. The Red Cowboy (his real
name is Vernon Stafford) loves glaciers; he has studied them for some
ten years, first at Harvard, then at various universities in this country
and in Europe. He has traveled to many of the existing glaciers of the

world, has camped for weeks on their backs, has descended icy crevices into the very core of their bodies and emerged alive; and, fortunately for me, he has spent a few weeks at Scratch Flat walking over the land and describing to me the events which must have taken place.

According to geologists, Vern Stafford included, about 15,000 to 16,000 years ago the "summer" seasons began to lengthen, the long advance halted, and the glacier began to draw back. As it did so, it released into the world untold cubic miles of water which had been stored in its body. Among other things, that water caused world sea levels to rise dramatically. It also created innumerable lakes which endured on the North American continent for centuries after the glacier retreated. It appears that one of those lakes, a rather small one, sat over Scratch Flat for a period of time—exactly how long, no one is able to say.

The glacier was not a monolithic front stretching east and west for thousands of miles. There must have been a front, obviously—that is, a general latitude where the snows melted every year—but current theories suggest that there was so much variation and there were so many ice ages or mini–ice ages during the great glaciations of the past fifty thousand years that it is difficult to say any one thing about the whole process. During the final millennia of its existence however, that is, during the recessional centuries when it did most of its handiwork on the land, at its forefront the glacier seems to have been nothing more than a series of towering blocks of ice, some of them as much as 100 to 200 miles square and others no larger than a ten-acre pond. For centuries, for a thousand years, for who knows how long, it appears that one of these blocks sat on top of Scratch Flat, slowly wasting away. Vast rushing streams poured down the face of the block of ice and rushed out from underneath carrying with them sand and gravel, boulders and similar debris. About twenty miles south of Scratch Flat this detritus created a dam of ice, gravel, and rock so that water backed up creating a shallow and lifeless lake.

My friend the Red Cowboy says that the tops of the glacial fields were not necessarily smooth stretches of ice or snow. There were crevices in the melting surface and, among other things, there were deep gurgling holes, swirling with water, which would sink into the nothingness of the body of the glacier. Nineteenth-century geologists referred to these holes as moulins or mills, after the tub mills of the period. The Red Cowboy has a more graphic term. When I pressed him for a description, he thought for a minute. "You know what a toilet's like? Well imagine a huge toilet. Only this toilet is stuck and keeps flushing, flushes maybe for ten years, maybe a hundred." According to the Red Cowboy these toilets or moulins played an interesting part in the creation of part of the local landscape.

Scratch Flat today is more or less surrounded by water. There is the wide stream to the east and northeast, there is the lake to the north and northwest, and in the middle there is a geological formation known as a drumlin, an elongated hill of perhaps a half a mile, with its steep end to the southeast and a sloping end to the northwest. The lake to the north is a remnant of the glacial lake and the stream may be a remnant of a large outwash stream that rushed out from beneath the block of ice. But there are a couple of anomalies in this simplified description. One is a series of mounds or hills on the west edge of the stream, and the other is a sharp, almost conical formation that once sat on the floodplain of Beaver Brook.

If you look at the old maps of Scratch Flat, you will see, marked in the wonderful old hand of the eighteenth- and nineteenth-century scribes, a place at the edge of Beaver Brook called Cobble Hill. One day in 1960 a couple of men in boots and khaki approached Ted Demogenes, the man who, according to twentieth-century legal documents, "owned" Cobble Hill. The men in khaki were from the Massachusetts Division of Public Works, and after some negotiation and discussion, they offered to buy Cobble Hill outright, buy the gravel and the sand, that is. It seems that a major highway was coming through, and the engineers needed the gravel for the roadbed. Before the bulldozers and the payloaders moved in, one of the engineers stopped the work for a while and called a geologist to have a look at Cobble Hill—there was something about it that was interesting. Ted Demogenes, who told me this story, didn't know what it was, didn't think to ask, or couldn't remember what they said if he did. But after a little research, my friend Vern thinks that he has figured it out. He did so by looking at earlier geological survey maps that show Cobble Hill.

Basically, he said, the conical hill was created by one of the moulins, and were it still in existence, would be known technically as a kame. The detritus of rocks, sand, and gravel that was flushed down the toilet of the glacier was deposited in the place that was Cobble Hill in a regular form. Kames often occur in the outwash plains of the glacier; there are similar formations to the south of Scratch Flat and there are others to the north. Vern says that if you look carefully at the maps, and if you know what to look for, you can see the actual footprints of the glacier as it tracked back across Scratch Flat to the north and northwest, flushing its icy toilets all the way.

The other curious geological formation on Scratch Flat is a series of mounds maybe fifteen yards high and twenty or twenty-five yards in circumference. These mounds occur irregularly along the banks of Beaver Brook on the eastern edge of the stream and are covered over with a thick growth of white pine. One wet March day while the Red Cowboy was staying at our house I managed to get him down to the mounds to have him explain them to me. By that time he had come to know the geology of the area fairly well; and once he had made a few preliminary digs, he was able to say how the hills were created. Conveniently, there was a woodchuck hole on the top of one of the hillocks; the Red Cowboy took advantage of it, began to dig deeper into it with his trenching shovel, and after a few minutes reached in and pulled up a handful of fine sand, as clean and white as the sand on a Florida beach. He rolled it around in his fingers for a few seconds, took out a lens and looked at the grains, then stood and looked across the wooded landscape at the random scattering of hills and mounds. "Dunes," he said after a few minutes, "you all have got some fine sand dunes here."

What had happened, he explained, was that the dam that created the lake had broken and the water had drained out, leaving a wasteland of mud, sand, gravel, and jumbled rocks. The open treeless landscape was exposed to the wind and as the lake bed dried, fine particles of sand were picked up, swirled across the flatlands, and deposited in a line along the edge of the outwash stream. He told me that he could tell that the sand was wind-deposited because the grains were small and uniform; had there been diversity of grain size or if the mounds had gravel in them, they would have been something else, he said.

With the receding waters of the lake, the place that is Scratch Flat was, for the first time in fifty thousand years, open to the sky,

and the land onto which so much human and natural history was to
play itself out was formed. You can see the resulting hills and ridges
as you drive past on Route 495. Beaver Brook winds twice beneath
the highway, and the flat lake bottoms surround the drumlin that sits
in the center of this little world. All of these land formations are
subtle. This is no country of dramatic vistas, great scarps, or rushing
cataracts. Everything is rounded and smoothed, worn down by ice
and shaped and reshaped by human hands. Time, not space, is the
dominant feature of the landscape in these parts: the place is defined
by human perceptions and human use.

   This version of the creation of Scratch Flat is not quite as simple
as I have described it. There were elements of guesswork involved,
and in fact some of the geologists I have talked to dispute the Red
Cowboy's interpretation of the maps. But then there are other geologists who will dispute his critics. The more you question, the more
confusing the story becomes. There is, however, another version of
the formation of Scratch Flat, one that is completely at odds with
what the Red Cowboy and all the other geologists tell me.

   There were human beings living on the American continent at
the time of the retreat of the glacier. These people begat descendants
who are still living in the place the Europeans came to call America.
Nompenekit is one of these people, through him I have met others,
and it was from one of them that I learned about these alternative
versions.

   One of Nompenekit's friends was a woman named Linda Waters, a Wampanoag who had gained respect in the Indian community
as a shaman or medicine woman. Linda Waters was about forty-five
years old when I first met her. She had rounded features, brownish
skin, and a thick braid of oily black hair running down her back. She
was slightly overweight, dressed in shopping center clothes, and in
spite of her mystical leanings, used to smoke a lot of cigarettes and
apparently used to drink a lot of whiskey. She once worked in the
mills at Lowell, but was unemployed when I knew her and would
receive money from the federal government to support her one child,
a teenage boy named Steve who liked fast cars, who also smoked a
lot of cigarettes, and who expressed little or no interest in Indian
affairs. Steve's father had left Linda when Steve was about a year old,
and had yet to return, although divorce proceedings were never carried out.

Linda spent her childhood on Cape Cod and had been steeped in what was left of Wampanoag traditions by her grandmother. When she was younger, she said, she loved nature, would spend days in the summer picking blueberries with her grandmother and listening to the old legends and stories of the Wampanoag people and other Indians. After her husband left her, Linda began to think more about her past, went back to Mashpee on Cape Cod, and began, as she explained it, "to walk alone." "One day," Linda said, "I heard my grandmother's voice in the pine trees. The voice said, 'Linda, don't forget what I told you.' I didn't know what that meant then. But later I knew that I am Wampanoag, and I knew that she was saying that I had special powers. My grandmother could talk to birds."

After her experience, Linda came back to Lowell and took a job in the mills. She began attending meetings of a local Indian affairs group and attending ceremonies and festivals of some of the Indian groups around New England. Nompenekit told me that at one point people began to worry about her again; she was dancing a little too hard, living her Indianness a little too intensely; and then in the midst of her "rebirth" she disappeared. When she came back a second time, she said that she had visited her uncle, an old man in Maine, and had had a vision. She said that she had been given power there, and now could "see through things," or as she told me on another occasion, "see into things." She changed her name to Tonupasqua, or Turtle Woman, and, according to Nompenekit, calmed down considerably.

I met her one night at Nompenekit's house in Lowell. I had asked him specifically if he knew anyone who could travel in time, go back into the past and see things as they were then. He said, in his enigmatic way, that maybe he did and maybe he didn't, and one afternoon a few weeks later, he called and invited me to come up to his house. There were a lot of people there sitting around the kitchen table drinking beer, some of them dressed in cowboy clothes such as you would see at a cheap western outfitter shop. I was introduced and in the course of the evening got to ask a lot of questions about the Indian view of time and history, how people might have lived, and how a place like Scratch Flat might have come into existence. Tonupasqua was there, but she stayed with the other women and never contributed to the discussion. Just before I left, she came up and asked me why I wanted to know all these things. I told her that I wanted to write an account of the way things really happened; I said I knew one version of the history of the area, but that I wanted to make sure that I included everything about the place, and that since it appeared from what I had learned so far that Indians had lived in the area for a long time, I wanted to get that part too. "Well, I can see different times," she said offhandedly and gave me a napkin with a telephone number on it.

I got to know Tonupasqua after that and would meet with her on occasion, sometimes at her house, sometimes in Nompenekit's kitchen; and whenever I wanted an alternative view of history, I got into the habit of asking her. Sometimes she would become subtly abusive of white people, white versions of history, and indirectly of me. She would rail at the archeologists, who "steal" her people's tools, or the anthropologists who dig into her people's secrets. Usually she lumped me grossly with all the other white exploiters, but since I must have given her the sense that I was simply interested in everybody's version of history, white, black, Indian, and anyone else who cared to share information, at least she came to tolerate me.

One day after fairly elaborate arrangements, I got her to come down to Scratch Flat. I wanted to get her to walk over the land with me, look at some of the sites where, according to the records, Indians had once gathered. We ended up driving around the land in my car, stopping at various points while I described some of the events that had taken place. Sometimes she would get out and look around, but mostly she sat in the car, smoking cigarettes and grunting positively at my stories. "I know, I know," she would say, or "right, right." She spoke as if she had seen it all before and was bored or anxious to get back to Lowell.

I called her a few days after her first visit and asked her if she had thought at all about Scratch Flat and how such a place might have come into existence. I had already told her the story of the Red Cowboy and the glacier and wanted to know if she thought that's what might have happened. She said that she was thinking about it, and that she would call me when she had "seen." Late one night she finally telephoned to say that she had the story and that I should come up the next day if I wanted to hear it.

"This Red Cowboy?" she asked me when I got there. "He is a man who has read a lot of books?" Yes, I said, he read books and even taught geology at a university in the West. "Well he don't know things. He don't know everything. I talked to my uncle about this and I can tell you now how that place there came to be like it is."

Turtle Woman explained that Scratch Flat was created long ago, in a time when a thing called the stiff-legged bear walked the land, and Crow and Wolf played hide-and-seek in the hills. She said there was a "being" who lived there with the people, whose name was Glooscap. Glooscap could do a lot of tricks, she said, and sometimes he helped the people, although sometimes, too, he played tricks on them. One day a horrible thing came out of the earth, a monster snake. This snake came to the village of the people who lived near Scratch Flat. If anyone strayed from the village at night, Snake would eat them, and the more people he ate, the hungrier he got, so that sometimes the people could see his head swaying over the top of the stockade that surrounded the village. All the people were worried about Snake, so they called a council and decided to send for Glooscap to see if he could help them. They sent Crow over the hills, above the head of Snake, to fetch him. A few days later Glooscap came to the village and the sachems told him about the monster. Glooscap could make things of metal, Tonupasqua said, and he taught the people to melt rocks, and from the melted rocks he made a thing like a bell. One night Glooscap took the bell out and tied it to Snake's tail while he was asleep. Then he stabbed Snake in the tail with a spear, and told him to run. Hobomacho, a terrible monster who also stalked the forests in those times, was right behind him, Glooscap said, ready to eat Snake alive. Snake slithered off, but as he moved, the bell rang out like the voice of Hobomacho. Snake slithered faster and soon he was moving so fast that he dug a groove in the ground. Finally, in desperation, he forced his way into a cave and disappeared into the earth forever. Tonupasqua said that the groove that Snake dug is now the course of Beaver Brook and the hole that he went down became the lake that lies on the north side of Scratch Flat.

A few months after I began to think of the glacier in terms of human history, it occurred to me that I too am a descendant of a people who hunted along the edge of the glacier during its recessional years. These people lived on a different continent and were of a different race than Tonupasqua's people and, over the past few hundred years, my people have developed another means of understanding time and events that took place in what we call the past. But that is not to say that Tonupasqua and Nompenekit and my people are different from each other; in fact, since we both experienced the realities of the glacier, the long winters, and the joy and terrors of the hunt, we may be more alike than we believe. Only recently have we gone our separate ways in terms of our views on time; and so when Tonupasqua told me one night that it is possible that I once personally visited the glacier that sat over New England fifteen thousand years ago, I was willing to believe her.

When I was about seven years old, I was given, I think from my two older brothers, an all too graphic description of a hideous entity known as the glacier. It was a great wall of ice shaped like a huge curving snowplow, caked and pitted with chunks of stone; and, what is more—and this is the terrifying aspect of it—the thing moved. I was told, in all honesty, that it moved slowly, but to my mind "slowly" meant about as fast as you could walk, and of course if you ever tripped or got stuck, it would sweep over you. It was immense and unstoppable; this plow of ice would crush whole houses, crumple automobiles, snap trees and fences, crush dogs, cows, bicycles, toys, and anything else that was left in its path. And, of course, it was coming back. It had come before, I was told, and it would return; it was just a question of time.

Such is the stuff of nightmares, and inevitably one night I had a dream about the glacier. Fortunately, it was not really a nightmare; it was more of a universal dream, filled with a sublime, though terrible, landscape. I was standing at the very top of the edge of the glacier, high above the surrounding land. Behind me I could see the ice fields rucked and pitted with jagged uplifted slabs of ice interspersed with smooth plains of snow, and all of it flat, flat beyond imagining, and stretching interminably backward. Ahead of me were houses, streets, dogs on the sidewalks, and everything else that is a part of the world of a seven-year-old; behind me was the ice, stretching backward into darkness. That, fortunately perhaps, is all I remember, except for one other thing, and that was the inevitability of this dream, the underlying reality of the return of the glacier.

I related the dream one night to Nompenekit and Tonupasqua and asked them what they thought about it. I described to them the incredible clarity that had characterized the experience.

"You still remember this thing?" Tonupasqua asked.

"Yes," I said, "I can still see the fields of ice."

"Well it may have been a dream. But my uncle would say that if that happened to me, I was there. You can travel in your sleep, you know. You live here now when you are awake; but then, when you sleep, you can go away to other times. This has happened to me. One night I dreamed that I could talk to the birds like my grandmother. I say I can talk to birds now. So maybe you went there to this glacier in dreamtime. Maybe you saw all these things."

"But you believe I was there?" I asked.

"I believe you could go there. You believe what you want," she said.

A few years ago, armed with a lot more knowledge of what the actual glacier was like, I went back again in time. I am in the habit of walking out in Scratch Flat in foul weather; I find that the old adage about the weather being bad only from the inside holds a certain amount of truth, and so periodically, during sleet, or snows, or rain, I get dressed in the proper gear and venture out. One January night about three years ago, after a particularly heavy snowfall, I strapped on some snowshoes and waddled down the east side of the drumlin to the marshes of Beaver Brook. In spite of the fact that the snow was a foot and a half deep, it was crusted over and it was easy going all the way—I was, after all, headed downhill. It was one of those crystal nights that sometimes occur in New England. There was a brilliant ice cold moon, a clear black sky, and a biting wind that swept down out of the northwest with a deep-throated growl. All around me the trees were cracking and swaying and little drifts of snow were working themselves loose in the open hayfields and stacking themselves up against the windbreaks of the stone walls. It was an exhilarating night for a walk, and all went well for the first half hour or so. Then about a half mile from my house, in a field about at the edge of the marshes of Beaver Brook, I stepped suddenly into a wilderness that might as well have been ten thousand miles from the nearest human settlement. I did not go abruptly into that wilderness of night, I went there in a series of excruciatingly slow steps. The strap on my left snowshoe broke, and somehow, before I was aware of it, came off altogether and got buried somewhere behind me. I went back to look for it, but although I found part of the strap, the critical crosspiece was lost and I found myself one-footed and alone in the emptiness of winter. My first reaction, of course, was to go home, so I turned around and began to make my way up the hill toward the house. I set as my first goal a large glacial boulder that sits in the middle of Charlie Lignos's hayfields.

It was hard traveling from the start. The crust broke through with every step and I would sink to my shins in the deep powder. I found that I could move forward, after a fashion, by pushing off with the snowshoe, stepping into the deep snow with my other foot, and then repeating the process, but it was slow going, and by the time I reached the shelter of the boulder, I was exhausted and somewhat concerned. I was warm enough, to be sure, the effort of walking had seen to that, but in the near-zero-degree air, I began to chill quickly and got up to move again. About a hundred yards uphill from the boulder, something like panic flashed in. I realized that there was the distinct possibility that I might not make it home at this rate, that I might die no more than a mile from my kitchen stove. In a half hour's time I had traveled maybe two hundred or three hundred yards; I was close to total exhaustion; I was cold, my cheeks were beginning to sting, and I still had at least a half a mile to make. It wasn't exactly panic that I felt; it was more a sense of excitement or revelation. But fear was at the root of it, a deep, primal fear. Ahead of me was the huge nothingness of drifting snow, behind me was the dark line of the woods with the open marshes below. There were no roads, no trails, no fellow human beings out for a stroll; there seemed, in fact, to be no life at all, as if I had been thrust back into the very heart of the glacial reign. I witnessed then, briefly, the essence of timelessness. I saw Scratch Flat as it must have been fifteen thousand years ago, saw the fields of ice, the heartless whip of blowing snow, the endless winters, and, at the base of it all, the insignificance of the human experiment. The place that I saw, the Scratch Flat that had endured for some fifty thousand years, was neither cruel nor kind; it was simply inhuman, totally devoid of meaning. Never mind that on the heels of this revelation I realized that it was easier to go downhill than it was to go up, and never mind that I half slid, half dove down to Beaver Brook and managed to walk to the Great Road on the wind-cleared ice. The essence of the experience, brief though it was, was that I had seen into the heart of the glacier.

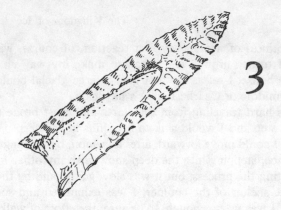

3

AFTER THE DELUGE

There is a small rise of high ground just to the northeast of Beaver Brook, and just beyond that ridge, like a natural extension of the streamside marshes, there is a section of half-submerged land known technically as a bog. Dotting the landscape of this one-acre plot of land you can see small black spruce trees. These are not the massive white pines and hemlocks that can be found in some parts of Scratch Flat; the trees are no more than four or five feet tall, in spite of the fact that some of them may be as much as seventy years old. If you walk out among these stunted trees, you will find yourself on tenuous footing; the very earth will sink beneath your feet, water will well up around your boots, and, if you jump up and down rhythmically, the bog will spring in slow motion like a giant trampoline. It is an unlikely place for a meditation on the quirks of time; you are, in a sense, strung there between sky and the lower depths, held up by a porous mat of vegetation. And yet, squatting there on a June morning amidst the dwarf black spruces, with the blue empty sky arching over me, I am able to glimpse a flicker of the realities of the past.

This is no idle speculation. The plants that grow in the bog at Scratch Flat are the same species that grew in the area shortly after the glacier drew back and the waters of the lake drained off. Along with the glacial stream that has now become Beaver Brook and the lake to the northeast, there were hundreds of shallow depressions, temporary pools, and ponds in Scratch Flat in the centuries following the retreat of the glacier and the draining of the lake. Some of these were simply poorly drained areas where glacial water collected; some were formed by outpourings of groundwater; and some were created when huge chunks of ice were calved from the mother block and melted away, creating the sharp depressions in the landscape known as kettle holes. All of these lakes and ponds, in fact, all of the lakes and ponds that are still in existence today, are in the process of becoming dry land.

Even before the last ice had melted from the landscape, plants started to grow on Scratch Flat. They may have even grown on the body of the glacier. The Red Cowboy told me once that he had seen a whole forest growing on a glacier in Alaska, and there is a red alga which commonly grows on the snow fields of glaciers. It is likely that on Scratch Flat in the wet areas without an inlet or an outlet, sphagnum moss began to grow at the pond edges even while the ice block remained. Slowly over the decades, as the ice to the north melted back and the summers grew warmer, this absorbent aquatic plant grew out toward the center of the ponds, eventually covering the surface entirely. Hardy arctic plants such as crowberry, bearberry, and cranberry began to grow on this floating mat of vegetation, and windblown pollen grains from the coniferous forests that were growing south of the glaciated regions at the time probably settled there. Spruce, fir, and larch started to grow on the mat of sphagnum along with the hardy shrubs, but because the soil conditions are poor in boggy areas, and because of the enduring cold, it is unlikely that these trees would have grown to any height. Like the spruces that grow in the bog at Beaver Brook today, they would have been dwarfed, no higher than a man's head. In effect, the environment that existed in Scratch Flat was similar to the environment that exists in tundra regions of the Arctic today. The past at Scratch Flat is the present in Point Barrow or any other arctic region.

Not all the wetlands of Scratch Flat followed this pattern, however. At the edges of the deeper ponds with inlets and outlets, sedges, rushes, and grasses started to grow in the shallow waters. Slowly over the centuries these aquatic plants blossomed, died and sank to the bottom so that the floor of the body of water was raised. In time, the ponds became grassy marshes and in these damp areas small shrubs began to grow, and then trees, and then finally the ponds dried up altogether and became forests.

This process is not a thing of the past; although the vegetation is somewhat different, it is still going on today. Just below the large glacial boulder in Charlie Lignos's fields, there is a small pond surrounded by grasses and sedges which is no more than a foot or two deep. It is a good place to look for frogs and salamanders, and because it lies below the glacial boulder, where I spend a lot of time nowadays, I find myself thinking about that little body of water and how in the few years that I have known it I have seen it change. It used to be deeper, this little pond; you could skate there in winter, five or six years ago, and if by chance you fell through the ice, or if in spring you went out wading after pond life, you would go up to your waist in water at the middle. Now in winter, grasses pierce the ice and the skating is poor, and in dry summers, you can almost walk across the pond. You will get your feet wet in the process, but the point is that this little body of standing water is now more or less a wetland, and unless Lignos intervenes by digging it out, it will become a marsh, and then a shrub swamp, then a red maple swamp, and then a woodland of white pine and oak.

That is the normal succession of things in this part of the world; you can see the various stages all over Scratch Flat. There is, for example, a small red maple swamp above my house on the northwest side of the drumlin. The swamp was probably a pond sixty years ago, but now in summer, unless you know your trees, you cannot distinguish it from the surrounding woodlands. It is only in spring, when the groundwater levels are high, that the remnant of the ice sheet makes itself apparent. Then the waters rise around the trunks of the red maple trees and, after reaching a critical level, run down across the small meadow to the north of my house.

There were, in the postglacial period, no red maple trees growing on Scratch Flat—deciduous trees came in later, after the climate moderated—but there were, in all likelihood, larch trees, and they can still be found in the swamp on the west edge of Scratch Flat. Larch is a curious tree. It is a conifer; that is, like an evergreen tree, it bears cones, and like an evergreen, it has tiny needles for leaves. But unlike an evergreen, it loses its needles each winter as a deciduous tree does. The swamp makes a brilliant display as it goes through its seasonal changes. The needles of the larch hang on longer than the leaves of the other deciduous trees, and so in late November or early December when all the fields have turned a lion brown and there is no color beyond the muted grays and greens of the pines, the larch swamp flares a brilliant yellow.

It is always dark in this little grove, even when the needles are off the trees. The branches crisscross overhead in such profusion that they block out the sky, and yet there in the owl-haunted gloom, underneath the covering of the branches on the higher ground, you can find other remnants of the postglacial environment. Spruce trees grow in the larch swamp, club mosses can be found there, and a small gray-green lichen known as reindeer moss can be seen in the higher places, as well as a number of mosses that are related to sphagnum moss. Any of these nonflowering plants can be found in the woods of Scratch Flat, as a matter of fact, if you know what to look for. In their small persistent way, these humble and quietly beautiful species have managed to reassert themselves in spite of the vagarics of fifteen thousand years of a varying climate and the exigencies of late-twentieth-century America.

There is now one area on Scratch Flat where you can see the beginnings of history for the upland vegetation such as the mosses and lichens. In 1965 the New England Electric Company stripped a swathe across the northwest corner of Scratch Flat, cut down all the trees, and scraped off much of the soil that had accumulated since the time of the glacier, including several acres of arable farmland. In place of the natural woodland, the company put up a forest of artificial poles, constructed from fir trees cut in the northwestern part of the American continent and transported all the way across the country in trucks. Over these towers of wood, wires were strung, and now if you go to the area on a damp night, you can hear an ominous crackling, as if the night had been electrified.

The area beneath the wires contrasts sharply with the woods and fields on either side of the swathe. For one thing, from the high ground of the drumlin you can see out to the east and west for forty miles or more, so that if you don't mind the interruption of a few power lines, you can get a good view of the monadnocks to the northwest. It is, however, a noisy, somewhat degraded stretch of land. Trail bikes and snowmobiles sometimes race through the area, and at one point about five years ago, a gravel company dug an immense hole in a section beneath the power lines and carted the gravel off to build roads, leaving behind a pit of lifeless, dry land. The pit was the picture of desolation, raw yellow soil mixed with gravel, upturned tree trunks, exposed sections of bedrock, rutted truck tracks, and standing puddles of muddy water. And yet, within a few months, that is toward the end of the first summer after the devastation, I noticed that reindeer moss was growing there. The so-called reindeer moss is actually a lichen and is basically a pioneer plant. Not unlike sphagnum moss, it can grow in nutrient-poor environments, and like all lichens, it is a combination of two different plants, a fungus and an alga. The fungus is able to break down and release nutrients from rocks and poor soils, and the algal part of the plant is able to carry out photosynthesis—good insurance for survival in a hard climate. The Red Cowboy told me that sphagnum and reindeer moss were probably the most common plants on Scratch Flat in the recessional years of the glacier.

Although there are variations on this view of the postglacial environment, there does seem to be a general consensus among botanists and geologists that after the glacier withdrew from the northeast, there was a lot of water around, and that in time plants grew in the water, and that the wetlands and the ponds and the lakes are slowly drying up and will disappear, and that, furthermore, on the dry land areas, small heathlike plants would have grown shortly after the ice disappeared. What existed in Scratch Flat for one thousand to two thousand years following the retreat of the glacier was an open, treeless ground, pocked with numerous ponds, edged by the lake and the rushing stream that is now Beaver Brook, and the whole of it dominated by the heath-covered drumlin. Today if you walk over Scratch Flat in any season when the ground is open, you can see the evidence of this environment everywhere you look. It can be seen in the mosses and the lichens, in the little sand deposits that the ants dredge up from beneath the surface of the ground, in the marshes and the swamps, in the meandering course of Beaver Brook, and in the isolated spruce trees and the larches. But most of all, you can sense the past in the bog. There the landscape is as close to tundra as you will find in Massachusetts, a flat microcosm of that larger ancient environment, set with spruces and firs.

It comes as no surprise to me that in the bog, in the peace of hot summer afternoons, when the highway beyond the eastern ridge is silent and the human residents of Scratch Flat have all retreated to air-conditioned rooms, or on still autumn mornings, in the faded swirls of mist, the centuries roll back and I can sense another time. After all, bogs are traditionally associated with such time warps. They are the haunts of pixies, ghosts, and dank sucking grounds which swallow horses, carriages, lost children, and anything else that wanders into their murky environs.

But the reality of the postglacial age has other ways of reasserting itself on Scratch Flat. In general, the negative European attitude toward wetlands has been transported across the Atlantic and has lodged itself in the minds of the late-twentieth-century Americans. Until recently, when the crucial role of wetlands in flood control and water supply was realized, it was believed that the only good swamp was a drained swamp—to borrow an expression that used to be applied to the native people of this area. And in those areas on Scratch Flat where developers still refuse to honor certain geological realities, the legacy of the Ice Age inevitably rises to take revenge.

Several years ago Billy Sherman sold off a section of farmland along a small road that cuts south from the Great Road and leads, among other places, to the local dump. There are now 22 houses on this road, all lined up in soldierly fashion and most of them sporting well-manicured, landscaped properties. Except for the bean fields that run up to the property lines, and the brooding, wooded drumlin to the east, the street resembles any street in suburban America. But lurking beneath the surface of Scratch Flat, like some mythical presence, is that old demon glacier.

A few years after the development was completed, there was an immense snowstorm, followed by heavy rains, a freeze-up, and then another rain—not an unusual weather condition in these parts. Once upon a time, in the distant past, before the coming of the English mind, the land beneath the houses was probably marsh or swamp. It was undoubtedly a good habitat for salamanders and wood frogs, and later, after the land was cleared and planted, it was not a bad place to grow food. Billy Sherman, and his father before him, made a good living growing cauliflower, celery, and beans there. But former swamps and suburban streets do not mix well, and for a few days that winter it was not possible to drive down that street. Some of the cellars of the new houses filled up with water and the fire department had to come down with big hoses and suck them dry. Town road crews came in with heavy equipment and attempted to break the ice dams that had formed and to clear some of the icy slush, but every day the waters would return, more snow would melt, and the whole street would freeze up again at night, sometimes trapping cars and trucks in their driveways. The place looked to me very much like Scratch Flat must have looked in the warming years when the glacial lake was forming and Beaver Brook was a wild, gushing river. In time, however, the weather moderated, spring came, and at the town meeting that year, the residents of the street, who had been desperate to get the town to vote through the funds for an improved road even before the storm, managed to make their point. Voters agreed to spend the money to put in curbing and storm drains, no easy task in a New England town meeting.

There has not been a flood since the improvements were made, but when it comes—and it is, of course, simply a matter of time until it does—the engineers have arranged things so that the waters will be drained off properly, the cellars will remain dry, and the street, presumably, will be passable. This change is just one more stage in the evolution of Scratch Flat. It is variously defined as progress or an act of civilization or an improvement. Of course, for the frogs and the salamanders that used to inhabit the swamps and breed in the standing water at the edge of the field, it is a decisive end. And for the people who are attempting to encourage and restore the small farms of New England, it is also an end—one of many. And it is something of a defeat for the local environmentalists who claimed that a housing development should not have been put there in the first place. I withhold judgment. I can say, however, that in the red maple swamp above my house, in the larch swamp, in the bog, in the floodplain of Beaver Brook, the concept of "flood," of destruction by water, does not exist. There is simply high water and low water. The plants and animals that have been living here since the draining of the glacial lake have adapted quite well to such conditions and can endure the worst that the sky can pour out.

Although it is today possible, with a little imagination, to experience some of the salient realities of the geology and the botany of the world in Scratch Flat 12,000 years ago, there is, to my mind, a gigantic 2,000- to 3,000-year hole in the history that can never be seen again in the present. Most of the so-called higher animals—the birds and the mammals—that once lived on Scratch Flat have disappeared, many of them from the face of the earth. Whenever I am down amidst the spruce and the cranberries in the arctic environment of the bog, I have a distinct sense that something is missing there, some element of the reality of this place that cannot bring itself up onto the screen of the present. For months after I made this realization, I couldn't say exactly what that thing was. Now I think I know: it is a woolly mammoth.

Part of the interest for me in exploring time in Scratch Flat is the little realizations that you come across. I knew that woolly mammoths once roamed the earth—I think I learned that in sixth grade; and I knew that in parts of Siberia entire mammoths in perfect condition have been dug out of the permafrost. It never occurred to me, however, that woolly mammoths might have crisscrossed my own backyard. There is no evidence of this, although woolly mammoth bones have been found elsewhere in the Northeast; but given the fact that the drumlin sat above the drained lake bed and given the fact that woolly mammoths were grass feeders and that there must have been grass growing on the drumlin on which I live, it is a fairly safe assumption that at some point in the two-thousand-year period of time in which woolly mammoths lived around Scratch Flat, one of them, at least one, must have walked across the field or meadow behind my house. I prefer to imagine herds of them grazing there, their great swaying trunks twisting around the clumps of fresh sedges, their huge curving tusks rooting in the soil, lifting and heaving in fights, the wind blowing the dark brown topknot of hair above their reddish bodies. Sometimes on winter walks in the lingering evening light, I like to think that I can see a group of them standing at the woods' edge packed together tightly to protect themselves from the cold, shifting and swaying, facing me, their alert curious trunks exploring the air for my scent. It is not all fantasy; they were here in this place "in a time" as Tonupasqua would put it, "before this time"—not so very long ago as geological clocks run.

There were other species of mammoth in the Scratch Flat area. The smaller Jefferson mammoths undoubtedly grazed or browsed here; then imperial mammoths, the giant of them all, standing twelve feet at the shoulder, may have been found in the area; and later in history after the region became forested, the smaller mastodon appeared. There were other prehistoric animals roaming Scratch Flat along with the mammoths and the mastodons. Giant elk and caribou were common; there were giant beavers, six feet long; there were musk-oxen, moose, and bison; and there were two species of bear, an immense thing not unlike the Kodiak bear of the Northwest, as well as that enduring survivor of the Pleistocene age, the grizzly bear. (The black bear, one of the integral players in the Scratch Flat story, did not come to the area for another thousand years or so.) For a millennium or more, these prehistoric animals were the virtual rulers of the flatlands of the area. Along with the smaller species of mammals and birds, most of which have also disappeared from the environment, they filled every available ecological niche. There were grass eaters, there were shrub feeders, there were water dwellers, aquatic plant eaters, and of course there were predators—sabertoothed cats, the bears, and a fleet-footed animal known as the dire wolf. The bears, like the bears of today, were omnivorous, taking what food they could find, when they could get it, no matter whether it was vegetable or animal. The cats were stalkers; in all likelihood they lay in wait on the ledges on the southern end of the Scratch Flat drumlin, watching the flats below for young caribou, elk, musk-ox and moose. The wolves, also like the wolves of today, were pack animals. Periodically, I imagine, groups of them would streak across the flat sections of the area to run down any of the large grazers that fed on the vegetation of Scratch Flat. They may have even cornered and slashed at the heels of the young woolly mammoths and the mastodons.

These animals endured in this area for some two thousand years, four, perhaps five, times as long as the white man's brief sojourn so far. They were here, generation after generation, mating, birthing, feeding, dying, year after year, century upon century, as if there would be no end to their reign. But in spite of their abundance, in spite of the fact that they had successfully exploited and thrived in the postglacial environment, their time on this planet, their geological moment in the sun, was coming to an end. Part of their demise may have been caused by another opportunistic mammal species, a relative newcomer to the American continent who also moved into the ice-free territory of Scratch Flat and its environs even before the last ice blocks melted away from the region.

The first glacial advances that were to overwhelm Scratch Flat and New England began some 60,000 to 70,000 years ago. The earliest human records for the North American continent may be 70,000 years old, and that particular find is highly controversial. It is more commonly believed that human beings did not arrive until 30,000 to 40,000 years ago at most, and some archeologists suggest the arrival may have been as recent as 12,000 years ago. The first record for New England is no more than 10,000 or 11,000 years old. So Scratch Flat had an essentially nonhuman, ahistorical existence from the time that the first continental shelves rose up out of the seas to become dry land. But with the arrival of the first people—whenever that took place—the area becomes real, takes on a history, a mythology, and a folklore.

The general public and, to some extent, the Indian people that I know in the area have a way of clumping everyone who lived in America in the time before the coming of the Europeans as Indians or Native Americans. Archeologists and anthropologists who study such things are more specific about the people who lived here. The so-called Paleo-Indians who first followed the woolly mammoths and the caribou onto the grazing lands of Scratch Flat were a very different culture from the people who later settled in the general area. The Paleo-Indians were strictly a hunting people. They were not, as I understand it, hunter-gatherers, that is, they did not mix their diet with plant foods. They did not have to; game was abundant and easy to kill. Some believe that the mammoths and the caribou and the elk had never encountered an upright, two-legged predator which could strike from afar. Wolves and saber-toothed cats they were used to and had evolved defenses for. But the newcomers were so totally different from any predator that had ever existed in this continent that there was no fear, no built-in defense mechanisms in these Pleistocene giants. You could, if you were there, walk up to them, stick a spear into their heart, step back, and watch them die, or so it is theorized.

But even if that were not the case, the artifacts of these Paleo-Indians suggest that they were accomplished and efficient hunters. They had evolved their techniques somewhere in the West, had been at work hunting woolly mammoths, bears, caribou, and elk in the Old World for 100,000 to 200,000 years before they spread into the American continent, and had, to say the least, perfected their art.

Part of this efficiency shows up in their artifacts. The so-called fluted point, the spearhead of these people, has in the center of it a thin groove. Some have suggested that this was mere decoration, some suggest that it enabled the hunter to fit the point to the spear shaft more securely; but the commonly held theory is that the fluted point promoted bleeding. Once the animal was stabbed, the blood would rush out through the groove, the animal would die faster, and the whole process would be over without extended tracking, messy fights at cliff faces, and killed or wounded hunters. What is more, these efficient hunters had another tool at hand, namely, fire. They would, it is believed, drive the herds of grazers to the killing ground by setting fires in certain areas and herding them into bogs or other natural traps, or forcing them over cliffs. They would, in other words, do anything they could to obtain meat easily. And since there were a lot of animals, and since they were relatively easy to hunt, it seems that the Paleo-Indians did not bother to make use of the wild plants that grew in the region. They were hunters, and as such they were different from the people who lived after them in the Scratch Flat region.

The Paleo-Indians were essentially what sixth-grade history books used to refer to as cavemen. They wore the furs of the animals they killed; they had not developed the bow; they had no pottery, no arts or crafts, except for the tools associated with hunting and butchering—knives, scrapers, and the delicately crafted fluted projectile point. These people had no villages; they were continuously on the move, following the herds of grazing animals. Their equipment was light and portable, and their shelters were rock overhangs, caves if they could find any, and temporary huts covered over with animal skins and brush. Except possibly for one image, one single folktale, none of their mythology, their art, or any of their history has survived. There were not many of these people living in New England during the Pleistocene; records of their campsites are not common in the region, and it is thought that their population levels were never very high. But given time and the Paleo tendency toward overkill, even these limited numbers managed to cause the extinction of many of the large game animals, woolly mammoths included. Nothing escaped their ruthless efficiency.

There were, archeologists believe, other pressures on these animals. The vegetation changed slowly about two thousand years after the retreat of the glacier—the area became more forested, for one thing—and the postglacial era seems a period of great climatic up-

heavals, characterized by droughts, extended rains, and similar cata-
clysms. The great mammals of the Pleistocene were programmed to
deal more with a stable, albeit inhospitable, tundralike environment,
and when it disappeared, when it was disrupted, they too disappeared. But they were helped along, many believe, by the relatively
small two-legged predators with the unfortunate habit of killing
more than they could possibly eat.

Those species that survived the fluted spear points and fires of
the Paleo-Indians retreated northward following the edge of the glacier, and their descendants can still be found in the Arctic today—
the musk-ox, the caribou, and the elk. But the masters of the place,
the great woolly mammoths with the swaying trunks and red flowing
wool, the things that I wish I could see splashing through the half-
submerged landscape of the bog, have disappeared. Sometimes in
winter, when it is blowing, and the snow slopes are drifting, and the
woods make a dark line against the white of the open grounds, I miss
them. That is not to say that I do not rejoice at the arrival of these
Paleo-Indians. They have the singular honor of creating for the first
time an American history. No matter how obscure or how few they
were, they had discovered a world unpeopled for five billion years.

4

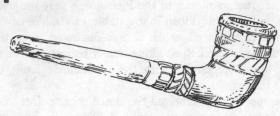

NIGHT ON
FORGE POND

Nompenekit and Tonupasqua do not accept any one of the chronologies that I have just set down; they would tell me that their people had been here always or forever. Tonupasqua in particular had a way of stating this that I used to find far more meaningful than her verbal expressions. "We have been here," she would say, and then she would drop her words and roll her right hand over and over in a circular pattern, extending her arm outward as she did so. The gesture was time. It said that there is no time; that time goes backward on occasion, forward on others; that it stalls out; that it skips around in a circle to catch you from behind; it is not now, or then, or to come; it simply is. All this was very difficult for me to comprehend, but it made easy history. Whenever I found a blank space in the Western version of the events that have taken place on Scratch Flat in the past ten thousand years, I would go to the medicine woman, Tonupasqua, and ask her what happened.

Since so little is known of the comings and goings of the Paleo-Indians in general, and of their time on Scratch Flat in particular, I once asked Tonupasqua if she could "see" this period of history. By now it was clear to me that what she meant by "seeing into things" or "seeing through things" was that she could, or believed she could, move freely in time. Both she and Nompenekit would speak in general terms when I questioned them about the past. They would rarely give me the kind of detailed information I want, and this was no less true for my questions about the Paleo people; but since this was, I believed, the only way of finding out anything at all about the period, I kept pressing for information, and finally one night I got what I was after.

There is, as I say, no material evidence of the Paleo-Indians, who undoubtedly, at some point in the two-thousand-year existence of this culture, stood on the drumlin on Scratch Flat and watched strings of game drift across the flatlands to the west. Paleo artifacts are rare enough in New England; burial sites have yet to be found, and indeed, it is possible that these people did not bother to bury their dead. They were, after all, continuously on the move, hunting, butchering, gorging themselves on great chunks of half-seared flesh, resting perhaps for a day or two, and then moving on to the next hunting site. But the apparent lack of religious artifacts, burial sites, or effigies does not mean that these people did not have a rich spiritual life. They had migrated out of an area that is rich in shamanistic ritual, and in the long hours while they rested between hunts, they undoubtedly told stories and recounted the ancient myths of their forefathers. One of these, the story of the stiff-legged bear, may have survived in the folktales of the Algonquian-speaking tribes that followed this primitive culture. The stiff-legged bear was just one more monster in the Algonquian pantheon, a terrible spirit-beast that lived in the dark places beyond the lighted campfires. It had long fur, giant, curving, tusklike teeth, and stood twice as high as a man's head. It was, in other words, very like a woolly mammoth, and it is not the only mythical creature that has survived into the present that seems to bear a resemblance to historical animals or events. There are many other similar creatures in Tonupasqua's folktales, and it has always seemed to me that somewhere in these stories there might be some evidence of the Paleo-Indians.

One year, after I had explained my predicament to Tonupasqua, she promised that she would go to visit her uncle in Maine to see if she could learn more about the period I was interested in. I didn't hear from her for a few weeks after that; then one June morning she called and invited me to her house in Lowell. She said she had visited her uncle and could tell me more about the people who lived in the place during the period which I had attempted to describe to her. Some of her friends would be there, she said, and they too could tell me things that I wanted to know.

This was one of those stifling days in late June, and when I got there that night a lot of people, some of them Indians, some of them clearly a mixture of black, Portuguese, and Indian, had gathered in a fenced area in back of Tonupasqua's kitchen and were drinking beer and talking quietly. Tonupasqua introduced me in a casual offhanded manner and explained why I had come; but it was clear that I represented some kind of intrusion, and the people fell into a somewhat prolonged and embarrassed silence. Nompenekit was there and I managed to get into a conversation on his favorite subject—current politics and radical, simplistic solutions to complex problems. Slowly, as I more or less melted into the group, the conversation picked up again and the formality began to fade. There was a lot of drinking going on among a small group of them, although Nompenekit, Tonupasqua, and a brownish young man with a long ponytail named White Bird Free at Last were abstaining. I sensed that these other people were fringe Indians, so to speak; they did not seem to share the abiding interest in Indian affairs that Nompenekit, White Bird, and Tonupasqua lived by.

After an hour or so, in spite of the heat, many of these fringe Indians moved into the kitchen, closer to the refrigerator and the beer, and the four of us stayed out at a picnic table in the fenced yard. The night drifted on; the conversation between us was light and somewhat disconnected, and I wasn't getting the information that Tonupasqua had promised me, but I didn't want to press her. Finally Nompenekit said that he would like to come down to this area I was always talking about. White Bird nodded at this and Tonupasqua gave me an odd and mysterious, almost angry look; clearly they had been talking about me. I invited them to come any time, we could have a lunch and walk over the land, I said, or even go out early and have breakfast in the woods. But they indicated that they wanted to go immediately in spite of the fact that it was now about midnight. After a few minutes, without telling the others, we left for Scratch Flat—Nompenekit driving his late-model Buick, Tonupasqua sitting beside him smoking cigarettes, and White Bird Free at Last lounging in the back seat. I had no idea where we were going on Scratch Flat or what we could do once we got there; but I didn't want to turn down an opportunity such as this.

Conversation fell off again during the trip; White Bird fell asleep, Nompenekit drifted off into a daydream, and Tonupasqua, her eyes wide and staring, began rocking forward and backward rhythmically, humming a monotonous tune over and over again as she did so. By the time we got to Scratch Flat I had made up my mind. I directed them past my house to a dirt road that winds through the pine woods to the point of land on Forge Pond where artifacts had been found and where, it is believed, Indians used to hold religious ceremonies. We had to walk through the woods for a quarter of a mile or so, through an area where there was no trail, but there was a moon, and the open stretch of the lake was clearly visible through the branching trees. I told them that this was an area where Indian people had gathered for thousands of years, "longer than anyone could know," I said. "We know, we know," Tonupasqua said. "It's all right here. We'll spend the night."

This was something I had not expected. I had thought they merely wanted to look over the place, and I was about to suggest that spending the night might not work out, since as far as I knew this was private land and we were more or less trespassing, but Tonupasqua cut me short. "We're going to dance now, okay?" she said, indicating that I should retire, get out of their way somehow, although I wasn't sure whether I was supposed to go home or just sit down and watch. White Bird Free at Last took out a packet of kinnikinnick or Indian tobacco, filled a pipe, and they all sat down in the pine needles and began to pass the pipe in silence. I walked off into the woods about twenty yards and sat down against a tree to see what would happen.

I should make clear that in spite of their names, these people, if you met them on the street, would not seem so very different than any other people in New England, except perhaps that their skin has a brownish color and their hair is straight and black and relatively long. They speak in English and, except for Nompenekit who grew up in Canada, they have the broad accent of any of the Massachusetts residents of their economic status, which is not what you might call elevated. They are working-class people in dress, habit, accent, and appearance; but they are also Indians, and they are proud of that fact, and, as far as I can tell, they are deeply religious. I mention this because it became clear to me later that the event that I witnessed that night was essentially a religious ceremony, no more exotic really than a Catholic mass or any other service. In spite of this, however, the ceremony had a decidedly nonwestern aura about it that seemed to free these people from the normal confines of reality.

It was now probably two in the morning, the night was hot, the screen of woods was impenetrable behind us, and the only sound was the slap of waves on the shore of the lake. Over the water I could see the glimmering lights of the village at the outlet for the lake, but here, on the point of land where many similar rituals may have been performed, we were separated from the temporal world, a mere island of four individuals afloat in time.

The pipe went around in silence for five or ten minutes, I could see its glow against the dark lake, and whenever Nompenekit dragged on it, the tobacco would flare up and cast a dull gleam over his wrinkled face. After a time, Tonupasqua began rocking again, moaning a low tune, which was interrupted by grunts and low mutterings from White Bird. Suddenly she rose to her feet and began to shift back and forth, her rounded body cutting off the glimmering lights of the civilized world across the lake. Nompenekit joined her, and after a minute or two, White Bird got up and began to shuffle his feet forward and backward. Then, abruptly, as if he had been seized by pain, White Bird threw up his right arm and crouched over, shouting in the high, unintelligible phrases known technically as vocables—meaningless words that traditional Indians use to accompany their dances. Crouching over, his right arm still raised, and his left arm crooked uncomfortably behind his back, he began to circle around the pipe, crossing his left leg behind his right and vice versa with short little stamps. Tonupasqua and Nompenekit swayed and shuffled for a minute longer and then they too joined in the dance, each of them taking up White Bird's long chant of vocables, interweaving the call with short grunts and shouts, and an occasional high whinny from Tonupasqua.

My first reaction was to join in; involuntarily, almost, I felt my arm go up as soon as Nompenekit joined in the dance. But with Tonupasqua's whinnying filling the air, I began to worry slightly that someone across the lake would hear the chanting and call the police. For about ten minutes I was too distracted to appreciate the spectacle, then slowly, once again, I fell in with the ceremony and would have joined the dance had I not felt that I might violate the ritual. I moved farther into the woods, sat down again to watch, and then, for some reason, began to feel dizzy and almost frightened. The reality of what was going on, the time scales that I felt I was witnessing, seemed too vast to comprehend, too much to handle at three in the morning. I felt that I was transported back into some indistinct period in the time before this time, when Menobozho, Hobomacho, the Bear, and the other mythological creatures walked over Scratch Flat. It was not an altogether pleasant revelation. What came to the forefront there was not the brilliantly lit Scratch Flat summer landscape, but the darker side of things, the horror and the mystery of the European Paleolithic death cults, rites of passage, and yet undiscovered rituals. Dark shuffling images flashed in front of me, unspeakable primal ceremonies, scarified, painted shamans, bear priests, wolf men and ritualistic sacrifices; and for a moment I thought I saw the actual form of a fourth figure dancing there. It was shorter, thicker than the others, and by the time I recognized the form as that of an upright bear, it had disappeared.

I realized then that I was not seeing Scratch Flat anymore. I had been carried back it seemed to an earlier period, transported somehow to the Mal'ta peninsula on Lake Baikal in Siberia where the tribes of American Indians are believed to have originated. Whatever I saw there was the same thing that Cotton Mather and the other Puritan ministers so feared when they first encountered the aboriginal Americans. It was the fiery worm that flew by night, the dark ecstasies and Satanic figures that lurked in the howling wilderness and tempted wayward European travelers. I found there, it seemed to me later, the most essential Paleo artifact of all, the spirit that was born in the mind of the Paleolithic hunters two hundred thousand years ago, nurtured on the Mal'ta peninsula, carried across the Behring Sea land bridge, carried across the American continent, carried through fifteen thousand years of American history, and then deposited on a point of land on an obscure pond in the drainage of the Merrimack River on the northeastern coast of North America.

This revelation (I would be hard-pressed to call it a vision; it was simply an exciting and intense understanding of the ceremony) lasted no more than three or four minutes and then subsided slowly. Within a few minutes I was worrying again about the modern-day police. But a hundred yards away, these survivors of the migration

from Mal'ta were still shuffling in a tight circle, the two men crouching over, twisting this way and that, crooking their arms back, and
Tonupasqua upright and staring outward into the emptiness, her
breast heaving and sweat rolling down her neck. She was like a
voodoo queen; all the trappings of white civilization, the polyester
pants and the light, store-bought blouse, had been seemingly stripped
from her and she danced there in all her primitive splendor, timeless,
earthy, regal, and even more unknowable than she was in real time.
Her whinnying had subsided into a series of short barklike bursts of
stifled little cries that rose from somewhere deep beneath her heaving
chest. Her braids had loosened; her breath, between the chants, came
in wheezing gulps; and although I could not see her eyes, they
seemed to be fixed in space and unmoving. The dance continued far
longer than any ritual I had ever experienced among white people.
They had been circling now for two, possibly three, hours for all I
knew. It was hard to judge time; the only fix I could get was the
sunrise.

The western sky beyond the lake turned a pearl gray, and
through the thick woods to the east I could make out a violet color.
With the lightening sky, White Bird Free at Last dropped out of the
dance and stood silently and erect a few feet back. Nompenekit
halted after a few minutes and then, still in a trance, Tonupasqua
slowed and stood where she was. Without a word, the two men came
up and faced her; the three of them joined hands, threw back their
heads, and raised their arms to the sky, still clasping hands, their
eyes shut tightly. This, I assumed, was some final ritual; but they
held this position for an interminable period. Around us in the
woods, the thrushes and the robins were beginning to call; somewhere over the lake a dog started barking; and yet they held their
position. The full dawn chorus of birds began then, first the long
screech of the great crested flycatchers, the comfortable "chewink"
of the towhees, and then the high buzzing of warblers. They held
while the outboard motor of a fisherman started up from the village
beyond us. They held as the wind came up, and they held while the
sky in the west turned from gray to yellow to violet and then, finally,
to blue. There was no end, it seemed, to this final prayer; they were
totally oblivious to their surroundings, to the dog, the motorboat, the
birds and even the rising of the sun.

Then suddenly, the prayer was over. They dropped their hands as a single individual, instantaneously, as if they had been counting in unison for all that time. With the prayer finished, the morning light around them, and the dance completed, we walked back to the car at the end of the dirt road. I didn't dare break their silence; in fact, I didn't dare walk with them for fear of interrupting something —I was, as you can imagine, in unfamiliar territory. I trailed along behind, pretending to interest myself in some of the wildflowers that were blooming along the way. We drove back to Lowell in silence; I picked up my car and drove home again.

After that night, Tonupasqua began talking more freely to me about Scratch Flat. I had always sensed with her a certain nervousness; I knew she mistrusted me—she mistrusted all white people probably, and I think she might have learned, through her Indian friends, to mistrust anthropologists and archeologists. But after our night on the point of land, she began to relate stories to me whenever I asked her about things. She became more friendly, joked with me from time to time about my curiosity, and once even went so far as to introduce me to a friend of hers as a "good boy." By that time, having seen what I had on the point of land, having seen back into the time of the mammoths and the Paleo shamans, I felt that I intuitively knew a little more about the people who followed the herds along the glacier fronts; and what is more, in her new state of mind, Tonupasqua volunteered a number of stories about her people without prodding.

One of the stories tells of how human beings came into the world. Her people were originally created by T'chi Manitou, the Maker, long ago in another time. People were a lot smaller then and perhaps more significantly, animals were a lot bigger. There were gigantic beavers, huge bears, and I am tempted to say long-furred, tusked creatures with trunks; but Tonupasqua didn't tell me that, she said that there were "other things, things with big teeth." The people that T'chi Manitou created were in constant danger from these giant animals, and it was clear that if things continued as they were, there wouldn't be any people left. So T'chi Manitou hid the people in a tree and sent Glooscap to help.

Glooscap is a character who appears again and again in Tonupasqua's stories. He is a traditional Algonquian mythological figure who is sometimes human in form, sometimes something else, and always full of tricks. T'chi Manitou told Glooscap where the people were hidden and said that when he was ready to take care of them, he should let them out. One of the first things Glooscap did was to go around the countryside reducing the size of all the dangerous animals. Then when he felt that the world was ready, he took a magic axe and split the great tree where the people were hidden. They all rushed out and in due time populated the earth.

Tonupasqua always had a way of telling me almost exactly what I wanted to hear. She seemed able to sense what I was after and would either make up the proper story, or had such a wealth of stories that she could draw them out, using the traditions of various Indian groups, and deliver up the one that best matched my version of history. That is how I account for the fact that Glooscap went around making all the animals small. There were indeed giant beavers in Beaver Brook at one point. Now the few that occasionally are found there are decidedly smaller. There were once huge mammoths and mastodons, and giant deer; now there are a few white-tailed deer and of course no elephants like mastodons. Furthermore, there is one Glooscap story which she told me which meshes perfectly with the geological events that helped to create Scratch Flat. Tonupasqua told me that long ago a frog monster had somehow tied up all the water in the world, or at least in one region where people lived. He had made great lakes for himself to live in; and because of all this water, there was no place for the people to hunt; they were confined to a few islands of high ground. Glooscap came into the country to kill the frog monster, but word got out and the great amphibian retreated under water and planned to eat Glooscap. One day the frog monster went to the cave where Glooscap was living at the time and hid inside while Glooscap was out hunting. The frog's plan was to surprise him when he came back and catch him with his great tongue. Glooscap came home that evening and sensed that something was wrong, so he called out, "Good evening cave, is anyone home?" Of course the frog monster didn't want to give himself away, so he remained silent. Glooscap called out again, asking if anyone was home, and then when the frog monster failed to answer, called out a third time. "This is strange," Glooscap said, in a loud voice. "Usually my cave answers me. There must be someone hiding inside who wants to eat me." Then he called out again, "Good evening cave, is everything all right?" "Yes," called the frog monster. "Do come in."

Then Glooscap rolled a big stone in front of the cave and trapped the frog monster inside.

Tonupasqua told me that Glooscap had another enemy, a giant bear who used to feed on his friends, the human beings. He told this giant bear that there was a cave on the west side of the frog monster's lake with a stone in front of it. Inside, he said, there were many people trapped, and if Bear was hungry, he had but to go and roll the stone aside. So Bear traveled to that country, rolled the stone aside, and out lashed the great sticky tongue. A monumental fight ensued, and in the process, both contestants were killed, and the battle so shook the ground that the impoundments that held the water of the lake were shaken loose and the lake drained off, exposing a fertile grazing area for the animals that the people liked to eat.

After my night on the point of land on Forge Pond, the obscure presence that I had always sensed in the isolated corners of Scratch Flat began to assume more of an identity and seemed to become more active. It became not simply a passive force to be sought, but a thing that was seeking recognition; it became a stalker. I would sense it behind me sometimes while I was out walking; I would spin around to meet it and it would not be there; I could not see it, and rational thinker that I am, I am not sure I even believed in it truly; but there was no question in my mind that I sensed something.

Part of the key to the understanding of this presence came from Nompenekit. He had become more interested in my project after the night dance at Forge Pond, and would occasionally come down to visit and walk to some site where I was convinced that Indians had had a fishing weir or a village or a camp. One of these sites is located on a low bluff of land which overlooks the marshes of Beaver Brook. The stream swings close to the bank at that point and is relatively deep and I had often thought that it might have been a good site for a fishing weir. One day Nompenekit and I walked down to get the feel of the place. We squatted on the bluff for a while, looking over the marshes, thinking, as usual, about the past and Indians, and about a man named Tom Dublet, who in the seventeenth century is supposed to have had a weir around here according to the white man's historical records.

I began to prod Nompenekit about some of these things, but he did not seem in a mood to talk. He squatted on the high ground, smoking cigarette after cigarette, simply staring out over the open marshes. I didn't quite catch his apparent need for silence at that point, and finally, exasperated at my eternal questions, he summed up what is, I believe, the essential Indian view of time and place.

"You know you're always so worried about the past," he said. "What does that matter, you know? What is it anyway? We don't believe that our people have ever gone away. We're right here now, you know what I mean?"

"No," I said, "I don't know what you mean," although I had an idea then of what he was going to say.

"The Indian people, we're all this, you see," he answered, and at this point he lifted his head sharply, indicating the marshes and the dark line of the pines on the hillside beyond. "We're made of this, the marshes here, the trees. No different, see what I mean? You don't understand this because you look on this world as something that is not you. But Indian people believe that we are no different than a squirrel or a bear, just a different form. We're all the same, squirrel, bear, me. Okay?"

He fell silent, lit another cigarette, and looked out again over the open marshes.

"One thing you got to know for this project. You've got some nice spaces here. You got marshes on this land; you got big hemlock trees back there behind your house; you got the brook; you got the big rock there; you got the lake. Long as you got those things, you got an Indian people here. I'm telling you this. You know that night we prayed here, well something else came out of the forest and danced with us. Tonupasqua called him out."

He stopped talking again at this point. He had made his point, but after ten minutes or so I asked him what it was that came out of the forest and danced.

"You wouldn't understand it," he said.

"I would. I believe."

"It was . . . it was a thing. One of our people."

"A ghost?"

"No. It wasn't no ghost; it was an Indian man. A spirit. He came out and danced. It was no ghost; this was a spirit man, some guy that used to be here and is still here now."

He was embarrassed, I could tell, but I kept pressing. I told him that sometimes when I walked in the woods at night, I felt something behind me, I had a sense of a presence, of a man or a ghost, and that I would like to believe that there really was something there and that I really was trying to believe that time could wind back on itself like a snake, as Tonupasqua said, that time past was time now. I went on and on with this little speech to try to convince him as thoroughly as I could that I wanted to learn to think in Indian time, that I was trying to understand white man's history by the Indian way of thinking. But even after my diatribe, and after a prolonged discussion of time and the Indian people, he was still reluctant to describe any further the thing that came out of the forest that night. Then I remembered my own experience. For some reason I had not at that point made the connection between the revelation that I had, and the thing or force that I had always felt on Scratch Flat.

"You know I think I saw something that night," I told him. "Something really basic, I didn't really see it, I just had a sense that there was something going on."

"Yeah, well that was it," he said.

"What was it?"

"What you saw, that was it."

"But was it a man? It looked like a bear, something halfway in between."

"You're telling me that you saw it?"

"No, I only sensed something, a very dark thing."

"All right."

"Well, what did you see?" I asked.

"Same thing."

"But you saw a man, you said, a spirit man."

"That's right. He came out of the pines there and circled around us a few times and then went away again."

"How was he dressed?" I asked. "What did he look like?"

Nompenekit looked over at me and shook his head as if to say, "You are really dumb."

"Doesn't matter," he said. "There was a thing there. He wasn't no different from me or Tonupasqua or White Bird Free at Last, except that he had been in the place before."

This last was delivered with a sense of total exasperation. Nompenekit and I are always very polite to each other. He is, notwithstanding his radical politics, a very gentle and quiet sort of individual, and in spite of my enthusiastic curiosity, the better part of my Anglo upbringing took over, I stopped making him uncomfortable and we never brought up the subject again.

5

ARCHAIC INTERLUDE

In the mid-nineteenth century the people living in the towns in the Scratch Flat area began to become aware of the fact that economic changes were taking place in the region and the old ways, the ways of their farming grandfathers, were passing. In order to counteract this, partly out of nostalgia and partly out of a genuine concern for the past, historical societies were organized and records, stories, and in some cases buildings were preserved. It is from these records, from the fragile notebooks of nineteenth-century romantics and stark official notes of the town fathers, that the events in the human history of Scratch Flat can be pieced together.

The historical society in the town in which most of Scratch Flat is located is hardly the most active in the state, and yet, over the past 150 years of its existence, its members have amassed a fair collection of artifacts and documents which are stored in an upstairs room in the town library. The room is kept under lock and key; the items collected there are not on public display; but it is possible to gain entry into this inner sanctum and explore at leisure the history that is put away there. The room is ill-lighted, hot in summer, and cold in winter; but inside, scrambled together with relics and records of seventeenth-, eighteenth-, and nineteenth-century American society, you can find the implements of a far more ancient culture.

There is a wooden case in the historical society collection that is about two feet square and covered with a glass front. Inside the case, all carefully labeled in the delicate pen of some nineteenth-century scribe, you can see an orderly arrangement of what are commonly called Indian "arrowheads"—known to archeologists as projectile points since the heads were used on spears as well as arrows. The points in the glass case were found near a pond at the southwestern edge of Scratch Flat, and unbeknownst to the man who collected them, they represent the first material evidence of human existence on the square-mile patch of land I am writing about.

In the center of the collection there is a projectile point which is about five inches long. In contrast to the triangular shape of the other points in the case, this larger implement is elongated and notched at the base. It is chipped from quartz, and if you look carefully at the edges, you can see the fine handiwork of the individual who made it. A series of delicate scallops or serrations runs down either side of the point and the whole thing flares slightly in the middle and then retreats gracefully to the notched base. The thing is too big to be the point of an arrow; it was obviously used on a spear; and if you took the time to analyze the differences between it and the other points in the collection, even without any foreknowledge of the subject, you would surmise that it belonged to a culture that was substantively different from the people who fashioned the other points.

This case was discovered, or rediscovered, in the attic of the town library in the late sixties by a man named Toby Beckwith, a descendant of one of the early settlers in this town and one of my intrepid guides through the confusing maze of the history of Scratch Flat. Toby Beckwith is a man who has been labeled by his acquaintances in the town as an eccentric. That is not to say that he is not liked, or that he is discriminated against—people in this community, if you live here long enough, have a way of accepting all sorts of behavior. Toby offers the people in the town—the highway workers who gather at the local diner for breakfast each morning, the women at the town offices, and the housewives, farmers, and petty officials of the town—something to talk about. He is about fifty years old and lives in a refurbished barn in back of his mother's house with a woman named Rosey to whom he may or may not be married—no one is really sure. He is a collector and a sometime salesman of precious antiques; he is a sometime farmer and gardener, a man who loves black coffee, good conversation, history, Indians, the theater, and the poetry of Robert Lowell. He has lived with or near his mother for the better part of his life and has, it is rumored, "an inheritance." In short, he is something of an exotic figure in comparison to the hardworking, if somewhat prosaic, people who now live on Scratch Flat. When Toby was about twenty-three years old, shortly after he graduated from Cornell, he left Scratch Flat for the world at large. He went to New York City and for a few years acted small parts in various off-Broadway productions. After that he drifted to Europe, lived for a time in Nice, tried his hand at the wheel in Monte Carlo, and then in the early sixties came back to this country and settled in the southwest. In Arizona he fell in with a group of Papago Indians, lived with them for a few years, and there developed his abiding love for Indian cultures. In the mid-sixties he returned to Scratch Flat sporting, long before it was fashionable in these parts, shoulder-length hair and a decided preference for the Indian way of life, that is to say, a closer relationship with and appreciation for the natural world.

It was on his return to the East, he said, that he experienced what amounted to an epiphany. He was fishing one day by the edge of Beaver Brook when he met an older man from Concord who said he was looking along the edges of the stream for Indian artifacts. The old man told Toby that this particular stretch of the brook had been, as far as he could tell, an important Indian fishing ground. Somewhere along this stretch, he said, Tom Dublet, one of the last Indians of the area, had had his fishing weir, and there were indications that the stream had been intensively used for centuries before.

This information broke over Toby's consciousness like a thunderstorm. He went home that afternoon in a daze. He had always known that there were Indians in New England, he had that drilled into him since third grade; but the fact that they had lived on Scratch Flat, within a mile of his house, the fact that there had actually been a people here not unlike the Papagos, came as a virtual revelation to him. After that he began looking for evidence of Indian cultures in the area. Each spring when the farmers around him would plow their fields, Toby would be there, shortly after the rains, walking patiently back and forth, his eyes forever searching the ground, looking for the little oddities amidst the small stones, a chip here, a triangular bit of rock there, anything that would reveal that what he was looking at had been fashioned by human hands. In the first spring, at the edge of Matty Matthews's cornfield, he found his first projectile point, a late Woodland culture arrowhead, triangular in shape and roughly chipped from a bit of quartz. It was after that, after many more discoveries, that he began his collection of Indian artifacts, many of the best of which he has given away to interested parties or to museums.

It was during this period that Toby took up the habit which has served to give him more of a reputation than any of his other preoccupations. Each spring, sometime around April, he removes his shoes and does not put them on again until the fall. He began doing this while he was looking for arrowheads; he said it allowed him to feel the presence of points; but in time he found it was easier to leave them off than put them on. The floor of Toby's pickup truck is littered now with odd pairs of sandals, sneakers, and boots which he carries in case he has to go into a store or restaurant. It was also about then, just about the time when it was becoming acceptable to have long hair, that Toby sheared his off. And it was during this same period—the late sixties—that Toby took up again with the woman named Rosey, an actress and singer whom he had known from his New York days. The two of them, working with scraps of recycled material, reconstructed his mother's barn into living quarters; and there, amidst the Indian artifacts, the spear points, the Papago blankets and rugs, and Rosey's impressionistic paintings of gardens, I first met Toby.

When I began to explore the past in Scratch Flat, I was told that if I wanted to know anything about the Indians of this area I should talk to Toby Beckwith; he was, people said, the ultimate authority on these matters. They also told me, some of them, not to believe a word he said. Armed with this foreknowledge, and willing to accept all the bits of information I could, I called Toby, set up a meeting, and have, in the course of the four years of our acquaintance, become his friend, his sounding board, and his straight man. I tell you all this as caveat. Most of the Indian history which I am presenting here comes from a variety of sources, and I present it without discrimination. But you should know that the professionals in the fields whom I talk to, the geologists, the botanists, and the archeologists in particular, do not always concur with the stories that are presented to me by Toby Beckwith and some of my Indian informants.

In 1969 Toby Beckwith was sorting through the collections of the town historical society when he came across the square case with the projectile points. The arrowheads had been collected in 1830 by a man named James Wilson and, other than an indication of the place in which they were found, came down through the centuries without additional information. By that time, Toby had a working knowledge of the various fashions and styles that appear in Indian points and was able to recognize immediately that the larger points in the middle of the case belonged to people known technically as Archaic Indians, that is the people who claimed Scratch Flat as their territory 10,000 to 8,000 years ago. It is, to date, the earliest artifact discovered in the immediate area, although Paleo points and other Archaic points have been found in the surrounding towns.

The spearhead in the historical society collection does not have the fluted notch in the middle that is characteristic of Paleo points. The people who fashioned it, by that time, had given up on the fluted groove and were making points that were in many cases smaller and less carefully crafted. This is a critical distinction, insignificant though it may seem. From this new construction style, this simple lack of a groove, you can read the whole story of the environmental and cultural changes that took place on Scratch Flat 10,000 to 8,000 years ago. I learned this fact from Toby Beckwith, but it is one of the bits of information that he has given me that almost everyone agrees upon.

It is a wonderful and a highly comforting experience to remove the Archaic point from its place and hold it in your hand. It seems miraculous, impossible almost, that this piece of stone was fashioned by human hands 10,000 years ago and that these people, although different in appearance and different in their way of life, were human beings not unlike any twentieth-century individual, no matter how sophisticated he or she claims to be. The Archaic people were born, nursed by their mothers, grew to adulthood, and then died. Daily time, presumably, did not move any faster or slower for them than it does for us. They would rise at dawn, and minute by minute, hour by hour, pass through a single day of life. They would do this for 365 days a year, for forty, fifty, in some cases eighty years; and then like all living things, something would flicker out and they would die. These people had their joys and their night terrors. They fell in love, they made love, they ate, they slept, they nuzzled their children, they spent a lot of time daydreaming about things, they played gambling games, they had sports, and they told stories. But there was one substantial difference between the Indian people that lived around Scratch Flat for most of human history and the people that live here today, and that is that the Indians were far more dependent on their immediate environment. Now, in Scratch Flat, the people tend to alter their environment to suit their needs; and in fact they could live pretty much in the same way anywhere in the United States. But the late-Paleo people who crossed Scratch Flat in search of bison and caribou and woolly mammoths did not have that opportunity. When the environment changed, they had to alter their way of life or they would not survive.

In those sections of Scratch Flat which are not now in farmland the predominant habitat is oak and white pine. Coming in from the east, from Route 495, or west along the Great Road from Groton, you will see the straight wooded ridge of the drumlin, lying on the horizon like a beached whale, its high head to the southeast and its tail tapering off to the northwest. On either side of this narrow ridge, the woodlands spill down from the crest in a dark irregular line. To the east they are broken by the low buildings of the so-called Beaver Brook Industrial Park and by Charlie Lignos's uncut hayfields. To the west they break into Jimmy Starkos's strawberry and corn fields, and here and there at the uncultivated edges of the farmlands, to the west of the drumlin, and especially in the uncut hayfields of Charlie Lignos's land, you can see the landscape of the Archaic period reasserting itself.

Nature in this section of the world abhors alteration. Cut back the forest for hayfields and corn, cover the land with hard-topped parking lots, or houses, or lawns, or roads, and then desert the area for even a few years, and you will see the ancient force of the late Pleistocene age wedging itself into the cracks in the asphalt. Down in the terraced farmlands below my house, the gray birches and the white pine seedlings are sprouting. The dogwood and the dogbane and the juniper are crowding out the timothy and other English grasses that have grown in these fields since 1752, when Jeremiah Caswell cleared off the Indian gardens here and planted his first crops for forage. Cultivation, the imposition of a European culture, civilization, is merely a thin veneer tacked over the past. Let it go for a year, turn your back on it, and it will break through and take over again. You can see it everywhere at the edges of the cultivated fields. Natural history is not only alive and well, it is coming back. All it needs is time.

The ecosystem that is striving to return to this area is itself a relative newcomer to Scratch Flat. The oak and pine forest and its accompanying flora and fauna began to grow here ten thousand years ago as the ice sheets drew farther north and the climate warmed. We know all this from another sort of record that was kept here on Scratch Flat, one that we only learned to read a few decades ago.

Bogs not only contain the remnant plants of the immediate post-glacial period, they also contain, deep in the layers of muck and peat beneath their surface, a record of the vegetation in any given period. Pollen is of course a major player in the sex life of modern plants. Trees, grasses, and shrubs produce tons of it each year in the proper seasons. The bulk of these vast clouds of pollen falls to earth each season and settles on the ground and on the surface of ponds, bogs, swamps, streams, and marshes in the general area in which the pollen-producing plants are growing. In time layers of pollen accumulate beneath the surface in boggy areas, and over the centuries they are buried in peat. Each species of plant produces a characteristically-shaped pollen grain, so if you bore down into the depths of the bog, and you can preserve the profile of the layerings; and further-more, if you know how to identify the characteristic species of grains (no small feat), then you can tell what plants were growing in the region in any given period.

No palynologist, or student of pollen, has ever taken a core sampling of the bog at Beaver Brook; but pollen counts from similar sites in the area have been studied, and it appears from these records that about ten thousand years ago the environment of Scratch Flat began to undergo a dramatic alteration. Within the space of a few centuries, the advance guard of conifers, which had grown sparsely here and there in protected areas of Scratch Flat in the first two thousand years after the glacier drew back, began to invade en masse. Cathedrallike stands of deep forest of spruce and fir, such as those that cover much of northern Russia and Canada today, began growing. This spruce fir forest lasted, it appears, from about 10,000 B.C. to 6,500 B.C.

Mixed in with these pollen deposits palynologists have found the pollen of jack pine, red pine, and toward the close of the period, the pollen of the white pine, which is abundant in the region at present. As usual, there are varying readings of this history. Some students of this transitional period believe that the forests of ten thousand years ago were nothing like the taiga or spruce fir forests, of today, and that growing along with the spruce and the fir, there were deciduous trees such as oak. In any case, it is generally agreed that about nine thousand years ago the white pine began to take over and that during this same period oak, hemlock, birch, alder, hornbeam, and plants in the bayberry family began to grow in lush profusion. The spruces and the firs declined and then about eight thousand years ago the vegetation which now covers Scratch Flat was established. Presumably it will remain with us—or attempt to remain with us in the face of encroaching civilization—until that time in the distant future when, for reasons yet undetermined, the glacier will return. At such time, it is supposed, the whole process will reverse itself; the spruce will begin to grow again, the tundra will return, and then finally, like a bad dream, the great sheets of ice will cover the region.

Not surprisingly, the animals of the Scratch Flat region began to change along with the vegetation, although they may have been helped along—herded, as it were—into extinction by the Paleo-Indians. The great woolly mammoths that fed on the hardy tundra vegetation were replaced by the grazing Jefferson mammoth which fed primarily on grasses, which in turn were replaced by the mammoths' more distant relative, the mastodon, which fed on trees and shrubs. The barren ground caribou gave way to the woodland caribou, the musk-oxen to herds of gregarious piglike peccaries. The bison, the ground sloth, the giant beaver and the great kodiaklike bear, the tapir, the wapiti or American elk, and an interesting combination of a moose and an elk moved up from the south into the forested areas of Scratch Flat.

Most of these new arrivals were decidedly smaller than the Pleistocene giants that ruled the region for the first five thousand years after the glacier retreated. They were, in all likelihood, more wary of their human predators, fleeter of foot for the most part, harder to catch; and perhaps most significantly from a human point of view, they did not supply the amount of meat that was available in the larger postglacial species. Whereas a woolly mammoth might supply a small band of hunters with food for several days, a caribou or an elk would barely provide enough meat for a single day. As a result, other sources of food had to be found, new hunting techniques had to be developed, and new tools had to be invented to deal with the changing environment. And that is the story that is written in the projectile point in the glass case in the historical society collection.

There is no data with the point in the glass case; all that is known is that it was found near Forge Pond along with some arrowheads about 1845, and that it hung around—probably in people's attics—for a few decades until it was donated to the historical society for safekeeping. Whether it fell from a wounded animal that was being pursued by Archaic hunters, whether it was thrown, missed its mark, and was subsequently lost, or whether it was intentionally discarded, can never be known, at least not by traditional means. But although the details are subtle, the spearhead is different from the fluted point of the Paleo people and, for that matter, from the triangular points in the case that belong to the Eastern Woodland culture that supplanted the Archaic people. The fact is that at the time that it was made, the people who fashioned the fluted point had disappeared from Scratch Flat and New England. Some archeologists believe that the Paleo people drifted north to tundralike environments, following the big game animals they were familiar with; but the current view is that the Paleo Indians simply evolved into the so-called Archaic culture. The changeover was slow. Between the classic fluted point of the Paleo people and the typical point of the Archaics, there are any number of transitional styles, attempts to come up with a working model. But slow though it may have been by modern technological standards, the change was completed and the finely crafted, delicately fluted Paleo points disappeared. They were replaced by smaller spear points with definite stems and a whole new array of tools associated with food gathering.

A tool known as the atlatl, or spear thrower, was developed during this period. By fitting a spear shaft to a notch at the end of a stick, in effect, the length of the throwing arm could be increased. The spear could be thrown farther and with more accuracy, and fast-moving, wary game such as the caribou could be killed. Harpoons with bifurcated, barbed points were created to hunt fish and aquatic and marine mammals. Adzes and axes were developed to shape wood, awls and needles to pierce and sew hides, and scrapers, bowls, spoons, and tools for preparing plant materials came into being.

This change in habitat in the Scratch Flat region and the subsequent change in the human culture that depended upon the natural habitat was hardly precipitous. The 350 years of European history in Scratch Flat would represent only a small percentage of the time spans involved. But the evidence of the change remains clear even today; you can read it in the vegetation that appears at the edges of the fields, in the pollen samples of the Scratch Flat bogs, and in the projectile point in the glass case in the town library. Scratch Flat is and was the world.

It is interesting to me that Nompenekit and Tonupasqua both more or less agreed with the history I have just described, although they described it in a different way. Glooscap's miraculous reduction of all the animals offers one explanation of the environmental changes that took place; but there is another story which seems to me more specific and which, among other things, gives an account of the manner in which the cranberry came to the world. Tonupasqua said that her grandmother used to tell her the story when she was a little girl and that she had more or less forgotten it until I asked her one night why the mastodon and the mammoth disappeared from the world.

The events which her grandmother described took place, she said, in a time that is almost forgotten. It seems that in those hard times T'chi Manitou put on earth an animal called Yahquahwhee in order to help his children, the Indian people. The Yahquahwhee was clearly a mastodon or a mammoth; it was huge; it had long hair, tusks and a nose like a snake. The T'chi Manitou intended Yahquahwhee to carry things for the people, but the great beast rebelled, refused to work, and became instead a rogue. It made war on the other animals and on its former masters, sometimes spearing them and lifting them high above the ground in its great trunk. The Yahquahwhee was difficult to fight; its skin was thick, and if you came near one, it would lower its head and sway its menacing tusks back and forth like long knives. Finally, the Indians and the animals decided to make war on the Yahquahwhee, and in the autumn of the

year a great battle was fought in a flat plain below a ridge of mountains. Tonupasqua said that mastodons and mammoths from all over
the world came to this battle; they came from the east, from the
south, and the north, and the west. They poured into the valley in
huge numbers, their ranks swelling with the arrival of each new
contingent. This was clearly going to be a decisive fight.

The battle raged for weeks and many animals suffered and died
there. It appeared after the first week that the Yahquahwhee were
going to be victorious; they were good fighters, Tonupasqua said, and
they were well organized. T'chi Manitou became concerned and descended from the sky and lay along the ridge in the form of a dark
cloud. Toward the end of the second week it was clear that the
hideous Yahquahwhee were going to win, but the apparent victory of
the great beasts became its downfall. So many animals died in this
battle that the valley floor was flooded in blood. The great weight of
the mastodons and the mammoths caused them to sink into the mire.
Many drowned and the tide of the battle began to turn; it appeared
that no one would win and all the animals and the people that T'chi
Manitou had created would disappear from the earth. So T'chi Manitou put an end to the war. He rose up in a thunderhead and cast
lightning bolts at the sides of the Yahquahwhee until finally only one
defiant bull was left alive. This great monster, the king of all the
Yahquahwhee, struggled up out of the bloody mire and escaped to
the north where, Tonupasqua assured me, he can still be found.

The valley where this historic battle was fought became a huge
marsh and to this day the bones of mastodon, barren ground caribou,
elk, dire wolves, saber-toothed cats, and other prehistoric animals
can be found buried in the mud. Some day, her grandmother said,
the white bone-hunters will find this marsh. They will dig into the
peat and find the remains of all the animals and know that the Indian
was right. But, Tonupasqua said, there is other evidence of the battle.
In the years following the great war, the Indian people had a hard
time living. There were no more herds of big game to hunt and the
people were forced to eat plants like grazing animals. T'chi Manitou
was disturbed to see his children in such distress and so, in his com-
passion, sent the cranberry to grow in the marshes. Each autumn, in
remembrance of the great war, he causes the coat of the cranberry to
turn blood red.

It is perhaps no more than a curious coincidence that both accounts of the history of the people who lived on Scratch Flat—the white European version and the red American-Asian version—tell essentially the same story. No matter who is telling it, the Indians begin as hunters and then, as the big game disappears, the people vary their diet to include more plant material. But the idea that prehistory is contained in the folktales and myths of the world is very appealing, especially when the stories reflect what we in the West refer to as "the facts."

None of these so-called facts can be determined from the few Archaic Indian artifacts that have been discovered on Scratch Flat; but that is not to say that the area has not been thoroughly picked over by amateur archeologists. In fact, a tradition of mostly erroneous Indian lore has been developed for the area as a result of some of these isolated finds. Ted Demogenes told me once that in the late 1920s intense young men in khaki and snake boots would come to his father's farm at the edge of Beaver Brook and request permission to search the area for arrowheads. The old man, an upright Greek immigrant with an eye on the future and a substantial footing in the present, would always give them permission, Ted said; but after they would leave, he would shake his head in something vaguely reminiscent of disgust or misunderstanding. "Goddamn pickers," he would say. "What's the use of arrowheads? You can't eat, you can't sell."

About one hundred years after the last living Indian disappeared from Scratch Flat, even before the science of archeology was developed, people with an interest in the past began to collect artifacts from Scratch Flat and the surrounding lands. Farmers had uncovered artifacts regularly in the decades before—they would turn up points, stone bowls, and pieces of pottery when they were plowing their fields in spring—and, inspired by these and lacking any accurate information, they probably invented and passed down some of the local Indian lore to their children and grandchildren. The white farmers of Scratch Flat, like the Indian people before them, were great storytellers, and some of the folktales—clear fabrications— have survived in oral tradition to this day.

There is a high hill east of Scratch Flat, about a mile beyond the floodplain of Beaver Brook. On top of the hill there is a large glacial boulder and on top of the boulder there is a shallow depression. One of the established patriarchs in the town, a man who delivers pronouncements on time and place with all the authority of an Eastern sage, told me that this place marks the site of an Indian village and that young virgins were regularly sacrificed on top of the boulder. The bowl would catch the blood, I was told, and the medicine man would wallow in it, drink great gulpfuls, and then dance through the village, growling and barking.

Needless to say, the story is apocryphal, but I do not doubt the truth of the legend. I mean that I believe that the story was told to the old patriarch by his grandfather, who in turn probably heard it at the knee of his father or grandfather. As you will see, there was a short period on Scratch Flat in the late seventeenth century when the Indians of the region were equated with torture, maimings, murder, and other unspeakable atrocities. They haunted the darkness beyond the doors of the first white settlers of Scratch Flat for decades after their disappearance and it is no surprise that they are associated in the local folktales with deeds of violence.

Nevertheless, by the mid-nineteenth century, white attitudes, comforted by the distance of time, began to moderate. One Scratch Flat chronicler called the Indians the "gentle brothers of the forest" and interested parties from outside the community began to actively search for evidence of Indian cultures. Over the past 150 years, along with the artifacts that have been collected, three important Indian sites have been located on Scratch Flat. One of these is at the outlet for Forge Pond, the other is the point of land on Forge Pond, and the third lies on the east side of Ted Demogenes's land on the floodplain of Beaver Brook. Unfortunately, none of these sites has ever been professionally analyzed and so there is no definitive information on the nature of the Indian cultures that used the areas, let alone the time periods in which they were used; all that is known is that from the so-called Archaic period onward, that is, from 8000 B.P. (before present) to A.D. 1774, there were Indians on Scratch Flat.

Professional archeologists are eternally plagued by isolated finds such as those which have been turned up on Scratch Flat. A projectile point or a bowl or a piece of pottery is all but meaningless unless it can be studied in relation to other artifacts in the same strata at the site. Fortunately, however, not far from Scratch Flat, a major Indian hunting camp was discovered in late September of 1978, and was subsequently dug and analyzed by the Institute for Conservative Archeology (ICA) of the Peabody Museum of Harvard University.

As a result of the National Environmental Policy Act, any construction that involves the use of federal funds must file what is known as an environmental impact statement which gives a full account of the local environment and the historical and archeological sites that would be altered by the proposed development. Because of this law, when a new ramp was planned for Route 85, not far from Scratch Flat, Fred Huntington of the ICA was asked to inspect the area for possible archeological sites. Directly in the path of the new section of road there was a large overhanging ledge of glacially deposited material. The rock face was oriented south-southeast, and it curved overhead, so that while not exactly a cave, it would at least have afforded some protection from the elements. It was, in other words, an ideal stopping place for small groups of hunters or for an extended family. Fred Huntington recognized the possibilities immediately. He made a test boring under the overhanging ledge and in the first hole found a selection of artifacts. There followed then what is known in the trade as a salvage dig. Construction of the ramp was halted and for six months, while the bulldozers and the blasters worked in the surrounding area, archeologists and students from the ICA measured, dug, screened, and collected, they believe, most of the artifacts and animal and plant remains from the site. Then, with the important material salvaged, the construction crews returned, holes were drilled in the rock face, and five thousand years of history was dynamited into oblivion.

It appears that this site may have been one of the more important archeological finds in the general area. For one thing, the shelter was used over a very long period of time. Samples of charcoal from the cave were analyzed and carbon 14 dates indicate that people used the site from approximately 4750 B.P. to A.D. 1300, about twenty-five hundred years in other words. Technically, this means that the people would have belonged to two different cultural groups, the so-called late Archaic and groups belonging to the Early Woodlands Indian culture.

But more importantly, perhaps, the rockshelter contained some of the best-preserved animal remains of any site in the Northeast. New England soils are naturally acidic, so bones and other organic matter break down readily and are rarely found in archeological sites. But the rock at Flagg Swamp contained a high amount of bicarbonate, which neutralized the soils. As a result, the bones of the animals and the remains of the plants that were used by the people had not disintegrated. Because of these remains, because of this particular find, it is possible to tell which animals and plants the Indians of the Scratch Flat area were using. In fact, since the site is so close to Scratch Flat and since it lies on the same general river drainage, it is fairly safe to assume that the people of the rockshelter also used the ponds of Scratch Flat, the marshes of Beaver Brook, and the forested drumlin between the brook and Forge Pond.

The late Archaic Indians who first came to the rockshelter were still meat eaters; but the animals that they were hunting were decidedly smaller than the animals that their early Archaic forefathers had hunted. White-tailed deer and wapiti made up part of their diet; but they were also hunting wild turkey, heath hen, muskrat, beaver, woodchuck, rabbit, and raccoon. Skunk, lynx, wolf, and fox remains were also found in the rockshelter, but these animals were probably not consumed as food. The Indians were also feeding on spotted and painted turtles, freshwater snails and mussels, and it appears, from the artifacts found and the bones, that they were accomplished fishermen. Trout, perch, alewife, tomcod and eel bones were found at the site.

The Flagg Swamp cave was primarily a cold-season shelter. Small bands of people would move into the shelter in November or December and then spend the winter there. But a fragment of a fishhook and a small notched stone which could have been used as a sinker indicate that the people were fishing with a hook and a line— probably through holes in the ice. The more common use of nets and weirs would not have been possible in winter.

Plant remains were also found in the debitage of the cave. Nuts, including hickory, hazelnuts, black walnuts, and oak acorns, were found along with the seeds of dogwood, hawthorne, bayberry, grape, and crab apple. The hickories and the walnuts and hazelnuts would have been eaten raw in all likelihood, and the acorns, bitter though they are, would have been soaked, then baked and then finally ground into flour. The seeds, fruits, and, in some instances, the bark of other plants found at the site were also eaten raw or, in the case of the sweeter fruits, thrown into the simmering Indian stews, although this custom may have been more the habit of the later residents of the rockshelter.

It is clear from these remains that the people who were living on Scratch Flat were resourceful food gatherers. They were mobile hunter-gatherers—eating both plants and animals. They appreciated, no doubt, the warmth of the winter sun as it poured into the inner depths of the rockshelter; and it is probable that by this time they were anointing their bodies with grease and oil to keep the flies away in summer, and cut the drying winds of winter. The remains of inedible birds such as screech owls and saw-whet owls were found along with the wild turkeys and the heath hens, and so it is also probable that the Indians were decorating themselves with feathers and mammal skins. Some of these decorative feathers may have been associated with religious ceremonies. And in connection with this, there was one other find in the Flagg Swamp Rockshelter which, to my mind, is the most significant of all.

One afternoon one of the students struck something hard with her trowel. She began to clear around the object and in a few minutes had exposed the top of a flat stone to the open air. She and another worker gently lifted the stone and there, carefully placed beneath it, they saw the skull of a large mammal. This was no ordinary find. The lower jawbone of the animal had been removed and had been placed on top of the head in a precise arrangement. Earth had been packed around the head and then the skull, with its detached jaw, was carefully covered with the stone. It was clearly a ritualistic burial of some sort. The students catalogued the position of the skull, then carefully removed it and packed it up for later analysis. Back at the laboratory at Harvard, the consulting mammalogist for the project identified the animal. It turned out to be a black bear.

It is clear from this find and from other evidence that bears figured heavily in the spiritual life of the Scratch Flat Indians. (They figured heavily in the profane life of the white people of the area too; but that story can come later.) Tonupasqua told me once that while it was T'chi Manitou who created the world and Glooscap who prepared the earth for the people, it was the bear who taught her people how to live. The full significance of all this came to me one evening in Tonupasqua's kitchen. I had mentioned the fact that Nompenekit had told me that another figure had emerged from the forest that night at Forge Pond to dance, and when she admitted, after some prodding, that there was indeed something else there, I asked her, almost in passing, if it had been a bear, or a bear shaman. She had a visible reaction. Tonupasqua has a way of glancing at you just before she is about to lie, a certain quick, almost surreptitious dart of the eyes, and for a while she denied that the figure, the "other man," had anything to do with bears.

"Wasn't no bear man there," she said, and busied herself with the salt and pepper shakers on her table. I could see the beginnings of a smile working over her face—always a sign in her that a truth or a good lie is about to emerge. I kept grilling her in our light, joking manner, and finally she told me the story.

"You got to understand," she said. "The bear and my people, we're no different, see. On this land where you live there were once a lot of bears. There was good hunting there. Back long ago there was a medicine man. He was a famous man, could do a lot of healing. This man's name was Pokawnau, or bear, and he had a lot of things he could do; but the best was that he could turn himself into a bear. So that's what happened. Pokawnau came out of the woods when we were there last summer and danced with us. T'chi Manitou was in him."

"Did he sing?" I asked.

"No, just danced. Round and round. Then he went back to the spirit world."

I asked her if Pokawnau lived in the forest around there and if he could be seen by anyone else, a white person for example, and whether he was a good spirit or a bad spirit.

"Well, I can tell you this," she said. "He is angry. See, something happened to him in that place, something happened to the bear, I think. I don't know what it was. But he lost power somehow. He lost something."

"What was it, did he tell you?"

"No, he don't talk in English. But he can communicate. There was a death, or something. A bad death maybe." She twisted her head slightly at this point, as if in remembered pain. "He is not happy," she said.

"Tonupasqua, how do you know all this after a few minutes dancing with some spirit form? How can you tell all this unless you know him better than you are saying?"

"I know things."

"How?"

"I know. Long ago, I know this," and at this point she rolled her arm outward to indicate the passage of time.

According to Tonupasqua's story, Pokawnau was one of those

shamans who have appeared from time to time in the legends and histories of the Indians of New England. If I have my chronologies right, he lived in human form about fifteen hundred years ago. "Before Crow brought corn to the people," is the way Tonupasqua told it—before the development of agriculture, in other words, which means over a thousand years ago. There is no white record of this shaman's presence, but Tonupasqua's uncle—her apparent source for most of the folklore—told her a lot of stories about his tricks. He could, for example, fly from the tops of trees; he never ate human food, and he could see events that had not yet taken place. Pokawnau was in his original existence a black bear. When he was still a young cub, a group of hunters captured him and carried him to their village. He was nursed there by a human mother and kept for one year as a pet. Then one day the people led him to a place outside the stockade and tied him to a stake. They circled him for a few hours, dancing and singing, and then, as the dance reached a frenzy, they shot arrows into him and killed him. His head was cut off and placed on a shelf in one of the huts and surrounded with knives, arrowheads, and other tools of the hunt. After that, a feast was held. The bear was "fed" with human food, and then the head was carried to the center of the village and placed on a pole and he was "married" to a young woman in the tribe. After his marriage, his head was taken down and carried out into the forest. The people dug a hole, broke off the lower jaw, and put it on top of his head and buried him. Now, Tonupasqua told me, he was ready for his journey to the southwest, his journey to the spirit world of his people.

Not long after this ritual, Pokawnau was born and lived with the people until his death. And even after he died, people would often see him in the forest. Sometimes he would appear to them as a bear, sometimes he would appear as a man; but in either form, he could impart information to the shamans who sought him.

"And did Pokawnau tell you anything that night?" I asked her.

"Yes, many things. He told me what I am telling you. He told me all these stories."

"I thought your uncle told you all this."

"Did I say that?"

"Yes. You said your uncle told you about Pokawnau and his miracles."

"Well, maybe I did."

"But who was it, Pokawnau or your uncle?"

"It was both," she said. "They are the same."

6

EATING
SCRATCH FLAT

It would be very easy, hearing all these stories of bear spirits from a distance of who knows how much time and space, to think that all these events are exotic accounts from a distant country and have no relation to our time or to the place where you happen to live. But the fact is, the place I am describing is no more than thirty-five miles west of Boston. Except for Scratch Flat itself, which because of the presence of the open farmlands has a definite character about it, this section of the Northeast is not discernibly different from anywhere else in the region. You can see in this part of the country what remains of the traditional New England village centers with their white church steeples; you will see, on the outskirts of the older village greens, the developments of newer houses, some built in the 1920s, some as late as the 1950s or 1960s; and beyond these, and still farther out from the village centers, you will see the newer developments; and in some communities, particularly in the nearby town of Acton, you will see apartments, shopping centers, and condominiums. Many of these are carefully landscaped, and at least some of them attempt to fit in to the general rural character of the region.

Most of the people who live in these dwellings have no knowledge of bear shamans or American Indian rituals. They rise in the morning; they drive to work in Boston; they drive home; they eat prepared dinners; they watch television, go to the movies, go to the theater, go skiing, or go to dinner parties; and then they drive home in the darkness of night with the black line of the yet-undeveloped hills beyond them, and rarely think about the fact that not so very long ago primitive hunter-gatherers, smeared in bear fat and clay paint, might have moved through those hills. I know all this because most of the time I do it myself. It is only because I consciously work at it, because I spent time poking around the forgotten corners of my land looking for history, that I am able to glimpse another perspective. Basically, the place that I am writing about is as firmly set in the realities of the late-twentieth-century as the busiest corner of New York City or San Francisco. The electronic media have seen to that. The people who live on Scratch Flat are heading blithely towards the twenty-first century, their hearts and minds filled with the eternal presence of the nightly news, as if this era in which we live, this little match snap of the present in the great darkness of history, is the only reality. But I am learning to think in Nompenekit's Indian time, and I can tell you from my limited traveling in this area that the world around here, the world in most places on the American continent, is turned upside down. The spirits of the bear shamans have not yet been evicted.

I take great comfort now in the presence of the pines and the oaks that grow around my house. There is a certain continuum that I can see there, a unity with the past five thousand years of history. The remnants of the glacial period, the boulder, the drumlin, and the bogs and spruce trees are real enough to me, but they exist somehow on a different plane. By contrast, the current flora and fauna of the place, the skunks and the foxes, all belong to our time—this little interglacial period known as the late Pleistocene. With the advent of the eastern woodland flora and fauna, some five thousand years ago, the erstwhile time traveler enters the brightly lit world of the Eastern Woodland Indian, an era which is well understood by archeologists and anthropologists and which marks, in its final years, the beginning of the European historical period.

I have never thought of Scratch Flat as the "country." That is, in spite of the fact that the place is characterized primarily by woods and fields, streams and ponds; and in spite of the fact that, on Sunday afternoons, people in city clothes and clean foreign cars drive out to the little valley where Scratch Flat is located to look at the horses and the cows, to shop at the farm stands, and, in autumn, to pick apples and pears from the many orchards in the valley; the place has always seemed to me a somewhat crowded, rural area in the process of becoming a suburb. This is, no doubt, partly due to the fact that before I moved here, I was taking care of a sixty-acre property on Martha's Vineyard, and that before that I had lived in the middle of some sixty thousand acres of state forestland in northwestern Connecticut, an area that was singularly lacking in housing of any sort—there were not even any farms in the region. At night, in any season there, you could step outside the door of the stone cottage in which I lived and hear, all across the hills, the wild yowling of owls, the rushing of streams, the sharp bark of foxes, and occasionally, the lonely yelp of the eastern coyote. It was all forest and brooks, and miles of hills, unhoused and well-suited for roaming. I would take off sometimes in the morning and wander at will until dusk, picking my way home through a dark, ominous landscape.

Although I was born at the cutting edge of New York City, I had become used to the immense stillness of those western New England hills and the dull night-throb of the Atlantic on the south shore of the Vineyard. To hear the hiss of a distant superhighway, to hear a power mower, no matter how far away, or to hear, in autumn, the whine of a chainsaw seemed to me the ultimate in overcrowding. I felt as if I had moved to a very busy corner of the world in Scratch Flat. It took me several years to get used to the noises around me; and I still am not able to experience here the wild sense of nothingness that I used to feel in the hills around East Hartland, Connecticut. This is probably the reason why I became interested in the history of Scratch Flat and began to explore that greater wilderness of time.

Having said all this, however, I should point out that friends and allies who come to visit Scratch Flat marvel at the rural feeling of the place (not the beauty, mind you; this is working farm country). And looking over the land surrounding my house, I suppose there is here a certain slack, uncared-for character about the fields, and the stream, and the woods. I once met a man from the nearby suburban town of Lincoln, an avid canoeist who described to me a beautiful creek of slow-moving dark waters which wound for three or four miles through high marsh grasses and crowning highlands. "It was like Africa there," he said. "Bird cries around you, grasses sweeping the canoe, not a single house, four miles without a human being." It took me a while to realize that he was talking about Beaver Brook.

There is a newer house just to the south of my home which can be seen when the leaves are off the trees. But behind my house, the pine forest stretches back for three quarters of a mile to the shores of Forge Pond. To the north, beyond a small overgrown field and past a deserted farmhouse, lies another dwelling, this one constructed in the 1750s by Jeremiah Caswell. South of the Caswell place, on the land now owned by Charlie Lignos, and east of my house there is nothing but woods and fields rolling down in a series of natural terraces to the marshes along Beaver Brook. The view from my kitchen window, from my plum grove, or from the hollyhocks in the gardens goes back four thousand years to the coming of the oaks and the pines. Over the drumlin to the south and west where the farmland lies, it goes back a thousand years to the beginnings of agriculture. The place is infused with time; everywhere you look, east or west, north or south, there is history; there are stories, and ghosts, and bear spirits. And if you look carefully through woodlands to the southeast, glimmering through the tangle of oak and pine, on winter nights you can see, in the lighted windows of the new computer companies that have come to Scratch Flat, the spirits of the future.

When I first came to Scratch Flat, I used to spend a lot of time looking for wild foods. I had learned the art of food gathering from a friend of mine in Connecticut and had come to enjoy both the act of foraging and the admittedly strong tastes of some of the wild plants that grow in New England. My friend the Red Cowboy is a forager too, a far more dedicated one than I am; in fact, he even depends on wild food for survival from time to time. On his frequent visits after I moved to the land, he and I would roam out over the old fields and the farmlands looking for food. It was about this time that I became interested in hunter-gatherer cultures, and during one of the Red Cowboy's visits, I got into a long discussion with him about the possibilities of surviving from the land in twentieth-century America. I was wondering then whether it would still be possible to live without buying food. He had thought all this through, he told me, and he declared that he would prove to me that it was possible; we would live for a week, he said, on foods that he collected within walking distance of my house. Fortunately, that experiment fell apart after the fourth day; but in the few days that we did spend foraging, I think I learned a lot about the early Woodland Indian people who lived from time to time on Scratch Flat. We were, after all, feeding off the same species of plants and animals.

Our food-gathering experiment took place in the summer (a fortuitous time for such a test, to be sure). Red Cowboy and I would get up in the early morning and, fortified with noncaloric drugs—i.e., black coffee—we would range out over Scratch Flat in search of breakfast. The blueberries were in season then, and since there was a profusion of berry bushes in a cutover section of pine woods on Jimmy Starkos's land, the Red Cowboy would always start there. We would pass through the stumps and old slash, quietly plucking berries, saving a few in our packs, but, true to form, eating most of them from the bush. Later in the morning we would go down to the bridge over Beaver Brook and fish for black bass, bluegills, or catfish. These the Red Cowboy would plank-fry over a fire we built in the woods behind my house. We were purists in the first day or two of the experiment; later we would use butter and a frying pan over the kitchen stove; and later still we would roll the fish in breadcrumbs and bacon bits. Most of the fresh greens, the new shoots of mustard for example, had grown old and bitter by the time of year in which we were collecting; but the Red Cowboy did manage to find some groundnuts growing on the southeast edge of Jimmy's land; and at the edge of Forge Pond I found a patch of hog peanuts, although there were hardly enough to supply us with one meal. By the end of the second day we were getting a little desperate. More and more the Red Cowboy would range along the edges of Beaver Brook looking for cattails, arrowhead tubers, and other aquatic plants. By the third day we didn't even bother to go into the woods and fields anymore. We went straight to the brook, gathered our quota of cattail stems and arrowhead tubers, and walked home to cook them up. Later that same afternoon, on a log about 50 yards up the brook from the bridge, I saw a group of painted turtles basking, piled one on top of the other in quest for the sun. I looked at the Red Cowboy and without a word he took off his pants and slid quietly into the water. I swam after him to help catch the escapees. Slowly, with his eyes just above the surface, the Red Cowboy swam or waded toward the baskers. They were alert to his presence, but every time it looked like the turtles were about to dive, the Red Cowboy would stop moving and remain quietly in the water until they relaxed. He knew that if one of them went, they would all go. When he was about five yards from the log, they splashed in, first an old one at the top of the pile, and then, one after another, the smaller ones. The Red Cowboy dove as soon as they dropped and I followed him. The water was murky, but ahead of me I could see the white body of my friend, his arms flying out in all directions. One of the turtles broke past him and swam toward the bottom. I made a grab, felt him, lost him for a second, and then caught him again. Red Cowboy caught two, not a bad haul, I suppose, for so primitive a hunting method. Later, although he admitted that he had never eaten painted turtles before, the Red Cowboy made a stew of our three captives. It had a dull pondlike taste to it, and there was very little meat.

"If only we could catch ourselves a nice fat whistle pig, we'd be sitting pretty," the Red Cowboy told me after the meal.

"What's a whistle pig?"

"You know, an old woodchuck."

I knew where there was a woodchuck hole in Charlie Lignos's lower hayfield and the next day, the fourth day of our experiment, I took him down to the hole. I have never known a man who is as patient as the Red Cowboy. Like an old terrier, he spent the better part of that morning waiting over the hole for the whistle pig to come out. He waited again that evening and then returned at dawn of the fifth day to try to catch him when he came out for breakfast.

"That son of a bitch has just got to eat sometime," he said.

In the meantime, while the Red Cowboy was watching the whistle pig's hole, I was assigned to gather more of our staple—cattails and arrowhead tubers. I was, by that time, getting a little bored of this game. Although the cattails had a fresh pealike taste, the tubers were dull and starchy; and since we were not using any spices and not adding any flour, or butter, or sweetener to our fare, the meals were becoming something of an ordeal. I am a man who lives to eat; but in those few days, I found that Red Cowboy and I were not only eating simply to live, we were spending most of our time trying to get the food. Except for the fact that I knew it was a temporary aberration, it was a rather dull and highly uncivilized existence—which, of course, was the whole point.

Red Cowboy returned that morning without his whistle pig. We ate arrowhead tubers for lunch, and then set out again to fish and hunt the marshes for more turtles, preferably a big twenty-pound snapper. We took my kayak this time, and gathered a boat load of arrowhead tubers and cattails just in case we didn't catch anything. About a mile downstream from the Great Road, I thought I saw what I was hoping for—an immense snapping turtle just below the surface. Without a word, I vaulted overboard and tried to catch it, but the thing escaped into the murky depths. Around a bend in the stream we came across a family of black ducks, a mother with a brood of seven or eight young ones. They were still flightless, but on our approach they churned into the long grasses and disappeared. We saw a great blue heron a little farther along, but he too ponderously rose up and flapped off before we got anywhere near him. We found birds' nests in the cattails, but they were all empty; and by the time we had reached the bridge at the lower end of Beaver Brook, we had found nothing out of the ordinary to eat, no more turtles, no birds, not even a frog.

This experiment was all terribly illegal; you are not allowed, at this point in the twentieth century, to arbitrarily eat herons, or turtles, or birds' eggs. But as far as I know, there is no law against eating insects; and so, at the end of the fifth day, having lost, by that time, about three or four pounds, and having suffered from a headache most of the time, and having lived with hunger like a constant companion, the Red Cowboy, somewhat to my horror, began to consider the possibility. We were sitting on my back porch eyeing a paper wasp nest at the corner of an arbor I had built across the back of the house, when he broached the subject.

"You know, Johnny, almost two thirds of the world eats insects," Red Cowboy told me.

I knew this fact already, and once or twice, partly as a joke, had eaten carpenter ants, but only one or two at most. I knew what the Red Cowboy had in mind; and before I could disagree, he had brushed away the slow-moving polistes wasps and brought the nest onto the porch. There we picked out the grubs and laid them on the table. We ate a few raw, and then, finding them tasteless, decided to fry the rest in butter. In the process, partly at the urging of my wife, who had endured all this with patient suspicion (not an uncommon state of mind concerning some of my projects), we added a clove of garlic to the wasp larvae, and then a little fresh thyme, and then, finally, just to improve things slightly, a dash of sherry and a little white pepper. We ate the grubs by candlelight to celebrate the end of our experiment.

"Sure do wish I could have caught that old whistle pig though," Red Cowboy said after the meal.

In spite of the lighthearted spirit in which our food-gathering lark was carried out, it was, in retrospect, a significant experience. The foods that we were eating and the habitats that we were foraging in were the same as the Eastern Woodland Indians had exploited. For one thing, I learned that the gathering of food, and especially the preparation of foods in order to get through a season of dearth, must have taken a considerable amount of time. Secondly, although we used shovels for the groundnuts, and a hook and line for the fish, it would take a great deal of skill in toolmaking, stalking, and fishing to actually construct all the tools and weapons from the natural materials at hand and then use them in a way to be certain to catch or kill whatever it is you were after. It is also significant, I think, that by the third day of our experiment, the Red Cowboy was suggesting ways to "improve" our habitat. He wanted to move the turtle log closer to high ground; he wanted to build a weir at the narrow neck at Beaver Brook (in an area where there may actually have been a weir two thousand years ago), and he was going to build a fire at one of the whistle pig's many entrances and smoke him out. It was no surprise to me when I learned, a year or so after our food foray, that the Woodland Indians of the region became adept at managing the land to fit their needs, and began—until their progress was rudely interrupted by history—to develop agriculture.

In connection with this it is interesting to note that, along with the nuts of forest trees in the remains at the Flagg Swamp rockshelter, the seeds of plants in the goosefoot family were found. These plants are common today in Scratch Flat; they appear with annoying regularity in my garden and along the edges of Jimmy-George Starkos's beet fields. Pigweed and other plants in the family prefer open, disturbed soils; they are not plants of the deep woods; and yet they were found in abundance in the floor of the shelter. This must mean that somewhere around Flagg Swamp there was open ground or disturbed soil, which would be expected if the Indians were practicing agriculture. The people who used the rockshelter were hunter-gatherers; but perhaps, even by that early date, they were reordering things somewhat, "improving" the habitat to encourage the growth of certain species of wild crops. All this is speculation, and my time frames are probably off; but at some point in the three-thousand year period between the first occupation of the rockshelter and the beginning of agriculture in the area, the people who lived around here must have been carrying out some sort of experimentation.

It is known that at the time of the arrival of the Europeans, the Indians were practicing a form of game management; and it appears from the records that the Nashoba Valley was one area that was intensively managed, which is to say that there has not been any untouched wild land here for at least four hundred years, possibly one thousand to two thousand years. The Indians of the early Woodland period were, as the bones in the rockshelter indicate, feeding on the white-tailed deer. In order to improve the deer herds, they would burn off the undergrowth of large sections of forestland. This would encourage new browse for the deer to feed on, would clear the ground of dry twigs and brush to make stalking easier, and would encourage the growth of another common Indian food plant, the blueberry. In our time the shoots of oak and pine, blueberries, and other small shrubs grow beneath the larger trees in the Scratch Flat woods and the forest floor is littered with fallen trunks and limbs, but this does not fit the early European descriptions of the region. Early records indicate that the woods in that time consisted of open stands of large trees, and one could see under the upper branches.

The Indians who moved through this open forestland in search of the white-tailed deer were essentially the same as the Archaic people; but not only had they learned to alter the existing habitat, to improve hunting, they had also developed a number of new tools to deal with the environment. The bow and arrow was invented in the Woodland period; the people used bolas to catch birds; ceramics came into use during this time; and the art of basketry was developed. Bowls, cups, platters, and spoons were carved from the malleable soapstone; nut stones or nut anvils, as well as the mortar and pestle, the mano and matate or grinding stones, and the stone pipe were developed during the same period. The late Archaic and early Woodland Indians were good woodworkers. Using stone axes, picks, drills, gouges, and similar devices, they were able to fashion not only spear shafts, atlatls, bows and arrows, but also bowls and dishes and other implements. But the final invention, the greatest revolution, was yet to come.

Some archeologists theorize that the changes that occurred in the late Archaic and early Woodland cultures were the result of events that were taking place far to the west of Scratch Flat and New England in the Ohio Valley. About twenty-five hundred years ago, the mound-building Adena culture of the region was invaded or overwhelmed by the Hopewell people from the west. It has been suggested, although the theory is controversial, that small bands of Adena people, displaced, or at least disgruntled with the new Hopewell customs, wandered east and became absorbed by the Indian cultures of New England. The Adena people brought with them the artifacts of their culture—tubular beads, rolled copper, small stones shaped like birds, bowls, and egg-shaped projectile points with extended stems. They also brought with them the art of ceramics, and—if the theory is correct—they quite literally carried with them the seeds of the most dramatic change that had yet to occur in Scratch Flat or anywhere else in New England. They brought with them the art of agriculture.

The Indian people in the area must have been ready for a system of organized agriculture; they were already practicing game management and, more or less by fiat, forest management; and it may even be possible that they recognized that by disturbing the soil they could encourage useful wild plants such as the goosefoot. How soon after the arrival of the idea of agriculture in the region the people of Scratch Flat began to clear the forest to create openings for gardens is not known. Nor is it clear at what point the flatlands surrounding the drumlin were cleared and planted. What is known is that the land along the floodplain of Beaver Brook and the bottom land on the west side of the tract is good for growing nonnative crops; and it is also known that the Indians were quick to take advantage of beneficial situations. Since it was already recognized as a hunting ground by the local people, it is likely that Scratch Flat was cleared and farmed fairly soon after the arrival of the concept of agriculture in the region.

The farming that the Woodland Indians practiced was similar to the swidden, or slash-and-burn, horticultural systems that are now used by primitive Indian cultures in the Amazon region. The men cut off the smaller trees and burned the larger ones at the bottom of the trunk, leaving the stumps in the ground. Working as a group, the men and women broke up the soil using hoes made of deer shoulder blades or clamshells. Later, the women pulled heaps of soil together, placing beneath each hill one or two fish. From April to June, the women planted corn; and, at the same time, squash and beans were set on the hill and allowed to grow up together with the corn.

Toby Beckwith, who has made himself something of an authority on Indian agriculture, tells me that this is a fortuitous combination. The beans, which are nitrogen-fixers, fed the corn, which is a heavy nitrogen consumer; the corn provided a climbing place for the beans; and the beans and the corn together provided the right amount of shade for the squash. Furthermore, the protein available from corn or beans is greater when the two crops are consumed together. Throughout the summer growing season, the women guarded the garden patch, keeping weeds, raccoons, squirrels, deer, and other invaders at bay. Toby told me that some tribes had tamed hawks that were tied near the garden patch to keep marauding blackbirds off; and, in some places, wooden towers were constructed and a boy was posted on twenty-four hour guard.

The harvested corn was either eaten green, boiled and then dried, or dried on the cob. All of the harvest that was not eaten immediately, which is to say, most of it, was stored in barns, or underground pits lined, in some cases, with stone. Toby says that one of these pits may have existed on Scratch Flat up into the twentieth century. There was, on the south side in the ill-fated Cobble Hill, a small section dug away, which was by tradition referred to as an "Indian house." Sometime in the 1920s when the Demogenes family first moved onto the farm, part of this pit was dug out. Toby questioned those who remember the place and is fairly certain that it was an Indian storage pit, although there is no way of really knowing.

A few years ago, as a part of his research on Indian agriculture, Toby decided to plant an Indian garden. He is not unfamiliar with gardening theories; his father was an orchardist for a while and his mother is a good gardener of the old school; and one year Toby successfully raised and sold in the Haymarket in Boston the produce from a 20-acre patch of land that he owns just beyond the confines of Scratch Flat. Nonetheless his Indian garden was a failure.

He religiously cleared off a small patch of land, dug the hills, fertilized them with fish, and then planted, in traditional Indian fashion, four kernels of corn in each hill, "one for each direction." Later he planted the beans, and then still later, when it was warm enough, he put in that queen of Indian crops, the pumpkin. Crows came and dug up his first planting of corn. Grackles got the next, and cutworms got a third. The fourth one survived to knee height, and the surrounding beans and pumpkins were growing well until borers got into his cornstalks and spread to the beans and then finally to the vines of the pumpkins. Toby went at them fanatically, digging out the grubs when he could find them; but before the summer was half over they had wiped out half of his harvest. His beans ripened before the corn, did quite well in fact; but squirrels began to make raids from the surrounding forest, and after them came, Toby says, "a veritable army of raccoons. Rank on rank, their generals in the fore, flag bearers and all." True to the Indian fashion, Toby had planted successive crops; but the squirrels got the first and the raccoons got the second and third. The pumpkins grew well enough, but they were a sad lot in comparison to the pumpkins of Jimmy Starkos, grown with nontraditional agribusiness technologies—chemical fertilizers, pesticides and all.

In his theatrical sort of way, Toby has drawn an all-encompassing conclusion from the failure of his garden. "It failed," he said, "because it was not grown by women." Long before the women's movement, before the advent of sexual politics, Toby had fully developed his theory of women. I will not give a full account of his theories because they do not necessarily pertain to the history of Scratch Flat, but basically he believes that in woman is the salvation of the world. Everything that has gone wrong in history is the fault of men, he says: wars, famine, plagues, the development of weapons, racism, and, of course, sexism. By contrast, Toby says, everything that has been right in the world—flowers, music, poetry, and so on—is due to the influence, either directly or indirectly, of women. All women have a basic nurturing, life-sustaining drive, Toby says; furthermore they are capable of producing life. "Men cannot have babies," Toby says grandly. "And so they make, instead, war. They tell the world that women are weak, that women cannot drive so simple a thing as a car, that they cannot function in the real world of finance because they have periods, that they cry, that they cannot run fast and that they are emotional. Men are jealous, don't you see. They can't have babies so they make a building or a bridge or worse, an idea, and then they tell you that this is more important than a life."

Women gave the world agriculture, Toby says, and to prove it he cites, among other events, the horticultural work of the late Woodland Indian women. The men cleared the land, "did the dumb work—ox or mule could have done it better," Toby says—the women did the rest. It was the Indian women who performed the early genetic experiments that increased the thumb-sized corn cob brought into New England to the full-sized ears that were given to William Bradford and the other early settlers at Plymouth. It was women who, long before the invention of soil chemistry and plant physiology, made the realization that the corn, beans, and squash grown together in the same hill would do better than the same crops grown separately. It was Indian women who learned about fertilization with fish. The fact that a man named Squanto taught this technique to the Pilgrims at Plymouth is, Toby says, one of the typical perversions of history. "Squanto probably had never put a herring in the ground in his life up to that point," Toby says. "He just knew about it because he had seen women do it." It was Indian women who drove off the crows, Indian women who weeded the gardens, and finally, it was the women who harvested the crops, ground the corn, and prepared the meals.

"My garden failed because the traditional Indian garden was a woman's art. I did everything right in that garden; but because I am a man, it wouldn't grow. It is a system that needs a womans' hand. There is some other element, you see, that we men don't know about."

There is, at present, a certain amount of discussion as to the name of the people who lived in the Nashoba Valley and Scratch Flat after the Archaic period ended. Generally, whoever lived here belonged to a larger group known as the Algonquian complex, which was basically a linguistic congregation of loosely related people. This larger group was broken up into tribes, which, in turn, were broken into smaller related groups, which may have been divided further into small extended family organizations. There is, as there often is in such cases, a lot of argument about how this system worked, and about which tribe lived where, and what group moved into which territory. But the general belief is that the Algonquians organized themselves by river drainage patterns; and since Scratch Flat is on Beaver Brook which, after many a turn, flows into the Merrimack River, it has been suggested that the people in this area were Pawtuckets. They might also, at any given time, have been Nipmucks, or Massachusetts; and at one point in history, rather late as far as this story is concerned, the people in this region may have been referred to as the Nashoba.

Generally it seems that the Pawtuckets who lived in the immediate area were a peaceful sort of people. On any given day in the thousand-year period that stretches from the beginning of agriculture to the arrival of the English, they would get up in the morning and, depending on the season, go about their various tasks. The women would prepare the stew pot and set it over the fire in the center of the wigwam; the men would work on spear points, and then the tribe would go off to work—the women to the garden in summer, the men to hunt or fish. During this period, agriculture was surpassing hunting as a food source. Whereas in the early Archaic period meat made up the greater part of the diet of the people in the area, even before the advent of horticulture, plants—all of them gathered by the women—were becoming a major source of nutrition; and by the time agriculture was established, the men were hunting as a supplement to the plant food, rather than vice versa.

In late fall, winter, and early spring, the men would hunt regularly, in some cases driving deer through elaborate temporary stockades and sometimes stalking them separately. Moose, elk, bear, lynx, bobcat, mountain lion, and other large animals were hunted either for food or clothing, as were smaller game such as beavers, woodchucks, rabbits, skunks, and raccoons. Like the Archaic people, the Woodland Indians fished through the year; fishing holes were pierced in the ice at Forge Pond and in ice-free seasons the men made use of the net or the weir. There was an important weir on Beaver Brook somewhere south of the Great Road, apparently a favorite fishing spot that was passed down from generation to generation. There was another weir at the outlet of Forge Pond that was also "owned" and passed down through the ages. Net sinkers have been found at the edge of Beaver Brook and Forge Pond, and arrowheads and other artifacts have been found on the flats between the pond and the drumlin, and along the Beaver Brook. Tools such as the adze and steatite bowls have also been found in the same general area, indicating that there must have been villages, or at least camps, in Scratch Flat throughout the Woodland period.

In spite of all these isolated discoveries, however, no major digs have been carried out in the general area; although, as I think I have made clear, all this means is that no professional archeologists have bothered to look. There is, however, among the Scratch Flat legends a Woodland Indian burial ground, in the northwest corner of the tract, where, according to word of mouth, many artifacts were once uncovered and many important Indian figures are buried. During Tonupasqua's first visit to Scratch Flat, when she had the grand tour by car, I parked as near to this supposed site as I could and tried to persuade her to trek through the woods with me to the place. I didn't tell her about the burial ground, I was, at this point, still more or less "testing" her, but I was very interested in her reaction. She wouldn't walk into the woods with me, but she did go off by herself along the edge of the wall beside the road and then stood for a while staring into the gloom of the hemlocks and white pines.

"You know this place around here?" she asked, after a few minutes.

"Not really, no, I'm trying to find out though."

"Well there's Indians round here somewhere."

"Buried you mean?"

"I don't know. I just think there was Indians here. Very near this place."

A few weeks later I went out to the site with a soil borer, planning to make a few test drills. I had been told that the site was located at the southwest corner of two stone walls, not far from the New England Electric Company power lines. It was one of those still summer days that sometimes occur on Scratch Flat, the type of day when there isn't any sound in all the world except for the quick buzz of a rising fly, and the high lazy call of the red-eyed vireos. I walked along the top of the wall, skipping from stone to stone, in order to not have to walk through the thick underbrush. I had a strange feeling as I moved deeper and deeper into the oak and hemlock forest. The air was close, primordial almost, and hot, and even though I didn't expect to find anything, I had a sense of exploration, a sense that I was about to step into some new and wholly comfortable territory where peace and stillness reigned. At the site, before digging, I sat on the wall for a while and listened to the stillness. It occurred to me that I ought to meditate, or close my eyes, or listen for some message from the grave in order to know where to dig; but the day was too relaxed for that sort of thing; this was merely an outing, one more excuse to be out on the land.

Not surprisingly, I started to think about the Indians who might be buried there. Gordon Lesley, the man who passed on the legends of the grave site to me, said the information about it had come from the various families who had lived on the farm on which the burial ground is located, which means, in all probability, that this wasn't really an Indian burial ground so much as a place where Indians happened to have been interred by white people, or at least so I figured. I began to think about the real people who were put in the ground. Were they old men or were they women, or children? Were they sloppy drunks who would sing and tell stories for a spot of rum? Or were they hardened fighters, who hid in the woods and lived off the land, hoping that this bad dream of the white man would disappear, and then only came out of the forest when it was time to die? I had a sense suddenly, not of the past, not a rollback of time, but of the reality of these late Woodland Indians—the theories they must have had to summon up to explain the presence of white men, the confusion they must have felt seeing the old ways pass and hearing the stories of the time before the time, when there were no white men and when everything progressed according to its way, the winter after the fall and the summer and the spring, and the beavers in the brook, and the deer at the forest edge. The past must have seemed to them, as it often does to us, a sort of golden age, a time before the world got turned upside down. I felt all at once a tremendous sense of sharing with these obscure Indians. They were very like us. Four hundred years ago they lived the essential twentieth-century experience, the conflicts wrought by abrupt and total cultural change.

Ever since that moment I have felt a closeness to the survivors of that terrible time in Indian history. And I realized the chauvinism of the act of digging up their graves, as if our time, our reality, and our culture, is the real thing and what we live now is all there ever was and all there ever will be.

7

A WOODLAND
NATION

Every year at Thanksgiving Nompenekit and a group of his native American friends get in White Bird's van and drive down Route 3 to Plymouth, Massachusetts. There, joined with people of a similar mind, they gather at the monument at Plymouth Rock and spend the day, not celebrating, but mourning that fateful point back in 1620 when, according to tradition, Bradford and company stepped ashore and established the first permanent European settlement in the New World. This great occasion in American history, this hard coming into the thankless New England November, will live forever as a day of infamy for Nompenekit and his people. It is symbolically the blackest period in their twelve-thousand-year reign, the literal end of an era.

Nevertheless it was inevitable; world history is littered with such invasions, although none quite so subtle. There was not one of them, on either side, who could have imagined the changes that would take place as a result of the founding of that small colony. Up to that point the changes that had occurred in the northeast were all but imperceptible to the people who lived in the region; they evolved over generations and are recorded only in the folktales of the aborigi-

nal people and the changes that archeologists note in the Indian
artifacts of the period. But after the arrival at Plymouth, within the
space of twenty years, the newcomers began to alter the lives of the
local natives and the forested environment of the continent. Plymouth was only a symbol. Given the conditions in Europe, the invasion would have taken place somewhere, and of course there had
been trade ("exploitation" is the word Nompenekit uses) for almost
100 years before the first colony was established.

The effect of this pre-colonial contact between the two cultures
can be seen in the metal axes, knives, glass beads, and other European goods that are found alongside traditional Indian artifacts in
the archeological sites of this period. On the darker side, another
import had appeared in the region about the same time, this one a
virus or a bacteria. Not long after the European trade began, a series
of plagues began to sweep through the American Indian populations
of the northeast. The plagues appeared in three successive waves and
in the end wiped out, it is believed, fully one-third of the Indians of
the region. Given the size of the native population at the time, this
was far more devastating than the various plagues of Europe and was
in effect the real undoing of the American Indian cultures in the east.
Plymouth was not the beginning of the end for the Indian; it was the
end of the beginning. By 1620 the work had been done.

Which of the many European explorers made the discovery that
eventually led to the destruction of the American Indian cultures is
under debate. Ever since the early nineteenth century, evidence has
appeared, carved in the rocks of New England and other sections of
the country, as far west as Wisconsin, suggesting the existence of
Viking colonies, of Celtic kings, hermitages of Irish Culdee monks,
explorations of Scottish princes, and even entourages of Phoenician
and Iberian explorers. Most of these fabulous discoveries, it turns
out, have been placed there by the imaginations of amateur archeologists; but local legend, substantiated in this particular case by at least
a few facts, suggests that an early Scottish explorer may have buried
one of his fellow knights on a hillside just to the northeast of Beaver
Brook. If it is true, this means that the first white man came to
Scratch Flat not in the early 1640s, as the standard histories suggest,
but in the fall of 1399.

From my sanctuary in the plum grove it is possible to look
down across the terraced fields of the Lignos land, across the valley

of the Beaver Brook, to a rounded eminence known as Prospect Hill. On the northeast side of this hill there is a shelf of bedrock that was scraped bare by the glacier and was grooved in the process by sharp stones and boulders carried in the body of the ice. Such glacial scratches, as they are technically called, are common throughout New England. On the bedrock on Prospect Hill, two of them are joined at one end by a series of small pockmarks in the stone. If you look carefully, you will see that the ledge is dotted with groups of these holes and that they seem to form patterns. Back in 1946 amateur archeologists from Connecticut thought they could see on the rock the image of a sword. One of these intrepid hunters, Frank Glynn of the Connecticut Archeological Society, made a tracing of the sword in 1950 and sent it to T. C. Lethbridge at the Museum of Archeology and Ethnology at Cambridge, England. Lethbridge identified the weapon as a fourteenth-century hand and a half-wheel pommel sword. Furthermore, he stated, in a letter to Glynn, that in England images of such swords generally appear in the hand of a knight. So Frank Glynn went back to the hill above Scratch Flat, stared at the ledge for a while, and then suddenly saw, in all its fourteenth-century splendor, the image of a full knight in armor, complete with sword and shield, falcon and helmet.

But how did this mysterious knight come to Scratch Flat some two hundred fifty years before the first settlement in the area and one hundred years before the official discovery of the New World? That part of the puzzle was fitted together by Frederick Pohl, a science fiction writer, popular historian, and sometime archeologist. Ironically, part of Pohl's answer involves one of the major players in the Native American version of the history of Scratch Flat.

Frederick Pohl cites as one of his prime sources for this history the *Zeno Narrative,* a document which some authorities believe to be factual, but which the eminent historian of these parts, Samuel Eliot Morison, considers part of the imaginative literature of sixteenth-century Venice. The Zeno Narrative is an account of the voyages of two Venetian adventurers in the late fourteenth century. The story was set down in the sixteenth century by a descendant of the two voyagers, a young man named Nicolo Zeno, who, according to Pohl, had trouble reading the handwriting in the notes of his forebears and as a result made a few errors in the transcription. These Pohl corrects in his story of the knight on the rock.

In 1390 one of the Zeno brothers sailed northward from Venice to Scotland and there met a prince who befriended him. Five years later the other Zeno brother, Antonio, sailed with this prince across the ocean and spent the winter in a brave new world. In the narrative, the friendly Scottish prince was called Zichmni, but Pohl claims that the man's name was Henry Sinclair and that the real name was obscured by time and the poor handwriting of Antonio.

Henry Sinclair was a historical figure. He was born in 1345 near Edinburgh and was the son of Sir William Sinclair. He died in 1400 in the Orkneys and was buried in Roslin Chapel near Edinburgh. He was above all a seafaring man, a great adventurer and a wild fighter. Like many of the adventurous seafarers of the period, he was always pushing himself farther and farther westward, until finally, on one of these voyages with Antonio Zeno as captain of the fleet, he reached Pictou Harbor in Nova Scotia, a place where there was a smoking mountain and a spring of boiling tar. Sinclair sent Antonio Zeno home and spent the winter in the exotic world without a ship to carry him out and with only a few knights for companions. After a year or so spent traveling inland in the coastal regions, he built a ship, coasted down the New England shore, and, after one more inland trip, returned to Scotland with his crew.

None of this American voyaging appears in the Zeno narrative. Antonio, as I say, had been sent home with the fleet; but by piecing together the Zeno accounts of the first landing and then using one somewhat questionable source, Pohl fills out the story of Sinclair in America. The sources that he uses are the folktales of the Algonquian Indians concerning a certain cultural hero, a man who came from across the sea, could swim up rushing streams, ride on whales, and trick his enemies. Citing a number of linguistic authorities, Pohl writes that the Micmac Indians who first encountered Sinclair would have had trouble pronouncing the r in the word earl, as in Earl Sinclair, and would have otherwise garbled the s and hard c in his name. For example, *Jesus Christ* in their pronunciation becomes *Sasoo Goole,* and *Earl Sinclair,* using the same general laws of error, would become something like *Kuloskap* or Glooscap.

With Sinclair identified as Glooscap, the rest of his voyages become easy to track. Glooscap, as you might expect, appears all over the northeast in his various forms, and performed so many miraculous tricks, was such an exotic character, that it is not difficult to rearrange some of these adventures to fit nicely with the possible adventures of the fourteenth-century hero.

At the end of his exploration, Sir Henry, according to Pohl, got caught in a northeaster and was blown southwest to the New England coast. While waiting for a fair breeze, he did a little inland exploring. He came, Pohl says, to the Merrimack River, and sailed inland until he came to a stream on the south bank. He and his men ascended the stream in their pulling boat until they came to a ford. Following the stream on foot, they came to a lake and then turned east and climbed a hill to view the surrounding countryside. The stream they ascended, according to Pohl, was Stony Brook; the body of water was Forge Pond; and the summit they climbed was Prospect Hill.

Sir Henry Sinclair, late of Roslin Castle, lord of the Western Isles, stood on this hill, his heavy armor gleaming in the autumn sun, and stared out to the west. There below him stretched the broad marshes with the stream that is Beaver Brook winding through it; beyond were the woodlands rising in a series of natural terraces to the crest of the low, whalelike hill. The woods were broken with the open patches of the gardens of the native peoples, the smokes of many fires curled in the azure autumn sky, beyond the drumlin to the west he would have seen the high hill called by the natives *Wassachusetts,* or 'big hill.' To the north of Wassachusetts he would have seen the lonely monadnocks of southern New Hampshire, and beyond that, and still farther to the north, if the day were clear, he would have seen the great heights of the White Mountains. Here was indeed, we can imagine, a glorious new world, uncluttered by plague, by refuse, by stinking narrow streets aswarm with crippled beggars, thieves, and rank street people. Here was no brutal English king, no well-armed enemies, no castle intrigues, no plotting Macbeths, no grimy North Sea skies. Pohl does not explain why Sir Henry turned around and went home. He had found a paradise.

But death stalked even in this happy world. Either on the way up, or on the way back down, one of Sir Henry's loyal knights was seized with calamity, a heart attack Pohl suggests, brought on by the exertion of the climb in full armor. Sir Henry grieved deeply, according to Pohl, and commanded that a memorial be erected to the man on the spot in which he fell. They had no tools to cut such a tomb and so, working slowly with an awl, one of the men cut what is known technically as a punch hole armorial in a ledge of soft stone on the north side of Prospect Hill. Following the natural grooves of the ledge, the man formed the dotted image of a head, with a helmet, the basinet raised. He formed the eyes, the shoulders, the sword, the beloved falcon, and the shield. On the shield he cut the heraldic emblems of Sir Henry's family crescent, a mullet, a buckle, and, at the bottom, a ship with a high bow and stern, not unlike a galley.

Then, with his knight buried, his explorations completed, Sir Henry set sail for home. Indian legend, via the Glooscap folklore, records his departure. Earl Sinclair gets in his great canoe (his whale in the folktale version) and sails eastward over the shining waters. He sings a beautiful, haunting melody as he sails away. Long after the vessel disappears over the horizon the awed natives can hear his voice; the song grows fainter and fainter until finally there is only the dull murmur of the waves on the stony shore.

There is one curious coincidence in all this, no matter how far-fetched the story may sound. With no foreknowledge of Pohl's theories on the voyages of Henry Sinclair, Lethbridge wrote to Glynn, after he had seen a full tracing of the knight, to describe the possible identity of the armor and heraldry. Lethbridge wrote that the emblems on the shield and the armor and the sword appear to have belonged to a North Scottish knight of the fourteenth century—a man who must have been "kin to the first Sinclair, Earl of Orkney."

My alternate source on all prehistorical matters shrugs off the story of Sir Henry with nonchalance. "Could have been such a man maybe," Tonupasqua said. "And it could have been that the Indian people back then were scared by this guy, didn't understand, so they made up stuff about him. People then, they were superstitious, anything different they would explain by way of Glooscap or some other spirit. My uncle told me about these two Indians back then. They were visiting a white man's village down around Plymouth, I think. They started back for their own place in the late afternoon and about three miles back in the woods they saw a man up in a tree. Only it wasn't no ordinary man. This guy was black. You got to understand; they had never seen a black man before, so they thought it was Hobomacho, the devil, the black devil. They ran back to the village. 'Hobomacho has come,' they said. 'Come quick and kill him.' The white men came out with their guns—didn't know what to expect—and there in the tree they see the black man. Only it's a slave—a white man's slave, and he was carrying a message or something and got lost, so he climbed a tree to see where he was.

"See what I mean? There could have been a white man came into the country of the Micmacs, but because they had never seen a thing like that, they decided that it's Glooscap. But Glooscap came first. I can tell you that. This white man Sinclair, he wasn't Glooscap. No way."

Nompenekit and White Bird Free at Last are more definite about the story. "This is what you call white racism," Nompenekit told me. "You have a whole culture in the Americas, you have a government, a form of democracy, the highest ideals of socialism, communism, capitalism, and democracy all put together in the Indian nation. You got a class of people who have learned to live with the earth, who don't exploit others. And what do you white people do? You say there isn't anything over there but wilderness and savages. Okay? So you send your people out to make up America. This story tells me that we don't exist, my people. We don't even exist until we get invented by whoever this guy is who made up this Sinclair story. It's probably not true, see? And if it is, who cares? Just one more black spot in our history, one more thing to mourn about. And anyway, who says all these markings weren't made by the Indian people."

I withhold judgment. I have been to the ledge where the image is carved and I see there a lot of glacial scratches and I see also a lot of little pockmarks spreading around in various patterns, and if I look long enough I can see there the sword and the triangular-shaped shield, and perhaps a head. But I can also see an Indian; and my children, whom I have also consulted, have seen a bird on the rock, a lion, a tall man, a penis, a tree, and, when I prod them, an Indian chief in full regalia.

There is another legend associated with the valley in which Scratch Flat is located, this one far more significant since it may be the origin of the name of the Nashoba. There is, in the historical society collection, an immense shoe. It is made of leather, is about sixteen inches long and about five inches wide, and is the last relic of a giant who lived about a mile south of Scratch Flat during the mid-nineteenth century. This giant was a gentle sort, according to local stories; he was forever using his strength and size to help free mired horses and wagons or to move heavy equipment. He would, as a matter of courtesy, walk in the street below the curb while visiting Boston so that he would not seem so overbearing, and he was so tall that his arms could reach the ground while he was sitting in his wagon. Henry David Thoreau, who would come to these parts from Concord from time to time, reported a meeting with this giant in his journals; and it is a great credit to the gentle man that he escaped the barbs of Thoreau's pen—he gets highest marks from Thoreau for his demeanor.

I once related the story of the giant to Nompenekit and some of his friends. There was a Wampanoag man there who expressed great interest, asked if I was sure he lived in the nineteenth century, and whether I had actually seen the shoe, and whether I believed that there really was such a man.

"Sure sounds like a white version of Marshopa," he said after he was convinced that I had not made everything up.

There is, it seems, among the folktales of the Woodland people, and especially among the People of the First Light, or Wampanoags, a giant who roamed the forest beyond the stockades. In contrast to the historical giant, Marshopa was in some versions of the story a vicious figure who would carry off women, flay men alive, thunder and growl, and shake the earth whenever he wanted to. There is a hill south of Scratch Flat which, even after the coming of the white man, used to emit rumbling sounds. Early accounts of the phenomenon report that the Indians believed that the hill would rumble because the four winds were pent up inside. But when I told this story to the Wampanoag, he said that it was more likely the voice of Marshopa. Later on, Tonupasqua told me that after a particularly nasty encounter with Marshopa, the local shaman called Glooscap to help. She told me that Marshopa was not all that bright a being, and that Glooscap, always quick to take advantage of any chinks in the mental armor of his enemies, challenged Marshopa to a digging contest.

"You go first," he said to the giant. "See if you can dig out the inside of that hill."

So Marshopa began to dig, and as soon as he had dug himself in a few feet, Glooscap began to fill in the hole behind him. Once the giant was deep inside the hill, Glooscap turned the hill to stone and Marshopa was imprisoned inside. For centuries after that the people in the area could hear him thundering in rage. To honor him, Tonupasqua said, the people named the valley after the giant.

"Why did Marshopa stop thundering after the white man came?" I asked Tonupasqua.

Nompenekit, who was with us at the time, looked over at me as if to say that I had just posed a very dumb question.

"After the white man came he died. We all died."

They were indeed dying after the white man came, and their giants and their wood dwarfs died with them. By the end of the sixteenth century Europeans were trading regularly on the Merrimack River, and it is likely that some of these adventurous sailors rowed, paddled, or poled up Stony Brook to the ford at Tyngsboro and then wandered upstream as far as Forge Pond. And even if they didn't physically make the trip to Scratch Flat, their artifacts did; and so, in all probability, did their noxious diseases, although generally the inland Indian communities were not as seriously affected by the plagues.

It is possible that the people of Scratch Flat may have been far enough inland to have avoided direct trade and contact in the first few decades of the seventeenth century. But after 1620, and especially after the establishment of the Massachusetts Bay Colony a few years later, they would have felt the presence of the white man and may have even seen a few in the flesh. Then in 1637 the first inland settlement was established at Concord, not ten miles south of Scratch Flat. The land was either traded, sold, or otherwise turned over to some of the English by Squaw Sachem and Tahattawan—two powerful sagamores who "owned" the area. The chief Tahattawan may have had his main living quarters in the Nashoba Valley, possibly in Scratch Flat itself, since it is known that one of his descendants was living here in the 1670s near the fishing weir on Beaver Brook.

But even before Squaw Sachem and Tahattawan traded Concord, the presence of the white newcomers started to change the appearance of Scratch Flat and the surrounding valley. The proficient Indian women horticulturalists would have welcomed any new crops, and early records of the valley report that before 1650 the region had been planted with apple trees. The women did not plant the trees for fruit. Indians of the region had no previous experience with alcohol, and early on, the native people seemed to have enjoyed its effects, in some cases to excess, although I have learned through

Nompenekit and his friends to suspect all early reports from the white chroniclers on the lascivious behavior of the local people. English apples of the time were used specifically to make hard cider which, along with beer, was one of the standard beverages of the white people, women, men, and children alike. The Indians quickly learned to grow the apples, press the cider, and ferment it to a bubbly, mind-altering drink. By the 1640s chroniclers write of prolonged drunken night dances in which the flame-lit figures of men and women dressed in animal skins and painted garishly, circle a great fire, crouching and leaping, the women wailing and the men grunting and slapping their thighs. As I say, I have learned to mistrust such reports; but on the other hand, I like very much the image of this festivity. For the first time, we get an image of the prolonged ecstasies that must have accompanied the Woodland, and Archaic ceremonies over the long stretch of Scratch Flat history. It was not necessarily the alcohol that made them dance; they were naturally inclined to dance, to make joyous gatherings, to gamble, and to experience excesses of any sort, including, it must be admitted, excesses of violent behavior.

The Eastern Woodland Indians were, according to some of the more objective European accounts, an open, happy, and friendly people. They were simpleminded, quick to burst into tears, or laughter, or rage; they were spontaneous, free, superstitious, fearful, and honest. They were also, it is reported in other accounts, very dirty, unclothed, limited in intelligence, and given to smearing themselves with greasy offal made from bear fat, painting their bodies, and tattooing themselves in lurid blue. In grief or joy or during any festive occasion, they would howl and sing, throw themselves upon the ground, and enter into paroxysms of emotion. The men were ruthless with their enemies, cruel to their women, kind to their children. They were drunken; they were insatiable gamblers; and they were notorious, uncontrollable thieves. Everything the Indians did, they did to excess; there seemed to be no limits to their behavior, no morality, no overbearing god or strict dogma governing their spiritual or physical life, and no strong political leader to set down rules, let alone enforce them. Their "kings"—the seventeenth-century English term for sachems or sagamores—were kings in name only; they had no real power. The council, subkings, princes, and shamans or spiritual healers each had control over certain areas. The shaman was consulted for spiritual matters, a subchief or sagamore for matters of war, and another sagamore for matters of village life, and so on. The only apparent law or center of power was the council, and the council included everyone, even women.

It is possible that never before in history had two such alien cultures, the Eastern Woodland Indians and the English Puritans, been thrown together. In contrast to the native Americans, everything the Puritans did, every aspect of their physical and spiritual life was governed by narrow-minded, unalterable laws and principles. There was no middle ground. These Puritan English, these hard-bitten seventeenth-century moralists, are much in disfavor in our time. And viewed from the perspective of twentieth-century concerns for human rights, for freedom of speech, freedom of press, freedom of religion, and behavior, and dress, not to mention a concern for Indian rights and the natural environment, they do not fare well. But that is a distorted view. Most of the world in that era was cruel, narrow-minded, and illiberal in relation to the twentieth century. The Woodland Indians themselves were not without prejudices and cruelties: the Mohawks and the Iroquois to the northwest, who were in those times making almost annual raids on the relatively peaceful Scratch Flat people, have a particularly bad record. They were, among other things, warlike, fond of torture and cruel mockery, and given to eating their enemies when they were done with them.

Since I am trying to take the long view in this account, I have come to see the Puritans as just one more set of players in the drama. They came on the stage, acted out their part, and then, in time modified their behavior and laid the mental foundation for the famous New England moral righteousness. They were the flower that would bloom in Concord two hundred years later, and one cannot blame them for having to live for a time as tight buds. In any case, it appears from the local histories that by the time these people came to Scratch Flat in 1656, they had loosened considerably. It is my opinion that the hard living, the intense physical labor that would have been required to carry out their way of life in the midst of the New England environment, served to moderate them. Clearing land, building wooden houses, and most particularly, picking up all those tens of thousands of stones, and boulders, and rocks that the glacier had left on Scratch Flat, was a prodigious undertaking. Accounts show that the first few settlers here got along well with the Indians who were living on Scratch Flat at the time.

It is certain that before 1637, when the inland community was established at Concord, there were Indians living on Scratch Flat. Everything about the place suggests that it was, and probably had been for perhaps as many as eight thousand years, a prime fishing, hunting, and, later, agricultural site. The lush marshes of Beaver Brook, the ponds and the presence of fish and waterfowl would have attracted Archaic people to the area. And upland game such as deer, bear, moose, and elk, as well as birds such as the heath hen, the grouse, and the wild turkey, must have been abundant in the woodlands. The flat fertile lands between the waters in all probability would have been cleared and planted not long after an agricultural way of life became established in the region. Everything—the environment, the weather, the soils, the physical layout, and finally, the number of artifacts uncovered—suggests that Scratch Flat was something of a center for native peoples.

But by the 1630s, the proximity of Concord, the existence of a white settlement no more than ten miles to the south, must have created a certain amount of consternation among the loosely connected, extended families that were living in the general area. By then it was known among the Indians that these white newcomers were not, as some Indians had at first suspected, gods from across the sea. News of harsh Puritan treatment of transgressors who broke the myriad Puritan strictures must have filtered up from Concord or down from the Merrimack to the Scratch Flat people. Later, after the Pequot War, when a whole village of Indians including women, children, and warriors alike was surrounded and burned to ashes, word of the fighting powers, the ruthlessness and cruelty of these white visitors must have struck terror into the quiet farmers of Scratch Flat. They must have felt a tremendous pressure from the presence of potential enemies. From the north the terrible Mohawks would make seasonal raids on Scratch Flat and demand tribute. The alternative to not paying was death at best, slow death by torture at worst. To the south, in Concord, and east in Boston and Salem, the Indians had the anomaly of the white man preaching to them of a terrible vengeful god, who if he were not prayed to properly would inflict a life of fire, an eternity of torture far worse than any that their Mohawk enemies could summon up. Even death could not save the

Indians from the jaws of this terrible monster. Compared to their pantheon, compared to Glooscap, the gentle T'chi Manitou, and even such terrors as Hobomacho and the wood giants, the Christian god must have seemed hideous and inescapable. The Indians of the area faced a dilemma such as they had never before encountered. They were surrounded, both physically and spiritually. It is no wonder that most of the people of Scratch Flat, broken by the pressure, decimated perhaps by plague, and squeezed by their traditional enemies from the north, gave up altogether and surrendered to the whites and the all-powerful being who ruled over them. Besides, they were told that there could be salvation; there could be, possibly, eternal pleasure, a happy hunting ground.

The man who brought them the good news of salvation was John Eliot, the so-called apostle to the Indians. Eliot was educated at Jesus College, Cambridge, and received his degree in 1623 with a reputation as a good student of ancient languages. In 1631 he followed hundreds of fellow Puritans to the New World and in 1632 was ordained as teacher at a church in Roxbury, near Boston. His interest in language and religion immediately attracted him to the "plight" of the heathen Indian, and by the early 1640s he was able to preach to them in their language and began work on translation of *Um-Biblum God,* the Algonquian Bible, the first book to be printed in the New World.

History has given Eliot mixed reviews. Nompenekit tells me he delivered the cruelist cut of all, he was a subtle master of deceit working on the last refuge of the native people, the freedom of the primal mind. He says that the people who followed John Eliot, the Indians who converted to Christianity, and especially the ones who became teachers and preached to their fellow Indians, were vicious traitors. Many white students of Indian culture tend to agree with this assessment, and ironically, even in his own time, the harsh Puritan establishment considered Eliot's missionary experiment and his continuous support of the Indian people during the hard years that were to follow, traitorous at worst and wasteful at best. The English establishment held that the Indians were savages, pure and simple, and if they would not convert on their own, then the Devil would take them. They were already, in the opinion of most ministers of the time, in league with the Enemy; let him have them, they said.

But John Eliot believed all the things he had been taught, believed that all men were equal, that the Indian was worthy, and that there could be salvation. He was called. He had the tools, he had the dedication, and somehow, throughout all the intrigues of seventeenth-century Puritan politics, he managed to gain enough power to get land legally set aside for Christianized Indians. In order to obtain this land, in order to hold forever property, houses, gardens, and fishing grounds, the Indian people had but to turn to God, accept the way of the Puritan.

Since the Indians had a relaxed attitude toward spiritual beings, it was perhaps not difficult for them to accept yet one more god. But Eliot and the Puritan mind complicated the plot. There were certain strictures involved in becoming a Christian. You could not simply say that yes, you believed in this god and feared him—as many Indians of that time did. In order to become a member of Eliot's flock, the locals were required to attend church—ad infinitum it must have seemed. They had to learn to read Eliot's *Um-Biblum God,* had to stop gambling, cut off their long hair, wear white man's clothes, shoes in particular, and—this above all—they had to banish the shamans, give up the healing ceremonies and the dances and the powwows.

Perhaps it is the result of an overly active imagination, or the ability to experience, at times, intensely realistic daydreams, but for some reason, this last law summons up to me a very clear image of an event that, for no good reason, I believe took place in the hemlock grove behind my house. It was brought on in part by something Tonupasqua told me when I asked her about the reaction of the shamans to Christianity, and in part by a leaf from Eliot's Bible that I happen to own.

Tonupasqua once told me that, more than anyone else in the Indian community, the shamans hated John Eliot and the Puritans. When the Indians of Scratch Flat, under the leadership of the sachem Tahattawan, turned to Eliot for safety (that more than anything else, she says), the shaman of the group, a man whose name she says she cannot repeat, became enraged. "He flew up into the trees and became a screaming hawk for three days and three nights," she said.

The page from Eliot's Bible came to me in an odd sort of way. In 1975 I was involved in the production of a book with the Nimrod Press in Boston. The Christmas after the work was done, I got in the mail a card from the press with a folder. Inside the folder, fitted carefully in four slots, was a page from the First American Bible. I have never asked how this apparent desecration came about—that is, why individual pages from a precious historical document were being strewn at random among the indifferent customers of a commercial press—but I kept the page, and from time to time, I meditate on it in an attempt to bring on the state of ceremonial time. It has about it all the beauty of an old book, the care in printing, the fine-quality paper, the wonderful old typeface of the era; but more than that, it has a close connection with Scratch Flat. It is possible that this very page was handled by one of the Christian Indians from this area. It is certain that the Scratch Flat people read all the words with care. They were, as you can imagine, worried about what would happen if they didn't read them.

One night after I had been looking over the page, I had an intense dream about a bear. The bear was in the hemlock grove behind the house, and it seems that he was dying. He was thrashing around, tearing at the ground, rolling in the needles, his fur clotted and dusty. Suddenly he rose up on two legs and I saw, instead, the image of an Indian shaman in an intense anger, dancing madly, throwing himself on the ground, screaming and gnashing his teeth, tears glistening on his cheeks. This dream took place, I think, *after* I heard Tonupasqua's tale of the bear shaman, and it was probably nothing more than a delayed response to the story. But whatever, the image has stuck with me and I find it easy to see the Scratch Flat shaman, whoever he was, biting his arm in anger, breaking limbs from trees, smashing his head against the trunk until the blood streams down his face. I see him, at times, racing blindly across the hills, plowing through streams and shallow waters at the edge of Forge Pond. I see him living at the outskirts of the Christian Indian village, yowling to his lost people in the night, stalking them by the day, the pariah of New England, angry and betrayed, confused, and tormented by the times. There is only one other image of this period that comes clearly to my mind, and that is a description I read in an early history of Concord, of the poor, broken Scratch Flat people, filing into the back of the church at Concord for Sunday services in their ill-fitted European clothes, their shorn hair and their uncomfortable shoes. Of the two images, I much prefer the anger of the shaman.

The Christian Indian village that was established in the area was given the name Nashoba by the local authorities, and the people who lived in the village were called the Nashoba Indians. It is not clear whether this is a general term for Indians of various tribes who accepted Christianity and moved into the village, or whether there actually was a tribe of Nashoba Indians living in the valley before Eliot and Tahattawan established the town there. If there was indeed a tribe, it must have been a splinter group of the Pawtucket Indians of the Merrimack region, although that too is arguable. The facts are that in 1654 Nashoba was legally granted to the Indians. There were in this village about 50 or 60 people under the general leadership and spiritual guidance of a teacher, or minister, an Indian convert named John Thomas "Goodman." In 1657 John Thomas's father was fishing for eels at his weir on Beaver Brook when something rustled in the bushes on the high ground and a small group of Mohawks stepped out, their hideous, shaved heads gleaming and their faces painted for war. It is likely that the old man knew immediately his fate. He may have at this point reverted to his old religion, put down his fish spear and started to chant his death song. He may also have resisted, or he may have prayed to his new god. Whatever he did, in some way he stirred the anger of the Mohawks. One of them stepped down the bank, raised his club, and smashed the skull of John Thomas's father. This marked, as I read it, the beginning of the so-called Maquas War, one of the many petty revenge wars that were fought with the Maquas or Mohawk Indians in that period. Because of this war, the town of Nashoba was deserted between 1657 and 1660. The records do not indicate where the people went, but it is likely that they moved down to Concord, or perhaps farther eastward under the protection of Squaw Sachem and the Boston Puritans. Protection from enemies was part of the unwritten pact that was made with Eliot. "We will worship your God, and you will save us from the Mohawks."

A large glacial boulder in the middle of Charlie Lignos's fields marks the northwest corner of the Nashoba plantation. It appears that Scratch Flat must have been the wilder, less settled section of the holding, since the main village, although it has never been officially discovered, seems to have been to the southwest not far from the hill in which the giant Marshopa was buried by Glooscap. I like to think that throughout the 30 years of the existence of Nashoba

Village, there were wild Indians living on Scratch Flat or on the outskirts. I am told that during this period many of the tribes broke up and that individuals or small extended family groups moved back into the woods, stopped farming, and took up the hunter-gatherer way of life of their ancestors, a life which they had clearly not forgotten. But the Indian culture was coming to an end. The Christians returned to Nashoba in 1660 and continued to live there until the next bloody war, a conflict that would end the twelve-thousand-year reign of the Asian immigrants on Scratch Flat.

By 1660 Indians throughout New England were beginning to feel the pressure of the increasing population of land-hungry English settlers. This was especially true in the Wampanoag territories in southeastern Massachusetts and Rhode Island. The Indian people of the area were pushed farther and farther from their homelands, and as a result, individual conflicts began to increase and the Indians became somewhat less friendly and more aggressive toward the white people they had once shared the land with. By the 1670s, under the direction of Metacomet or King Philip, the tribes in the area began to mobilize for war. They had, somewhere in the back of their minds, the idea that it would be still possible, at this stage, to push the English invaders back to the shore, where they would get into their winged vessels and sail again across the sea, leaving the world to the Indians. Philip and his allies felt that such an unconditional victory would be possible if all the Indian tribes in New England would rise up as a body and fight together against their common enemy. It was not an impossible dream. Although the Indians were outnumbered almost two to one by that time, they were good and stealthy fighters, and in fact they almost won and probably would have if they had all cooperated according to Philip's plan.

The inevitable conflict began in 1675 when Indians forced a group of English from their homes and set fire to the buildings. The war spread quickly throughout the region and early in the conflict turned in the favor of the natives. The isolated inland communities were all but decimated by raiding parties. The town of Groton on the west side of Scratch Flat was burned and deserted, as were other small towns to the southwest. Mount Wachusetts, in the Nashua River Valley to the west of Nashoba, became an Indian rallying point under the direction of a woman named Queen Wetamoo and a man named Netus. Throughout the course of the war, victory dances and revelries, as well as peace negotiations and prisoner exchanges, were carried out there.

There were, at the time, several English houses on, or very near, Scratch Flat, one close to the weir at Beaver Brook, one not far from Groton, and several others just to the north of Forge Pond. One night early in the war, a group of Indians from the Wachusetts camp came up to Scratch Flat and began to snuffle around one of the houses near Forge Pond, snorting like pigs and making "other obscene noises." The man of the house came out and did not return that night. In the morning his wife opened the front door and saw his head stuck on a pole in the middle of the clearing. Not far downstream from Stony Brook, which drains Forge Pond and the Beaver Brook, English soldiers hauled the wife and twelve-year-old son of a Christian Indian from a house and clubbed them to death with rifle butts. The war swirled around the area like a fire storm, and the traitorous Christian Indians, the ones who had sold their birthright in order to survive, were caught in the middle. They were hated by the unconverted Indians and, in spite of their good intentions and their willingness to cooperate, they were mistrusted and ultimately betrayed by their white protectors.

One of the Christian Indians caught in the conflict was a man named Tom Dublet. He was married to a woman named Sarah who was the granddaughter of Tahattawan. Tom Dublet lived on Scratch Flat near the weir at Beaver Brook and across the Great Road from one of the earliest English houses in the tract of land. He is described as a tractable Indian, a man who loved peace, and who was willing to endure the bad dream of the English as long as they did not disturb his fishing hole. He was, reading between the scanty historical lines, something of a cynic perhaps, resigned to his fate, but in the end willing to help the English work out their problems with the Indians, and vice versa. There were several incidents that took place near Scratch Flat in which the Indians carried off women and children. The women they would use for ransom; the children they would, if they could, keep with them; and Tom Dublet seems to have played a significant role in one of these incidents.

It is worth a small digression here, I think, to say something about the ransom of captives during King Philip's War because I believe there is a lot that can be understood about the character of the two cultures from the Indian treatment of the English children and the attitude of the children toward the Indians. The Indians would kill children and women as readily as they would fighting men, there should be no mistaking that fact; but they also—and even their worst enemies admit this—had a pronounced fondness for both their own children and the children of the English enemy. They would treat them well, and on several occasions, it is reported, after elaborate trade negotiations were carried out and it was permissible for the white children to return to their natural parents, the children themselves refused to go, or resisted, preferring instead the life of the Indians. The harsher aspects of Puritan ethic, ie., the hours spent on the cold winter benches of the Protestant churches praying to some unseeable being, the beatings for incomprehensible transgressions, the tight clothing, the attitude toward nature, all, to my mind at least, rub harshly with the natural human instincts.

By contrast, the Indians had a lot of physical contact with their children. Like primitive people the world around, they were forever nuzzling them, hugging and wrestling with them and spoiling them. The Eastern Woodland Indians believed that the hard time would come later. At age twelve or so, the children would be sent off into the forest to seek a vision and a name. When they came back, even though they might still have been children at heart, they were treated as adults. Given different attitudes toward children, given the choice, it is no wonder that the English children chose to remain with their Indian captors.

One of the children captured by the Indians was named Mary Shepard. She had been assigned to stand guard on a hill over a farm about a mile east of Scratch Flat while her father and brothers worked in the barn. A small group of Indians managed to sneak up on her, captured her, killed her father and brothers, and carried her off to the Mount Wachusetts camp. That night, if the legend has any bearing in truth, she rose from the side of her Indian captor, stole a horse and a blanket, and rode back to the family farm, crossing the icy Nashua River in the process.

The other ransom incident involved Mary Rowlandson of Lancaster. Her children did not fare so well; one of them was killed by the Indians and another died in captivity, although the rest of her family survived. Mary Rowlandson was the wife of the minister at the Lancaster settlement. She was something of a sporting type; she smoked four pipes of tobacco a day, she wrote, and spent the rest of the day longing for a fifth. After she was ransomed, she wrote down an account of her travels with the Indians during her captivity and from this record you can get a good sense of the privations that the Indians were willing to endure to win King Philip's War. They were, according to the account, almost constantly on the move, sometimes with food, sometimes without, and always in need of money or ammunition or more food to keep them going.

Early in the war the Indians recognized that their enemies would pay a handsome price for captives and so the custom of taking prisoners—especially women and children—became more common. When the Wachusetts-area Indians were ready to negotiate a price for Mary Rowlandson, they sent word to the Governor and council, and Tom Dublet was selected to work out the exchange; in fact, it appears that he volunteered for the job, even though his life would be at great risk. Dublet set out for Wachusetts in April 1676 and returned a week or two later with a letter from Netus and the other leaders saying that the renegades wanted two Indians to carry out further negotiations. So another Nashoba was sent down with Tom Dublet, a man named Peter Tatatiquinea or Conway, and this time the two of them managed to secure freedom for Mary Rowlandson.

There were still other prisoners at the Wachusetts camp, however, whom the Indians were willing to ransom. So Dublet went back to talk and then went back perhaps several other times and finally arranged a meeting and exchange which is believed to have taken place near his house on Beaver Brook, or, as the histories tell us, "between Concord and Groaten." Tom Dublet received no payment for his elaborate shuttle diplomacy, and in fact, little thanks at all. Later in his life he petitioned the court for some recompense and after eight years was finally awarded a settlement. The Great and General Court voted to give him two coats.

That was not an uncommon reaction to the services of the Christian Indians. King Philip never managed to unite all the Indian tribes and, in general, both Christians and unconverted Indians were willing to help the English defeat the rebels. But the English attitude toward the natives prevented them, at least in the beginning, from allowing the Indians to help. Later in the war, when Indians had demonstrated their unquestionable loyalty to the English, some Indian forces were organized; but the prevailing belief among whites was that all Indians were loyal only to Indians. As long as they were permitted to live freely amidst the white settlers, they would present a threat, it was believed. By the end of 1676, pressure to do something about the supposed potential threat from Christian Indians was building, and by winter many of the members of John Eliot's Praying Indian towns had been rounded up and forceably moved to Deer Island in Boston Harbor where they were interned for the duration of the war with scant supplies and little shelter.

The people of Nashoba, peaceful though they were, were not exempt from suspicion. Pressure began to build in the town of Concord, and one night, acting on absolutely no authority, a rogue captain named Mosely appeared with his men in the Indian village. The women and the men and the children of Scratch Flat and Nashoba were herded out into the cold, ropes were fitted around their necks, and they were marched to Concord to be shipped to Deer Island. A local intermediary, John Hoar, kept the Nashoba people at his house for a while, but the presence of Indians inside the very town made the residents all the more nervous, and in time, they were rounded up once more, marched to Boston, loaded in boats, and carried out to the open-air concentration camp where the majority of them died of starvation or exposure.

In effect, that was the end. After who knows how many thousands of years of habitation, the native people of Scratch Flat, in the space of one generation, through various means, had been removed from the land, opening the area for the new invaders. The end did not come immediately, but the internment on Deer Island, the forced removal of the entire village, and the subsequent breakup of the New England tribes after King Philip's War marked as clear an ending as anything. Some of the Nashobas imprisoned on Deer Island returned to Scratch Flat after the war. Tom Dublet came back to his fishing weir on Beaver Brook and continued to live out his time there, presumably a bitter, broken old man. The official histories of the town indicate that an old squaw named Sara Indian, or Sarah Dublet, either the wife or daughter of Tom, owned land south of Scratch Flat near the supposed site of the Christian Indian village. She lived until 1734 and was the only heir to some five hundred acres. By that time she was old and blind, and under the care of a family named Jones of Concord. In order to pay for her care, she sold or turned over her land to the two Jones brothers.

This was the last of the legally owned Indian property of the

Nashoba village. Even before the war was over, the rest had been divided. Some sections of Scratch Flat went to a man from Groton named Peleg Lawrence, who in 1683 constructed a house on the west side of the tract. Other portions of Scratch Flat went to families from the surrounding towns. By 1686, for the first time in history, Scratch Flat began to appear on maps, its natural boundaries cut and squared by the concept of ownership of land. Little by little, tract by tract, the general area was divided, and quartered, halved and quartered again, until by 1830 there was not a yard of it, not so much as a foot that had not been measured and walked over, and argued over. You will see, in the historical records of this area, eternal discussion over who owns what and where, which line runs to which rock wall, and whose wall is it, and where this or that town line runs and why. The Scratch Flat of the hunter-gatherers, the wide stream and the marshes, the grazing lands of the caribou and the mammoth, the wild open country of the Paleo-Indians had become a nation of quiet yeomen with an enduring capacity for work, a people without ecstasies and without demonic night rituals.

Even after the death of Sara Dublet, however, there were reports of Indians in and around Scratch Flat. These were, no doubt, unconverted Pawtuckets who had, even before the war, reverted to the ways of their Archaic ancestors. One of them is described simply as "a tall Indian." He appeared from time to time at the edges of the fields. People would see him crouching beside Beaver Brook, totally naked, not dressed in English clothes by any means. Whenever he was spotted, he would run in terror, and generally, he seemed to be a peaceable Indian, although later on he began to steal corn and later still became a housebreaker or cat thief. As late as the early eighteenth century, he could still be seen, sometimes by little children; only in these later reports he would stand quietly amidst the trees and would no longer run in terror, but simply fade from view. The children would see him, and when they looked again, he would be gone.

The other Indian who remained after the war years was not as gentle a figure. He would dress in the skins of animals, he carried a long spear, his hair had grown out and fell below his shoulders, and he had, in his eyes, a wild glare. He was not afraid of white people and would jump them whenever he had the opportunity, threatening them with his spear, growling, and gnashing his teeth, although he never harmed anyone physically. This figure began to haunt the people of Scratch Flat. He was, they reported, a demon Indian, a remnant of the rebel tribes. Parties of farmers halfheartedly hunted him in the forest, not really expecting to find anything, not really believing perhaps that he was even there; and, in time, he too faded into legend. And after him, there were none.

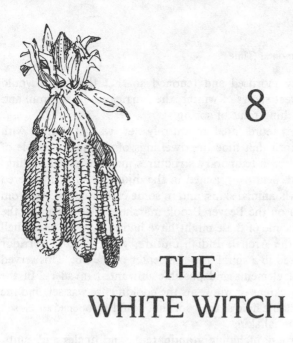

8

THE
WHITE WITCH

The earliest extant house in Scratch Flat was constructed in 1658 near Beaver Brook, although according to a number of different records there were several others in the area by that date, none of which are now standing. After the breakup of Nashoba Plantation, the house of Peleg Lawrence was built on the west end of the Great Road, and new structures appeared one after another from that beginning until the early 1800s, when there were, according to old maps, seven houses within the square mile and approximately five large farm holdings.

In the early years the houses were probably no more than rude cabins. In fact, some of them may have been mere hovels, holes dug into the side of a hill, shored up with timbers and covered on one side with planks. In effect the white newcomers had not advanced much beyond the stage of the Archaic rockshelter. But these hovels were temporary; they housed the family, and perhaps an indentured servant or slave, while the main house was under construction. And even the most modest of these early English houses were elaborate structures in comparison to the dwellings that were there before. The frames were massive—four or five times as thick as they needed to be; and carefully mortised and tenoned so that the house would withstand the great snows of winter, the hurricanes of autumn, and the eternal drenching rains of spring.

These houses represented an entirely new way of dealing with the world. Up until that time the dwellings of the native people of Scratch Flat had been temporary structures made from cut saplings set in the ground, bent over, joined in the middle, and then covered with strips of bark, animal skins, and in some cases mats woven from cattails collected on the Beaver Brook marshes. In the years of the Archaic period, some of these might have had the unique snail-shell construction of the Archaic Indian culture; you entered a corridor and then wandered in a spiral into the center of the hut. This served well to keep out elements and possible unwanted invaders. In the center of these wickiups or wigwams the cooking fire was set, and the smoke rose through a hole in the roof that could be opened or closed with a flap of animal skin.

A family group, including grandparents and uncles and aunts, slept in these small structures, although there may have been on Scratch Flat some of the larger houses which could hold more than one family or large extended family. The structures were perfectly fitted to the environment. They could be put up in a day—the women doing most of the work—they kept out the rain and the cold, and when they became old or dirty or, in summer, infested with fleas or other vermin, they were simply deserted and burned. Villages of these wigwams would have appeared and disappeared on Scratch Flat throughout history, here one summer for fishing, or a winter for hunting, or for no reason in particular other than the fact that Scratch Flat was recognized as good land. No one among these mobile people ever took their houses too seriously; they were merely shelters—what mattered to them was the family and food; housing was a secondary consideration.

But the English structures were built for time. Hard work, tedious fitting jobs, long delays because of the weather did not discourage these enduring craftsmen. They had a singular idea, and that was permanence. They had the wood, they had the granite for foundations, and they were coming to stay—or so they thought—and so they built to last. But although the houses were built for all time, they were as mortal as their inhabitants. There is only one structure left from the seventeenth century, and of the seven houses built in the eighteenth century, only two are still standing. In most cases, these older structures were undone by fire. The center of the town in which Scratch Flat is located is one mile distant; and even if there had been a proper fire department and efficient fire-fighting system, it is unlikely that the firemen could have mobilized and reached the burning structures by the time the fire was reported. As in most towns, the old houses that have survived in the community are near the center of town where the fire-fighting neighbors and equipment were close at hand. When a fire started in Scratch Flat, even if the news did get over to the town, it was generally too late.

What was true of the houses was true too of the farming methods that were practiced by the two cultures that shared Scratch Flat during the seventeenth century. The form of shelter and the means of food supply both reflected the cultural attitudes toward the land. The English farmers who moved into the area in increasing numbers by the end of the century began to re-create, as well as possible, the landscape of Kent, England, from which they had come. The first job of these stout Kentish men was to clear those sections of Scratch Flat that were not already opened by Indian agriculture. The white men began in the low grounds near their dwellings on the south edge of the square mile, clearing first enough ground to put in the kitchen garden or home lot where the women grew household vegetables such as turnips, carrots, onions, and parsnips. As soon as possible, outholdings were cleared where the men tended staple crops such as peas, beans, oats, barley, and wheat. At the same time, in the Scratch Flat area at least, fruit trees were planted. Kent was and still is the fruit-growing area of England; and it is not surprising that the Scratch Flat settlers attempted to continue the tradition in the New World, a tradition which, in this case, succeeded—apple growing is still a major industry in the Nashoba Valley.

The new settlers also brought livestock to the valley for the first time. As is clear from dog skulls that were found in the Flagg Swamp Rockshelter, the Indians had kept dogs for thousands of years. They used them to assist in the hunt, and ate them during periods of dearth; but the Eastern Woodland Indians were essentially horticulturalists; they kept no animals and still relied heavily on wild plants and hunting to supplement their vegetarian agriculture.

In contrast, the English were heavy protein eaters. Ideally, each adult would consume a pound of meat, cheese, or fish a day, and perhaps a quarter of a pound of corn or oats or barley porridge. These foods were consumed at two defined sittings, one at high noon and the other about seven or eight o'clock in the evening. This also contrasted sharply with the eating habits of the Indians, who would make a pot of stew in the morning and then eat all day long whenever they were hungry. The only meals they would share in the technical sense were ceremonial feasts, and these too consisted of little more than day-long and night-long eating bouts.

It is likely that one of the reasons why Scratch Flat was settled so early in the history of the region was the presence of the grassy meadows around Beaver Brook. The marshes would provide free forage for the cows and oxen of Joel Proctor, Peleg Lawrence, and the other seventeenth-century settlers; the animals would graze there during the growing season and the marshes would be cut for hay. I surmise that in Scratch Flat pasture lands and grazing meadows were not cleared until later in the century, as more settlers moved into the area. Pigs and goats were turned loose to forage for themselves in the surrounding woodlands. In fact, up until the nineteenth century, pigs were allowed to roam free in Scratch Flat and were rounded up in the fall to be slaughtered, having fattened themselves sufficiently on the acorns and hickory nuts of the forestlands.

The farms of Scratch Flat in the late seventeenth century were holdings of approximately sixty acres. Along with the arable lands where corn, barley, and peas were grown, there were wood lots where the farmers and their sons cut fuel and wood for the timbers of the houses and outbuildings. One of the most graphic differences between the two cultures is evident in this treatment of the forests. The Indians would clear only so much and then purposely allow the land to come back. But the Kentish men were out to remake the world, and slowly, winter by winter, year by year, the flatlands around the drumlin were cut off. All memory, all evidence of the previous ecosystem, was rooted out and destroyed. The shrubs were burned; the stumps of the trees were twisted and heaved free by teams of oxen; and the thousands upon thousands of rocks, stones, and movable boulders were thrown onto ox-drawn stone boats, then thrown off again, and then, in time, piled one on the other to create the running walls that crisscross Scratch Flat to this day. This alone, this clearing away the debris of the glacier, was a prodigious task, undertaken, I imagine, not in a lifetime, not even perhaps in a full generation. The stone walls of New England are veritable New World cathedrals, built over time, to stand against time, and constructed with the care and the grace—one might even say the love—that would go into some spiritual monument. It is not surprising, given the nature of these pragmatic yeomen, that these monuments served to mark property lines and to keep in sheep and cows.

The remaking of the face of Scratch Flat was not accomplished by the end of the seventeenth century, and even by the middle of the eighteenth century, when most of the major landholdings in the area had been stabilized, there were still some uncut groves of hemlock, oak, and red maple. But by the nineteenth century the place was devoid of trees for the first time since the glacier withdrew; and this treeless, rolling landscape of meadows, hayfields, and garden plots lasted for the next hundred and fifty years.

In the 1930s, as a part of a survey, aerial photographs were taken of the communities that surround Scratch Flat; and even in that late period, even after the hundred-year out-migration of the New England agriculturalists, the land was still treeless and thoroughly cultivated. You can see Scratch Flat in the distance in the aerial photos, its hayfields stretching north from the Great Road, its squared and angled croplands, its orchards, pastures, barns, and clean white farmhouses. It was, even then, the all-American ideal, a rural idyll of clean honest work, clean honest farms, and bright earth-scented mornings. There is a darker side to the Scratch Flat story; but superficially, God was in his heaven during this three-hundred-year agricultural period and all was right with the world.

One of the reasons why the English newcomers were able to go about the business of remaking the world with such diligence is that they had brought with them from Kent a very different attitude toward land than the people who had lived in the place before they came. The concept of wilderness, of a place apart, was totally alien to the Indian people. For them there was no delineation between that which was human and that which was wild. The world at large, although filled with demons, was essentially a garden from which fruits were to be plucked. The native people, as Nompenekit made clear to me, did not think of themselves as separate from the bears or trees of the forests. That was not the view of the English. The American land—sixteenth- and early seventeenth-century propaganda literature notwithstanding—was to them a wasteland to be subdued and Christianized. It was filled with frothing red-eyed beasts, dank inhuman forests, unwholesome, fetid swamps, and—the worst of all —wild humanoid creatures in service of none other than the worst enemy of the Puritan nation—the Devil himself.

There was a popular belief among the early Puritans—moderated somewhat by the time that people got to Scratch Flat—that while the Devil had been extirpated from the European landscape, he was very much alive in the cold swamps of New England and had assumed as his charges the services of the Indian. These savages were the Devil's agents and would attempt, whenever possible, to cheat, rob, and ultimately kill the pious Christian newcomers. For this reason, to kill an Indian, a servant of the Devil, was not necessarily a crime and in fact, could be viewed as a service to civilization. This attitude was by no means universal in the New England white community; but it did exist, had a number of advocates, and is reflected in the views of even the most liberal and moderate thinkers such as Roger Williams and John Eliot. The wars on the Indian, and by extension, the war on the natural American environment, was in fact no less than a jihad, or holy war.

This individual, the Devil, the so-called Black Man, was a very real entity for the early settlers of Scratch Flat. They believed in him as readily as we believe in the unseen scientific phenomena of our time, radiation, for example, or electricity. There was no question that he was about; and it is not surprising, given the state of mind in New England in the late seventeenth century, that the Black Man infected the minds of two girls on the Great Road in the early years of the 1700s.

Even before the Black Man came to Scratch Flat, there had been reports in the area of unaccountable accidents and occurrences in the general area. Most of these were attributed to the presence of the primitive Indian in animal skins who, although he may have been real enough in the 1690s and early 1700s, was, after the death of Sara Dublet, believed to be a troublesome ghost. By 1720, however, another sort of spirit, a European form, began to appear on Scratch Flat. The events began, as these sort of things often did in those times, with the odd behavior of two young girls, Thankful and Virtue Pease, who lived along the Great Road. Thankful Pease was about fourteen years old and, by all descriptions, a beautiful young country girl with clear green eyes and healthy skin. Virtue was two years younger and appears to be something of a minor player in all this, but a willing one. When she was about thirteen, Thankful began to act in a strange manner; she would spend hours by herself, apparently daydreaming, sometimes rocking back and forth and avoiding work whenever possible. Then in the spring, about the time that her father's apple trees began to flower, she and Virtue were seized with dementia. They would sometimes howl like dogs, chirp like birds, or mew like kittens. They would crowd themselves into the corner when their mother came to investigate, hissing and slashing out with crooked fingers, like fighting cats. On other occasions one of the girls would come and summon help from the mother or some other adult. The grownups would find the other girl floating in the middle of a nearby pond or perched high in an apple tree, or on top of the barn. It was all very strange, but there was an explanation: the girls were clearly under the spell of a witch.

On the east side of Beaver Brook, near the town, there was a farm belonging to a certain Mr. Thomas Dudley, an upright citizen of the community who had a young wife identified in the history books simply as Mrs. Dudley. This young woman was, like the Pease girls, something of an odd individual, although by no means spiteful and harmful; in fact, she seems to have been simply one of those people who appreciates the natural world. Mrs. Dudley was given to wandering. She would sometimes cross Beaver Brook and spend the day in the woodlands on the hill, returning, it is reported, after nightfall, carrying with her wildflowers, birds' eggs, and bright stones. When the news of the actions of the Pease girls reached the town, rumors concerning the behavior of Mrs. Dudley began to spread, and soon it was believed that, over on the dark side of the hill on Scratch Flat, that is, probably in the old hemlock grove on the northwest slope, there was a coven. At night, it was said, Mrs. Dudley would fly to the place, strip off her clothes, and dance around the fire, her eyes wide and glaring.

All of this was mere rumor, of course. No one did anything about the witchery. The trials of Salem were over and it is possible that the reaction to the Salem hysteria, the doubt and suspicion surrounding the whole event once the emotion was over, was still prevalent. Besides, Mr. and Mrs. Dudley were both upstanding citizens; and except for her strange nature rambles, she was well liked by the other housewives. Nevertheless, when pressed to confess who was tormenting them, the two Pease girls identified Mrs. Dudley as the cause. From that time on, the witch began to appear more often in the girls' lives. She would come to the farm disguised as a bird, break into the house, flutter around the room, and then leave, throwing the girls into spasms. They would choke and spit, lift their dresses, writhe on the floor, and finally, in a fit of ecstasy, faint.

About this time, an old woman named Goody Bartlett, who lived alone on the far side of town away from Scratch Flat, announced that one night she had followed Mrs. Dudley and found her on the hills across the brook. There, said Goody Bartlett, Mrs. Dudley met with a dark man with whom she had congress and whose child would be, said Goody, a bane to the town. Toby Beckwith, who related some of the finer details of this story to me, after I dug them out from the town histories, described this announcement graphically, crouching over to imitate the old hag, his tongue darting between dry, thin lips, like Quasimodo in the tower.

"She had congress," Toby whined in his theatrical voice, "and now she will release into the world a creature most foul."

It appears that no one would accept Goody Bartlett's story; but it was true that, at the time, Mrs. Dudley was known to be pregnant —"in a delicate way" is the wording that the nineteenth-century histories use. Pregnancy notwithstanding, she continued to plague the Pease girls. On one occasion there was a rush of wind in the kitchen door and the girls fell to the floor screaming, "Mrs. Dudley has come. Kill her. Kill the witch." At this point, perhaps half to calm the girls, Mrs. Pease swung a frying pan through the air, the rush of wind disappeared, and the girls recovered. The same thing happened about three weeks later. Mrs. Dudley came in the door in the form of an invisible bird and began fluttering around the kitchen. The girls began to scream again, and once more Arabella Pease went for the apparition, this time with a knife, jabbing here and there in the air. "She is there," the girls would shout. "No, over here. There, see, stab her, mother. Pierce her heart." Suddenly Arabella Pease felt the knife slip into something. It was not air, and it was not flesh, the reports say; it was something in between. At the moment of this incident, Mr. Dudley and his wife were walking toward the meetinghouse in the town, when suddenly Mrs. Dudley felt "her bowels fall out." She began to bleed, was taken home, and died a few days later, apparently of a miscarriage.

After her death the seizures stopped, and years later the two girls claimed that they had made up the whole story. At least that is what the official account says. Legend of the event, the story passed down from generation to generation and told to me by Toby, is that the two girls left Scratch Flat abruptly after this incident and were never seen again. He says that he was told that down in the section of the town known as Hog End, Goody Bartlett lived to be more than 150 years old and, after the events of the Scratch Flat witchery, assumed a certain peace, smoking her pipe beside her door, getting older and older in the spring sun. She outlived all the players in the drama, Toby said, and would herself in later years recount the events, adding, where she could, more lurid details about Mrs. Dudley and exonerating her own role in the story. Whatever happened to the girls is not recorded; but about that time Goody Bartlett got two fat hogs that grew old with her. It was claimed that she cut pork chops from the living flesh of the two pigs and thereby supplied herself with food for the rest of her life.

The story of Mrs. Dudley does not end in the eighteenth century. Like many of the Scratch Flat histories, it loops around on itself and gets replayed from time to time. Some years ago in the early mornings, I used to see a black-haired woman walking a black dog along Forge Village Road. She had a distinctive style of moving —slow, almost languorous, although she walked with direction and purpose. She was clearly lost in thought, yet it was obvious that she knew exactly where she was at any given moment and knew exactly where she was headed. She was a very early riser. On my way out for my morning jaunts over Scratch Flat, I would often meet her on her way home, and after a few such meetings—she and I were the only ones about at that hour—we fell into conversation and, quite abruptly, with very little small talk, got down to the basic issues.

Like many of the people that live in the newer houses on Scratch Flat, she was something of a transient. She grew up on a dairy farm in Wisconsin, moved to Milwaukee, married, moved to Chicago, then to Reston, Virginia, and then finally, after a short stay in Worcester, Massachusetts, moved to Scratch Flat. She told me that she had a strange sensation when she first came here, a sense of having seen it all before. There was something in the woods, she said, "something comforting, as if I had come home."

I noticed immediately that she was a different sort of person than the average Scratch Flat resident. For one thing, although she was rather plain from a distance, close up I noticed that she was almost exquisitely beautiful. She had silky black hair, clear gray-green eyes, arched eyebrows, and well-defined, almost chiseled lips, as if she were a bit of a marble sculpture. Her face was almost classical in appearance, a face that seemed to assume the characteristics of all western cultures throughout all time. And as it turned out, her face more or less matched her inner self. She was one of those women whose age is hard to judge. Her face was young, between thirty and thirty-five, but there was something older about her, a sense of experience, or pain, or deeper knowledge. There was nothing on the surface that would indicate this; it was something that was apparent in her carriage or demeanor.

She told me that her family had lived in Wisconsin for more than four generations, having moved there from New England sometime around the beginning of the nineteenth century. She said she never knew where her ancestors had lived in New England, and in fact, she had never cared much; she was, she said, more interested in other things, spiritual matters, for example, or animals and plants. She did not fit in well in Wisconsin. Ever since her childhood, she said, she had felt that she was different, that she had a power or a sense or feeling about things that other people did not share or understand. Early in her life she developed a sharp sense of connection with trees and animals. She told me that she felt that she was able to communicate with other living things and would often have strange experiences associated with animals. For example, once she was lying on the floor in her house in Virginia when the clear image of a beautiful tabby cat appeared in her mind's eye. She stood up and, for no conscious reason, went to the kitchen and opened the back door. There on the porch was the same cat, a stray whom she took in and cherished for years. She said that in times of pain or struggle in her life, inevitably, in the depths of her agony, a beautiful wild bird would come to her and she would know then that her pain was temporary and that her life, or her time in this life, would move on and things would be smoother for her.

I asked her if she actually spoke words to animals and plants, and if so, whether they would speak back to her. She said that whatever communication she had was at another level; it was deeper than a verbal exchange, at the level of thought or feeling, something so obscure sometimes that she was unable to understand it thoroughly; she simply was aware of the transfer of information.

This sense of communion was also extended to the land. She said that in Wisconsin she felt a close connection with animals and plants, and when she was in Virginia she felt close to the people, but alienated from the land and the animals. But when she came to Scratch Flat, something was very right; she was able to feel the connection with the land and the animals and did not feel alienated from the people. Before she arrived she had developed a strong sense of what she termed "safe spots." She said that when she was in one of these places, no harm could come to her. She would lie down and sleep, and although the surrounding woodlands might be filled with bears or wolves, or, even with murderers and rapists, she would be protected as long as she stayed in the safe spot. She said that she had found many such safe spots on Scratch Flat and that she and her dog would often visit them during her predawn walks. "Sometimes I spend hours there," she told me. "Hours? I don't know, maybe whole days. I lose track of time in the safe spots. The world is different inside them."

She said that she did not usually tell people about these powers or abilities that she felt she had, but she said that there were certain people whom she knew she could trust and knew she would share her life with. "You are one of those people," she told me. "I knew immediately I could trust you."

I felt the same sort of connection with her, or at least sensed immediately her openness to ideas about time and space, and in our very first meeting I began to tell her about Scratch Flat and my project and Nompenekit and the Native American concept of ceremonial time. She seemed to understand, but when we talked further on another day, I learned that in spite of her mystical leanings, she had a very western concept of time.

At one of our meetings, I began to talk about our western bias concerning the structure of time. I said that she and I think of time as linear, flowing from past, to present, to future like a river, whereas Nompenekit thinks of it as a lake or pool in which all events are contained.

"But I can tell you about time," she said. "I have seen its shape and it *is* linear. It is like a huge band or bar that stretches infinitely backward and infinitely forward. I am a cubicle in that band. Sometimes the cubicle that I am in rises above time and I can see that now, in the present, I am in this year, at this point. But I can also be in any other point in the band at other periods. My cubicle was, and will be."

"You have lived before?" I asked her.

"I think so. Yes. Egypt I think. I have this strong sense of Egypt, some connection there. Greece too. And also here. These woods and hills. I know them already. I could tell that when I first came here. I was replaying something."

A few years after she moved to Scratch Flat, after she had experienced the sense of replay, she made an incredible discovery that finally gave a purpose to her life, or at least to her presence in this time and place. She said that her mother had given her a sampler with the family name inscribed on it along with a little homily about farm life. The sampler had been given to her mother by her mother, who had received it from her mother, and so on back into history. My friend had carried the sampler with her and, knowing that she had ancestors in New England, decided at one point, even though she was not overly interested in genealogy, to see if she could trace her family. She happened to meet a woman at her work who was interested in local history and knew how to find her way through the maze of documents and birth records, and through her, she began to track down the name sewn into the sampler.

"What was it?" I asked her.

"Mary Louise Dudley."

"You knew then?"

"I wasn't surprised. I knew. Yes. Should have known."

"And you know the story of Mrs. Dudley?"

"I know that story, yes."

"And you believe she was a witch?"

"I can't say. I believe she was different; believe she had powers. I also believe there was a terrible injustice somehow. I had a view once, about a year ago, of an event. My cubicle or my person was above this great band of time and I could see two people, a man and a woman, standing near a graveyard, and there was pain. Some sort of banishment, or expulsion. I am not a Christian, you know, not religious, and I could sense pain in the woman. I could share something about not being a Christian with her. He killed her."

"Who?"

"Her husband. I think he murdered her, either psychically or physically. I don't know which. But I think I know now why I am here in this place in this time."

"To find out?"

"No, it's a debt I have to pay. There is some reason. Something that has to be fulfilled. I don't know how, don't know what it is. But I am here for that reason. It's why I've come back as this person in this place. It's the reason for the accident of my moving here."

She turned away for a second or two then. I noticed just before she turned that there was a slight twitch at the corners of her mouth. Although her eyes were clear, I could see that she was deeply moved.

"It could be you," she said. "It could be meeting you. I don't tell people all this because I am afraid that they would think things about me, think I'm crazy. But you I trust. I feel right telling you, and I don't mind that you tell others."

It appears from the records that there is a connection between Scratch Flat and the town of Ipswich on the North Shore of Massachusetts. Some of the houses that were constructed on Scratch Flat in the early part of the eighteenth century were saltboxes of a style that was common in the Ipswich area. They were, like all saltboxes, constructed with a long sloping back roof which faced generally to the northwest to deflect the prevailing winter winds; they had a central entrance, and four upstairs rooms surrounding the massive center chimney. The Scratch Flat saltboxes had a window over the center door, however, which is a construction detail that appears only in the saltboxes built around Ipswich.

Only one of these houses is left on Scratch Flat; the others were either burned or dismantled during the late nineteenth century. The Scratch Flat saltbox was built by a man named Jeremiah Caswell, who moved to the area from the North Shore in the mid-1700s. Jeremiah was the grandson of Richard Caswell, who was born in East Coker, Somersetshire, about 1602. Richard came to America in 1638 and settled first in Salem, and then moved to North Beverly where he purchased a tract of land and became a successful farmer and an outstanding member of the local community. His name appears in 1653 on a list of 21 subscribers to Harvard College, and he was one of the founding members of the Wenham Church. His first son, Thomas, born in Beverly, inherited the family farm and was, it seems, also an upright citizen of the community. In the early part of the eighteenth century, Thomas Caswell's third son, Jeremiah, came west to the territory north of Nashoba and, sometime around 1750, built the saltbox about a quarter of a mile north of the Great Road, just above the boulder that marked the northwest corner of the Christian Indian plantation. The original holding of the Caswell farm was about 60 acres; but over the years, Jeremiah appears to have expanded his empire, and by the early 1800s, when the property was sold to another party, the farm extended over the hill and down the other side to the shore of Forge Pond, and east to the marshes of Beaver Brook. At a narrow point in the brook there was a ford which connected the Caswell farm with another large holding east of the marshes. This means that the hills to the east were, in all likelihood, cleared of forest by the mid-eighteenth century.

Jeremiah Caswell was what might be termed a hard-liner. He was prosperous, strict, economical, upright, forthright, not given to light moments, and above all he was a man of his word. Furthermore, he expected those in his family to follow his example. Caswell had two children, Adam and Eve, and may have had a slave, a man named Mingo, whose name appears from time to time associated with the Caswell family. When Eve was about 16 or 17, she met a young man named Enoch Pratt who was the son of a farmer from a nearby community, but who was, for some reason, living or working on the Lawrence estate on Scratch Flat. On warm evenings, Enoch would walk up the west slope of the drumlin and, according to some accounts, wait in Caswell's apple orchard for Eve. On the excuse of some minor chore, Eve would slip out the door and meet Enoch on the hill. The nineteenth-century records of these meetings do not provide the details of the encounters, but it is clear that the meetings involved passion. Enoch was a 21-year-old visionary who was forever thinking of a world without the grind of subsistence. What stories he communicated to Eve in the darkening orchard, what dreams, or whispers, or kisses, or whatever heated moments of love they shared, are not set down; but it is obvious that there developed between them one of those transcending relationships. This was no affair of convenience—a worthy match between a hardworking farm boy from over the hill and a good, honest dairy maid—their love, their attachment, was ethereal; it was beyond work, beyond practicality and the hard realities of life on Scratch Flat. In time they made their love known, and it appears that, in spite of Enoch's romantic tendencies and his dreams, old man Caswell approved, and Enoch and Eve were betrothed.

Exactly when this affair took place is not clear. Some of the notes in the historical society suggest that the story was played out around 1775, just before the American Revolution; but there are earlier records which indicate that the events took place during the French and Indian Wars. The earlier record may be the more accurate since it is known that one of the boys in the Lawrence family—joined by Enoch in all probability—went off to the war in 1758 and was presumed dead, and then returned a year later after having been held captive by Indians in Canada. Enoch Pratt was not so lucky, although in his own way he, too, returned.

In the orchard the night before he left for the war, Enoch met Eve. It was another one of those intense, thoroughly passionate encounters. According to Toby Beckwith, who related this story to me and supplied his characteristic drama, Eve pleaded with him not to go; she grabbed him around the neck, held tightly, and when he tried to extricate himself, made him swear to return to her, no matter what.

"Swear it," she whispered to him.

"I swear."

"I mean to God. Swear it."

"I swear to return," he said.

"Again."

"I swear to return," and then, his breath coming harder, "in body or spirit, I swear to return."

"And I will meet you," she vowed.

Sometime after Enoch left, word came back to Scratch Flat that Enoch was dead, killed by Indians somewhere on the western frontier. Eve went into shock, but seems to have recovered sufficiently by the end of the year after his departure to have resumed her daily chores. Early one evening, in the late spring, she was milking a cow in the yard when she saw a figure standing beyond the home lot. She walked toward the man, realized it was Enoch, began to run to greet him, and then suddenly turned and raced into the house screaming in terror. It was not the Enoch of the flesh that appeared in the evening light; it was some spirit form, either Enoch, or the Black Man. Still shaking from the encounter, she reported the event to her father, who delivered at this point one of the first lines to be recorded in the folk history of Scratch Flat. "If you vowed to meet him, Eve, you must meet him, in the flesh or in the spirit," he said.

Toby Beckwith graphically presented to me the results. "She went back to the orchard," he said, "her lower lip quivering, and there in the darkness consummated her marriage." Enoch appeared throughout that summer and whenever he called her, she would come to him. But by the fall, it was clear that she was dying. Slowly, over the winter, she wasted away, and in the spring, two years after the affair had begun, she died. You can see her gravestone in the old burying ground in the town.

Enoch was not satisfied. From that time on he appears on Scratch Flat searching for Eve, sometimes calling her name. He was regularly seen in the lower fields along the Beaver Brook, wandering in the evening light in the years following her death. A report of him appears about fifty years after the event, and by 1800 he was seen regularly and often could be heard calling her. Barnabas Barnes, who moved into the Caswell estate in the 1820s, reported his presence in the Caswell house, and he was seen off and on up through the 1950s in the general area. In the spring of 1975, Tommy Prescott was cutting through Scratch Flat to Forge Village after his car broke down on the Great Road. He walked through the woods on the southeast side of the tract, broke into the open fields of the Lignos farm, and was skirting the edge of the pasture when he passed through a rush of cold air that stopped him in shock. At the edge of the field, in clear view, he saw a man in colonial dress, his black hair pulled back and made fast at the nape of his neck. The man was about twenty years old, and had no discernible expression on his face; he simply stared at Prescott in silence, and then stepped back into the woods and faded from view.

Tommy Prescott, fifty years old, is a rural jack-of-all-trades: a car mechanic, a woodcutter, a welder, and above all, a pragmatic realist. But the apparition at Scratch Flat shook the very foundations of his philosophy. After the incident, he began to believe in spirits and extrasensory perception and finally, after reading a number of popular books on the subject, he became convinced of the fact that extraterrestrial visitors had appeared on Scratch Flat throughout history. He tried to convince me that Enoch Pratt was somehow involved not with the past, but a brighter future, that he was an agent of a race of superbrains, and that he had caused a number of unexplained mishaps that had occurred during the construction of one of the industries in the Beaver Brook Industrial Park.

I am an agnostic when it comes to such matters. I have yet to see Enoch Pratt or any other spirit; but if I happened to meet such a presence, I suppose, given the priming that I have had in recent years from the likes of Tonupasqua and Nompenekit, that I would at least try to accept the thing as real. I would welcome such a visitation, and, in fact, have half heartedly spent a number of hours wandering over the lower fields in Scratch Flat, hoping to see or hear the presence of Enoch Pratt. One night I was coming back from the marsh through an old orchard that once belonged to the Barnes family. No one has taken care of the orchard for years, and winter storms and high March winds have littered the ground beneath the trees with a tangle of fallen limbs and hanging branches. I was picking my way through this maze when, just behind me to the right, I heard a strangled screech or scream, as if a woman had been frightened by something, started to cry out, and then had been throttled in mid-scream. It was instant flight-or-fight. The hair went up on my neck; I spun, heart slamming, and stared into the dark branches, trying to see whatever it was that had invaded the reality of the night.

There was nothing to be seen. No Enoch Pratt, at least. I have seen and heard barred owls in the pine woods beyond that orchard and I became convinced after a few minutes of reflection that the noise was an owl scream. Barred owls are capable of the most unworldly screeches and caterwauls and have no doubt accounted for a number of the demons that have inhabited the wooded areas of Scratch Flat in the past three hundred years. But Tommy Prescott, Toby Beckwith, and some of the others to whom I have described the events are less critical about my experiences.

By contrast, Tonupasqua said that she doubted that the spirit was the ghost of Enoch Pratt although she did not doubt that there was a presence on Scratch Flat.

"They're all seeing something else," she told me. "They're all seeing the Pokawnau, the bear shaman. That's what I believe. We are the people of that land there and this Caswell woman, she goes out and meets Pokawnau in the hemlock grove. That's what happens. Wasn't no orchard; wasn't no soldier. She's out there with Pokawnau and he killed her. That's what I say, and that's what my uncle told me."

I am beginning to suspect that she might have a point. If length of time is any factor in the endurance of spirit forms, then certainly Pokawnau has the advantage. In connection with this, I had two experiences which, while certainly not convincing, at least suggest that there could be other forces at work in the area.

There are nights in Scratch Flat when the whole world goes silent, when the traffic on the highway beyond the eastern ridge dwindles to nothing, and trains do not pass on the Portland-Ayer lines to the west, and all the dogs on all the farms beyond the drumlin fall quiet. On one of these nights in winter, for no good reason except that it was still and snowing, I walked back through the woods behind our house to the hemlock grove where Mrs. Dudley supposedly met her coven. It was a genuinely beautiful evening: the cloud cover was light in spite of the snow; behind the clouds there was a full moon so that the woods were better lit than they usually are; and I could perceive the forms of individual trees, the white floor of the woods, and above, the nothingness of the white-gray sky. Halfway to the grove, I sensed that the stalker was following me, the old presence that I sensed when I first came to Scratch Flat. And the more I thought about it, the more real the thing became. There was no fear in this knowledge, and I did not turn around to see what it was. I knew from many such experiences that the act would only serve to drive the thing away. I stopped to listen for it for a few seconds and, as is always the case in these situations, it stopped too, and waited, only to continue tracking me when I moved on. I was, by this time, very tempted to turn, but I resisted the temptation until I got to the stand of hemlocks. Once there I spun around quickly and saw what I thought was my dog standing on a stone wall about 20 yards beyond the grove. Nothing odd about this, except that he had disappeared two or three months before under rather odd circumstances.

On the night of the first frost that year in Scratch Flat, I stepped outside and could hear all across the hills the yelp and howl of the farm dogs. You can often hear distant barking on Scratch Flat, but on this night there was a decided increase in activity. I was on the phone later that evening with Toby Beckwith and mentioned the fact to him. He said he had noticed it too. "Means one of them is going to die tonight," he said. My dog was, at the time, about fifteen years old, a terrier mongrel and a veteran of any number of fights, collisions with cars, and similar scrapes. He was ripe for death: his teeth were broken, he was going deaf; he was blind in one eye; and on cold mornings, he would limp around stiff-legged for a few hours before he limbered up. I let him out that night not thinking much about Toby Beckwith and his superstitions. He didn't come back that night, nor the next morning, nor the following day, not an uncommon occurrence in his case. When he didn't show up at the end of the third day, we began to look for him; and by mid-winter, after a fruitless search, he was presumed dead.

The thing on the wall turned out to be, not our old veteran rover, but a young dog exactly like him. He approached slowly when I called him, but when I made a move to pet him, he turned, tucked his tail between his legs, ran off a few paces, mounted the wall again, and looked back at me. I followed him, and he repeated the performance, moving farther and farther back in the woods, until finally, he broke into a trot and disappeared. I walked back to the hemlock grove, spent a few more minutes watching the snow filter through the trees, and then walked back home by way of the red maple swamp.

"You look for tracks?" Tonupasqua asked me when I related the story to her.

"What do you mean?" I asked.

"You should have looked for dog tracks in the snow. Then you could have told what it was. Me, I would say, there was no tracks of that dog."

TIME TRAVELERS

During the nineteenth century Scratch Flat was dominated by four large landholders, the Proctors, the Lawrences, and the Browns along the Great Road, and the family of Barnabas Barnes on Forge Village Road. Barnabas Barnes in particular seems to have enjoyed flush times during his long life on Scratch Flat. He appears again and again in the town records, first as overseer to the poor, then as selectman, and then again in various smaller offices. Among other things, he expanded the Caswell holdings in his time; on a map of 1830 his orchards extend over the drumlin and down the west side to the Lawrence and Brown farms, and east and south to the marshes of the brook. He moved into the Caswell house in the early 1800s, and he and his family took over two other houses that appeared along Forge Village Road about this time. One of these is the house I now live in. It is a small farmhouse that once belonged to a man named Peter Farwell. Farwell's death notice appears in the town records in 1840, and it is likely that Barnabas Barnes's daughter, Hannah, moved into the house shortly afterward.

According to the family history, old man Barnes was a raconteur. Nightly he would entertain his children, and later his grand-

children, with stories of the Indians of Scratch Flat and of the ap-
pearances of the ghost of Enoch Pratt. Even in those early years, the
past was darkening for the people of the area, and the legends of
Tom Dublet, the rich Indian lore of the peninsula at Forge Pond
were already providing much of the material for the folklore of the
tract of land. Barnabas was an upright, religious citizen, but in the
family history, he appears as something of an actor. The Barneses
had inherited from Jeremiah Caswell the leg bone of a British soldier
from the Revolutionary War, which Barnabas kept hidden in a chest
in the kitchen. From time to time, to liven up the stories of the war
and of the Indians, Barnes would disappear from the fireside, and
then return carrying the leg bone in his mouth and dancing mania-
cally, his eyes flashing. It seems that one night he was seized by the
fantasy of his act and could not stop himself. He raced through the
rooms of the house, turning and crouching, snorting hideously, and
finally collapsing on the floor, the spittle glistening on his lips. He
was put to bed, given herbal tea; and not long after his recovery, his
wife buried the bone behind the beehives in the orchard.

The two Barnes sons inherited the place and lived on in obscurity, presumably working dawn to dusk, year in and year out, until
they died and the farm was sold to a descendant of the Brown family.
But Hannah, unmarried, energetic, and something of a visionary,
went on to make it into the local histories. She had dark quick eyes
and black hair, the result of some apparent mixing of Massachusetts
Indian blood in her family after the family's arrival in the New
World in the mid-seventeenth century; and was, from all reports, an
ambitious woman who was interested in reading and art and later in
teaching. Early in her life she fell under the influence of Michelangelo. He became a constant subject of her conversation and later her
school lessons—he was to her the paramount human spirit, the man
above time and above place. Local legend has it that Hannah never
married because she had, in her mind, taken Michelangelo as a husband and lover. But whatever the rumors, he was clearly fixed in her
mind, and her infatuation for him as a man as well as an artist
endured for all of her life.

The histories do not say so, but it is likely that Hannah was, at
this time, associated with the events that were taking place in Concord in the 1840s and 50s. This period in the history of Scratch Flat
—the mid-nineteenth century—was a veritable age of enlightenment,

something that had never occurred before there, and that has yet to occur again. The town had by this time established its lyceum—the educational lecture series that many New England small towns were developing in those years. Intellectual curiosity began to flourish among the simple, hardworking farmers of Scratch Flat. Books were read and discussed, and people who generally thought only of cows and hay began to think of poetry and art. The concept of something beyond simple productivity began to affect them. Ralph Waldo Emerson lectured on several occasions at the town lyceum; poets and travelers, philosophical theorists, and, it must be admitted, a number of nineteenth-century quacks, weekly delivered programs for the lyceum.

In Concord, the radical educational theories of Bronson Alcott and Margaret Fuller must have attracted the attention of Hannah Barnes, and she may have brought something of their enthusiasm for learning up to the intellectual wilderness of Scratch Flat. In 1845 a school was built just north of the Great Road not far from the town poor farm, and for years, for most of her life in fact, Hannah Barnes was the teacher there, as well as superintendent of schools for the town, bringing news of the Renaissance, of Michelangelo, Leonardo, and all the hopes of education to her humble, narrow-eyed pupils.

There is a very interesting reference in two different sources on Hannah Barnes's schools which tells you something else about the comunity in those years and which points to what I feel is the real history of the place. The square-mile tract was dominated in those years by the four large landholders, but large families of the period notwithstanding, it is not likely that these landholders could have farmed the entire Scratch Flat area without assistance; and here and there in the records, and particularly in a record of the students of Hannah Barnes's school, you can get an indication of who these people were. There was a poem composed about Hannah Barnes and her school by one of her students which makes reference to the "sea" of towheads of the students, and the black island of the "fuzzy heads of the darkies." In another record it is stated that there were ten "colored" children in Miss Barnes's classes out of a class of 25 pupils. Here, I believe, is the real history of life on Scratch Flat.

These workers came, it seems to me, from all races and all parts, Yankees on the down-and-out, Irish immigrants, and later, in the early part of the twentieth century, hardworking Greeks. Here in the unwritten records, in the side references and the indifferent notes of the white Anglo-Saxons who wrote the histories, you will spot this other side of history and you will hear and read the folklore of their lives.

Many of these stories were collected by the woman who was for some seventy-five years the unofficial historian for the town. Margaret Lacey was born in 1887 in a house that lies just south of Scratch Flat. Except for a short period in the 1920s when she and a cousin made an extended trip to Arizona, she lived in the community all of her life. Even before she was twenty years old, she developed a keen interest in the past; and for the next seventy-five years began taking notes on the history of the town and its houses and interviewing some of the old people who had been alive before the Civil War. By the end of her life she was walking history. Any house, any family, or any event, no matter how obscure, she could relate to you without reference to her notes; and she never tired, even in her old age, of telling the stories to her pilgrims—whether high school students or arcane explorers such as myself who came to her seeking enlightenment.

She was, when I knew her, a frail old woman, almost a living skull, with crinkly white hair and blue eyes that could freeze the sun. She was ever polite in her accounts of the old times, ever so careful not to slander, even if that individual had been dead for a hundred years; and in order to get the stories from her, the real stories I mean, you had to work carefully. She was almost loath to talk about herself and her past, would make only slanted references to the fact that, yes, she had been here when the first airplane flew over Scratch Flat, and, yes, she did remember the arrival of the first automobiles, and the laying of the electricity wires, the hardtopping of the Great Road, and other momentous events. In spite of the fact that I became, or must have become, one of her most willing students, she never acknowledged that I was anyone any different from the half-bored high school children who came there on assignment, simply because she was old and their teachers had said she could tell them a story or two. She never knew that I was searching, through her, for something other than history; never knew how confused she made me when she would say that she had seen things that it will never be possible to see again in our time, and that she had carried these events from her past to our present. I never attempted to question her about the dilemma of time—the fact that somehow the past had been lived, had died and dispersed, never seemed to disturb her little universe. She was unflappable, a stiff old schooner beating through the incredible storm of history and refusing to take in sail.

Margaret Lacey experienced what I consider the best of all possible deaths. She used to hold forth from her couch in the cool living room of the house in which she was born. Her pilgrims would come to her and sit in an overstuffed chair beside her couch while she reminisced, talking on without notes and without the long asides and diversions that sometimes obscure the plot when old people talk about the past. In the fall of 1981, not two days after I had visited her, a high school girl came to interview her on some aspect of the nineteenth century. The girl was diligently taking notes when the steely voice halted at a natural stopping place in some account or other. The girl looked up and saw that Margaret had fallen asleep, as old people sometimes do. She waited politely for her to wake up from her nap, and then, after a few minutes, rose and went into the other room to ask the caretaker if it was common for the old lady to fall asleep in the middle of an interview. Margaret Lacey had experienced, of course, the longest nap of all: a clean break. There was no struggle, there was no unpleasant choking, no horrifying flash of the reality of what was happening; she just "passed away."

In the late spring of 1915, in the time when the roses were blooming around the Scratch Flat farmhouses and the peonies were just going by and the sun was warm, Margaret Lacey and Henry Brown took a walk over Scratch Flat. Henry Brown was, at the time, about eighty-five years old; and given the fact that the two of them covered almost three miles that day, stopping only for lunch and a tea break, he must have been in very good shape. After the walk, Margaret Lacey went home and wrote down an account of Brown's stories, and it is because of these notes that some of the events of the nineteenth century have survived.

Most of Brown's tales were of the families that had lived in houses that were mere cellar holes by 1915; but a number of personalities emerged as well. Among these was a man named Uncle Peter Hazzard, a figure of almost legendary proportions. Peter Hazzard was a black man and, like many of the black people that make their appearance in the early history of Scratch Flat and the town, was not particularly discriminated against. In fact, it appears that somewhere on the south side of Scratch Flat Peter's brother had a substantial holding in the 1850s, and later in the century a black man named Hazzard was elected selectman in the nearby community of Ayer.

Peter Hazzard was an excellent fiddler and would often play for dances in the town meetinghouse, a great cavernous structure with a suspended upper floor to improve the bounce of the contra dancing that went on there every Saturday night. Hazzard could play grace notes like no other fiddler in the region; he could seize a whole hall full of dancers with his ceaseless, ramming downbeats and his sparkling melodies and improvisations. He would, Brown reported, go into a sort of trance toward the end of the evening, playing madly, as if he were possessed of some other being; and the stalwart Yankee farmers, stamping around the floor of the hall in their orderly contra dance lines, would sometimes halt altogether just to listen to Uncle Peter's playing. Brown notes that on other occasions the people would become so affected by the music that the dancing would assume, in his words, "an unwholesome energy"—whatever that means. Peter was also a composer, knew how to write music, and would, from time to time, entertain the lyceum with his compositions. He never wore shoes, even in winter, and the soles of his feet were thicker than the hide of an ox. One winter his sister made him a pair of mocassins to keep the snow off; but they hurt his feet, and for the first time in his life he got sick that winter, so he never wore shoes again. He was an immense man, from Brown's account, about six feet five inches, very black, and very handsome, with a broad smile and darting black eyes. He was not fond of work, it appears; and in spite of the fact that this must have been, in those times of the Puritan work ethic, a sin greater than murder, he seems to have been tolerated. Brown never explained to Margaret Lacey how it was that a man like Peter Hazzard could live as well as he did in Scratch Flat, enjoy the respect of all the Yankees, and yet never work. She became interested in this fact later in her life and in her diligent way dug out what she believes to be the answer.

The Lawrence family had three rambling boys in the 1830s about the time that Peter Hazzard was a teenager himself. There was a gristmill just to the west of Scratch Flat and apparently the pond for the mill was a favorite swimming hole for the local children, black and white alike. One summer day William Lawrence took his sons to the mill pond for a swim. Peter Hazzard was there at the time, either helping old man Lawrence or helping out at the mill. In any case, the boys were diving from the mill dam into the murky water, trying to retrieve a coin that was supposed to lie at the bottom of the pond. Peter watched from the shore, not sure, says Margaret Lacey, that the game was all that wise. Old man Lawrence must have had the same reaction and called the boys back to the wagon. "One more dive," the older boy is reported to have called out; and, disobeying his father, he raced back along the mill dam, dove into the muddied pond, and did not rise again. The old man was seized with shock; he stood up in the wagon looking into the dark waters, his knees shaking and his lips pressed to a thin line. The two younger brothers began racing around the shore wading in to their waists, but were reluctant to dive into deeper water to retrieve their brother. The old man let out what Margaret describes as a strangled plea; but before it cleared his throat, Peter Hazzard dove off the dam, clothes and all, and disappeared beneath the surface. The ripples of his dive moved outward, the waters smoothed over, and then suddenly like a breaching porpoise, Peter surfaced, dove again, and then reappeared dragging the naked body of the boy. The four of them managed to revive him, loaded him onto the wagon, and started back for the farmhouse, leaving Peter at the mill. Shortly after the horses started up, the old man braked the wagon and came back to Peter. "I have gained a fourth son," he said. "I will be beholden to you for the rest of my life. But not a word of this." The whole incident lasted no more than a minute or two. It was an almost thoughtless act of bravery on Peter Hazzard's part, but it set him up for life. The Lawrence family supported him until his death.

There is another story that appears from Henry Brown in which black people were the major players; and this particular anecdote, it seems to me, is disturbingly related to some of the events which Tonupasqua told me about Pokawnau and his anger. In the early part of the 1800s, there was a black couple named Johnny and Millie Putnam living in what is described as a hut in the woods somewhere on the drumlin off the Forge Village Road not far from the Proctor homestead. Free blacks were sometimes given poor land outright in New England towns in this period; and it is likely that in this case, the holding, what there was of it, was granted to Johnny Putnam by Joel Proctor, since Proctor appears as a player in the events that were to follow.

The land in the region had, by the turn of the nineteenth century, been fairly well cleared of what the people of that era would call varmints, meaning, among other animals, wolves and bears. There is, or was, an inscription on a rock in a valley just to the southeast of Scratch Flat which announced proudly that one Josiah Whitcomb had killed a bear in that valley in 1756; and this attitude, this war on nature, was carried on without remorse throughout the eighteenth century. But it appears that there was still some wild land in the early part of the nineteenth century and, from time to time, the remnants of the howling wilderness of early periods would show up in the region.

One night early in the fall, during a light snow, Johnny and Millie's dog scratched desperately at the hut door; and when it was let in, it raced to a corner and spent the night shivering and whimpering, its hackles raised. In the morning, Johnny went out and saw in the light snow the tracks of a large animal circling the house. Leaving Millie and the dog alone, he walked down to the Proctor farm and told Joel Proctor about the tracks. Joel was apparently something of a famous hunter in the area, and arming himself with his best rifle, he walked with Johnny back to the hut. The tracks led off in a northwesterly direction, and the two men, trailed by the dog, began to follow them. Whatever it was had circled one of the Lawrence barns a few times and then backtracked to the northeast and ended in the hemlock grove on the back of the Caswell holding, presumably the same hemlock grove with its two-hundred-year-old trees that now stands in that section of the tract. Johnny Putnam and Joel Proctor halted outside the grove and attempted to get the dog to flush whatever was inside. Failing that, they went in themselves.

The snow had not quite covered the ground in places in the grove, and in the gloom and the bare ground, the two men lost the tracks and stood there trying to decide what to do. It was at this point that Johnny, fatigued from the sleepless night, sat down with his back against the tree and either took out a chaw of tobacco or began to pack a pipe. Proctor was about to join him when he happened to look up and saw, not five feet above Johnny, the great triangular head of a huge bear, its eyes fixed on the white man. Proctor slowly raised his rifle and, with the bear still steadily fixing his eye with what Henry Brown described as an almost resigned expression, took aim and fired. The bear's eyes narrowed slightly and then without struggle he fell on top of Johnny Putnam, who, though stunned, managed to crawl out from under the body. Proctor decided to go back and get an ox team to haul the bear home, and he left Johnny there to watch over the body, taking the gun with him. Johnny sat down again against another tree to smoke or chew.

Time passed in the hemlock grove, and the events that followed may have been as much a figment of Johnny Putnam's imagination as truth; but the account does have a curious resemblance to some of the stories Tonupasqua told me. Johnny noticed suddenly that the body of the bear was twitching. He was about to get up and run when the bear experienced a violent spasm, jumped to its feet, and stood there swaying menacingly, coughing up blood, with its seemingly intelligent eyes fixing the man. Johnny was frozen by fear, but it was clear that the animal was dying. It began to shake again and cry piteously, half whining, half growling in a humanlike voice. Several times it jerked its head back as if it were trying to lift its body off the ground; and at one point it succeeded in rising up on its hind legs. For a long time the bear remained aloft, stumbling around the small clearing, shuffling and swaying, jerking its head back violently, coughing and choking. It was the most hideous death Johnny Putnam had ever witnessed. It was not the simple spasm that he had seen in dying pigs and oxen, nor the jerks and leg kicks of the rabbits he and Proctor had hunted together. This death, Brown reported, was something far more ominous, far beyond normal, as if this bear were dying for all bears. For five, perhaps ten minutes, it reeled around the clearing, crashing into trees, spewing out blood, and then finally, almost tragically and peacefully, it sat down—literally sat like a man—directly in front of Johnny and died upright, its eyes staring blankly at the black man.

Johnny Putnam's life went downhill from that point on. For two weeks afterward he lost his voice and when it came back, he was loath to talk about the event. Partly, perhaps, to shake the memory, he joined up with a local man from the town and went off as his servant to join in the War of 1812. Millie never received word from him and, after a year, was courted by another black man from the Scratch Flat area named Mr. Harrison. Daily, the tall, well-spoken Harrison would come to Millie's hut and encourage her to forget the crazy ruin that was her husband. He was dead anyway, said the man, and in time Millie relented and moved in with Harrison. About a year later, Johnny showed up again, somewhat improved in spirit, and confronted the situation. Johnny and Millie finally went to a magistrate in the town to let him decide how to resolve the triangle. The town official stated that Millie must choose between the two men and that the men must live with her decision. Millie struggled for two days and then announced that she would live with Mr. Harrison. Johnny went back to the hut on Scratch Flat and lived alone until he died.

Brown's father and young Henry would often visit Johnny's hut; and there, in his last years, he recounted again and again the story of the events that had taken place in the hemlock grove, although according to Brown, it was not until he was on his deathbed that he released the critical part of the story. "Wasn't no bear died that day," he told Brown's father. "Was a man."

Apart from Margaret Lacey's record-making walk with Henry Brown, there is another document which—by reading between the lines—can give an account of the unrecorded history of Scratch Flat during the nineteenth century. In the early part of the 1800s, towns throughout New England were voting through funds to develop what were then known as town farms or poor farms. The idea of the poor farm was twofold. On the one hand, the intent was to house the paupers of the community who had no families to take care of them; and on the other hand, to house the many vagrants who would appear from time to time in any given community. Both types of social outcast were found in Scratch Flat and the surrounding towns during the period. The farms provided temporary seasonal work and a certain amount of shelter in the barns and outbuildings; and the changing economics of the times had created a fair number of paupers. In 1825 the town built a poor farm just above the marshes of Beaver Brook on the east-facing slope of the drumlin. It is still standing, a sturdy federalist structure with a massive granite foundation, some sixteen or twenty rooms, and a separate room in the cellar fitted with an iron door and barred windows to house the drunks and the occasionally violent vagrants who would show up in the town periodically. The poor farms in any community were expected to pay for themselves; they were working farms, equipped with the tools and livestock necessary to farm the land and live-in farm managers.

There were certain problems associated with this. Many of the residents of the town farms were not capable of work. The "paupers," as they were called, were often older women, and there were usually a number of cripples as well as a high number of retarded or semiretarded individuals. Residents were given room and board, but in exchange, they were expected to work on the farm, as were the vagrants who boarded there for shorter periods. In spite of these physical limitations, since the farms were intended to be economically self-sufficient, the overseers and the appointed town officials kept accurate records of income and expenditures—how much each item cost, and then in another column, how much each "resource" was sold for. All these details were set down at the end of each fiscal year and entered into the town records, where they can still be found.

I have spent many winter afternoons poring over these entries. Although they are somewhat boring on the surface, if you read between the lines, you can see written there a segment of the history of Scratch Flat in the nineteenth century—which crops were grown, what items were used on the tables, the medical care employed, the tools and the construction materials used, the fuel that was burned and the cost of that fuel. Everything that was eaten, or grown, or sold, or purchased, everything that was used in any way, was recorded in the fine old hand of the accountants, whoever they may have been. In 1873, for example, it is clear that the poor farm had a good dairy herd. Along with apples, pears, potatoes, eggs, chickens, pork, corn, beans, and hop poles, you will see, heading the income side of the ledger at $1,213.83, the words "milk sold."

You will also see there, fairly far down the list and selling for a mere $5.25, the entry "cranberries sold." This is hardly earthshaking information, needless to say. In that same year, elsewhere in the world, there was a financial panic in New York, a republic was established for the first time in Spain, and the machine on which this book was written was invented in the gunsmith firm of E. Remington and Sons. But if you know how to read the message, and if you know something about the events of the period, you can read in that simple entry the news of the world, in the history of Scratch Flat.

The lesson of the cranberry is an example. As any sixth-grade history will tell you, the 1850s were a period of major economic upheaval in New England. Whole families were deserting their farms and moving westward; and those that stayed on were hard-pressed to wrest a good living from the land. This was not necessarily the case on Scratch Flat; this little section of the region had—and still has—good soils, and farmers of one race or another have done well here for more than five hundred years. But that is not to say that the local farmers were not influenced by the agricultural experiments that were going on; and since the appointed overseers to the poor were farmers themselves, it is likely that some of these new crops would have been tested on the poor farm. It is a fairly safe assumption that sometime after the 1850s, John Madson, who happened to be the farm manager during this period, walked his charges down to the Beaver Brook marshes below the town farm. There they scythed the native vegetation, ditched a section of the marsh, put in flood control gates, and, once the ground was prepared, set out cranberry runners. One year later the runners would have produced the first crop of berries and these the farmhands packed in berry boxes purchased from the nearby Shaker community in the town of Harvard—the group responsible for the mass production of these containers. Then, with the berries cleaned and packed, John Madson sold them at the local store. In the year 1873 he received, for all of this labor, a total of $5.25.

What is not recorded in the town farm ledger is the price of the labor. That entry appears in another section of the town reports under the heading "Marriages, Births, Deaths." On the poor farm, as you can imagine, it was mostly death and very little marriage and birth. You must juggle the two reports to read the story, but it is quite clear once you put the entries together, "Timothy Stebbins, black man, died July 8, 1853. Town farm." "Medical services, Town Farm, $2.19." "Dacey Willis, pauper, d. Town Farm April 12, 1849, kicked by horse." "Dead vagrant in Town Farm, June 1, 1854."

They came to that place at the end of their tethers, old women, cripples, the mentally retarded, the down-and-outers, immigrants cast adrift in the New World, walking, some of them, west to New York, to Ohio, and later to California, and all points in between. They were carted there in farm wagons from their hovels in Hog End; they were delivered there by distant relatives who could no longer afford to pay their upkeep; they came in from other towns in the area, settled for a while in boardinghouses, and then, too sick to remain, were moved over to the poor farm. And they came on the underground railway, up from slavery to slavery, although some of the local free blacks may have been given the poor land on the hilltops in the town. The residents of the poor farms were the broken frames of the nineteenth-century social structure, cracked and knotted and hardly supporting the building. Their presence and the existence of the town farm in that area meant that on Scratch Flat you could witness the entire social scale of the community—from the stalwart large landholders to the vagrants and the retarded.

There is some indication, although it is by no means certain, that Henry David Thoreau may have spent some time on Scratch Flat. He came there in 1853 to visit Bulkley Emerson, the retarded brother of Ralph Waldo Emerson. It is not clear what was wrong with Bulkley Emerson, but it was obvious that he was mentally deficient in some form or another. He would become loud and boisterous at times, and although it appears that he was sometimes capable of caring for himself, generally he was boarded out somewhere, either in private homes or in institutions in the area. It is known that for a while he lived in the house of Reuben Hoar in the town in which Scratch Flat lies; but he was apparently removed from there after a year or so, and was placed either in the town farm or in another private home in the general area. When Emerson's mother died, Thoreau came up to Scratch Flat and fetched Bulkley to take him to the funeral. And it seems from this that he may have visited him there before.

Toby Beckwith, an imaginative Thoreauvian, claims that Thoreau would regularly come to talk to Bulkley, that he would often seek out the opinions of the simpleminded; and that here on Scratch Flat, there were deep discussions between Thoreau and Bulkley on the nature of the universe, on life, and on religion, and the art of making do. Toby cites Thoreau's portrait of the French Canadian woodcutter in *Walden* as an example of Thoreau's interest in simple people.

"We'll never know what vast issues he and Bulkley worked at down there in the fields beyond the poor farm. But I know they were there. I know they talked about the world, Bulkley shouting out his opinions in his gruff voice, Thoreau pondering all, no matter how stupid," Toby said.

He went on to describe to me the long walks by Beaver Brook, the insights that Thoreau gained, the alternate view of things; all of which is perfectly plausible, I suppose, except that if such conversation did take place, it seems likely that Thoreau would have set them down in his journals. I said as much to Toby one afternoon.

"He did," said Toby. "He set them all down, but he didn't give Bulkley the credit. Out of the mouths of babes and sucklings; my good man, out of the mouths of babes. I think Thoreau was nothing more than an early new journalist. He was an excellent reporter, but he was nonobjective and he was very bad about his sources."

Toby Beckwith has supplied me with other accounts of the town poor farm and the people who lived there who do not appear in the official records. For one of these accounts he cites as his source a man he once met who claimed to be a reincarnation of an Irish laborer who stopped for a night at the poor farm and then stayed on to work for a season. Toby, as I say, worked in off-Broadway productions for a few years and it is likely that his account is more the product of his theatrical mind; but I set it down here anyway, just in case it's true. If nothing else, it is a fairly accurate story of how things were toward the end of the century for the down-and-out.

On a moist spring morning in 1969 Toby and Rosey, having nothing better to do that day, set out to walk the perimeter of Scratch Flat. They began early in the morning from Toby's mother's place on the southwest end, just beyond Bill Sherman's bean fields. They walked through the woods over what is known as Proctor's Hill (the south end of the drumlin), and then crossed the Great Road and continued up the edge of the marshes of Beaver Brook. They were in no hurry, Rosey had brought water and tea and a sterno stove and at the edge of the old hayfields below Jeremiah Caswell's farm they kicked down the grasses and settled in to make tea. They were just finishing up when they saw a man in English tweeds emerge from the woods and poke along the edge of the hayfields. When they saw him lift into a jump, click his heels, and carry on jauntily with his arms behind his back, they knew they were onto something.

"A true eccentric," said Rosey.

"Well, we can't let this go by can we?" Toby said.

They hailed the man, offered him a cup of tea, and settled in to hear his story.

The man was not quite properly attired in period clothing, that is, his tweeds appeared to be a store-bought American version, his shoes were unshined black leather of a style that industrial workers sometimes wear, and he spoke in what Toby said could have been a fake Irish brogue. But he was doing his best, Toby said. He was also clearly psychotic or at the very least suffering from some sort of character disorder.

"I've been travelin' in toime, here," the man said after the introductions were finished and the small talk had been completed. "I've been looking over some of me old haunts."

The man explained then that he had been in some strife in his life, had had some hard times, and finally had come to realize that he had once been alive before and that the other life, his former life, was struggling to get out. Now that it was in the open, he was exploring some of the places he had once known. It appears that he had done a lot of research on his earlier life because he had some facts about the history of the area, specifically about the town of Ayer, that he couldn't have known unless he had lived back then, or done a fair amount of homework.

"He was an exquisite liar," Toby said, "but that is beside the point."

The young gentleman, Peter Riley by name, had arrived in Boston in 1882 with the understanding that the city streets were paved with gold. When he found out otherwise, he headed west where he had heard things were better. With twenty-eight cents to his name and a good pair of shoes, he began walking toward the afternoon sun, sleeping in people's barns and from time to time stealing chickens from henhouses. He took a job as a day laborer on a farm in Concord for a while and when that failed, walked west to Hudson, where he heard there was work in a mill. Not finding any work, he walked north again, until he came to the pig farms in Hog End. There he stayed for a few months during his first winter, sleeping behind a stove in one of the sheds, rolled in rags and such blankets as he could scramble together. He got a hold of a little whiskey at this time, and he and a fellow worker, "a great porker of a thing," got into a fight and Peter lost one front tooth and half of the other. He had come up to the center of the town to get his mouth cleaned up, and then, thinking things might be better to the west, as he had heard, he walked out the Great Road to Scratch Flat. He knew about the poor farm and put in there for the night, offering to pitch a little hay in the morning if that were necessary. They took him in, put him in an upstairs room with a hollow-eyed man who snored and coughed the night long; and then the next morning, true to his word, Peter put in some time in the dairy barn. The rooms were clean in the poorhouse, the food was hot and more than adequate, and, his mouth still hurting, and with no better prospects in mind, he decided to stay on for a while.

"I became a great worker there," he told Toby. "The hero of the farm and the only able-bodied man in the whole place."

The manager must have welcomed him if what he says is true, and Peter says that he was "promoted" to assistant farmer. He stayed there a full year, herding the cripples and the "idjuts" around the place, cutting the hay, pruning the apple trees, grubbing potatoes, and eating plateful after plateful of solid food. "Three squares a day and a clean bed. What more could a travelin' man ask for."

But Peter Riley was twenty-two years old and, from time to time, there would rise in him darker passions. "Needed a woman, my good man. I needed, ah, but how would they say it in those times? I can't remember that part."

Peter Riley said that there was a "colored girl" living on a nearby farm in those years, a high-toned woman with good cheekbones and a come-hither air—probably someone in the Hazzard family. In the summer, when his chores were done, Peter would wander over to the farm and spend the evening there courting the young lady. Race in this particular case seemed to be no object. But there was another suitor, "a black scoundrel with a gimpy leg and yellow eyes," and one night on his way back from his courting, Peter stopped by a trough on the Great Road to cool his passion. Out from the bushes stepped the black man and clouted Peter "up the side of me head," as Toby expressed it.

Peter spent that night by the trough and then crawled to the poor farm for rest and recovery. He went back to work as willingly as ever, but he didn't forget the slight, and about three weeks later went out for revenge. Armed with an axe handle and fortified with a pint of whiskey, he walked to the black man's shack, over on the south side of Beaver Brook, and called for a fight. The black man and his brothers came out and once more, with a single blow, knocked Peter senseless. This went on throughout the summer, Peter calling for a fight and getting beaten up, coming back for more with the same results. Finally, late one night, strengthened again by whiskey, he and a group of his friends walked over to the black man's house, set fire to his chicken house, shouted a few racial epithets, and ran off before the brothers could mobilize. An hour later, realizing what might result from this rash act, he went back to the poor farm and packed up his meager belongings.

" 'I wasn't making any money there in any case,' " Toby quoted.

Peter walked west again, found work as a paid hand on a farm in Groton, and then worked on a farm in the hill town of Ashby for a while. In those times, farmers in Scratch Flat used to drive their heifers and young bulls up to the high meadows in Ashby to graze for the summer. Peter got word there that the black man was dead, and came back that fall with the cattle drivers to see what had happened to his girl. "Black bastard wasn't dead, by any means; they tricked me, the Yankee sons of bitches. He was waiting there with a big knife, married to that young she-goat, and waiting to draw blood from the likes of me." Peter retreated without confrontation.

The Scratch Flat segment of the story ends there. Peter went on to become a policeman in the town of Ayer, and although he got in a few scrapes in his early years, rose to a high rank in the force. He died in Ayer, a respected citizen, in 1922 and was born again, according to his account, in 1927. He was raised in Ayer, and even in his childhood, was plagued by a strange feeling that he had seen it all before. He began drinking with a group of ruffians in the town, worked for a while in the mills, and then suffered, he said, a nervous breakdown and was institutionalized. It was while he was in the hospital that he came to the realization that he had been reincarnated; and armed with this information, he made a speedy recovery, was released, and had been, he said, "a toime traveler ever since."

As are we all.

10

THE PEOPLE'S PLACE

Around the turn of the century many of the farm families of Scratch Flat began to break up. The Lawrences disappear from the history books; a new house, built by a Proctor family, was constructed near the early Lawrence homestead in the late 1800s; and then about 1889 the old saltbox, probably the first English house in the area, was torn down. Another house, farther west along the Great Road, was empty at this time and either burned or was torn down, and the Barnes estate on Forge Village Road was taken over by a family named Peters. The estate was broken up at this sale, and a Levi Case moved into the small farmhouse where Hannah Barnes had lived. The Proctors, who had owned several of the houses along the Great Road, sold some of their holdings to other families; and with the institution of social welfare laws in Massachusetts, the town farm was disbanded and sold in 1909. All this is not to say that farming stopped on Scratch Flat. The soils were still good, and in some ways, in spite of the decline of agriculture at the turn of the century, the farms of the tract were about to come into a period of flush times. Quickly, within the space of 20 years, many of the farms changed hands again; and then in the 1920s, the families that now own the farms along the Great Road moved onto Scratch Flat. James Demogenes, a Greek carpenter from Dracut, bought the former town poor farm in 1927. A local farmer named Matty Matthews took over the newer Proctor house on the west end of the Great Road, and Fred Sherman moved up from southeastern Massachusetts and began to work the former Brown farm. A fine old plaster-ended house, possibly the home of the Hazzard family, was torn down at this time, and one night in 1925 there was a fire in Hannah Barnes's one-room schoolhouse. Outside in the snow, tracks were seen leading off into the orchards to the north, and a month or two later, old man Matthews died, under questionable circumstances, possibly the first of several suicides that would take place on Scratch Flat in the coming years. Rumor spread that he had gone crazy in his old age and burned the schoolhouse. His son-in-law David, better known as Matty, took over the farm at age nineteen and is still holding out.

It was, in some ways, the best of times. Fred Sherman was a perfectionist of a farmer, a man who would plow under a whole row of cabbages if one single head was not to his liking. He had come to Scratch Flat because the soils were good, and he was in business to make money. James Demogenes had five sturdy sons and, although he was sickly himself by that time, had a determination to make his new project work and to shape a good life for his children. The boys took over the dairy operation while the old man supervised from the porch, occasionally hobbling around the dairy yard pointing out little projects that had to be done. Within a few years the herd grew, a truck farming operation was started, and the boys began to win coveted agricultural awards. His son Stevie, with Fred Sherman's son, Billy, spent one winter in Homestead, Florida, studying advanced growing techniques that were being used on some of the new truck farms that had been established in that area.

James Demogenes had two daughters, Winnie and Elizabeth. One year, hearing that there were Greeks in the area and that there might be part-time work on the Demogenes farm, Jimmy-George Starkos, a young immigrant fresh from a small town near Salonika, showed up and offered to help out. He was taken on, or rather taken in, and that summer began to court Winnie. It was all tentative at first; Winnie spoke no Greek, and Jimmy spoke only broken English, and they would linger after milking in the dairy barn, laughing with each other, sometimes wrestling, but not talking much. It was all seemingly light and playful, until one August night when Jimmy-George, tears in his eyes, sank to his knees, hugged Winnie's thighs, and asked, in his way, if they could marry.

It was a good match. Jimmy was a willing worker and with the financial help of James Demogenes, they managed to buy a stony unproductive farm that had once belonged to the Brown family. The two of them began dairy farming at first; but with the coming of the Depression and falling milk prices and no money to buy food, let alone amenities such as furniture, it was clear that the farm was going to fail. It was not the best land on Scratch Flat. The farm is located on the west side of the drumlin where the glacial soils are rocky and thin. But it was better than the land that Jimmy-George had left behind in Greece, and there was a lot more of it—sixty acres all told. He and Winnie, working sixteen hours a day sometimes, planted a large kitchen garden in one of the hayfields and began clearing rocks from the other fields. They were still without furniture, making do with orange crates for tables and sleeping on bare floors in the upstairs rooms. But in the second season there, with care, the beets and the lettuce, the sweet corn and the strawberries began to flourish in the heavily manured soils. If nothing else, they would at least eat well in summer.

One August afternoon, just as the corn was coming in, on an inspiration Winnie hauled two orange crates out to the Great Road, placed a board between them, and set out a few piles of corn. Late in the afternoon a black limousine heading west for Groton pulled up in front of the makeshift stand. Winnie came out nervously, drying her hands on her skirt. A uniformed chauffeur stepped out and bought the entire table of corn. He stopped again two days later and bought all her green beans, and then again the following day to buy more corn. For the next twenty years the same limousine would pull up during the summer months and buy Winnie's produce. It was clear that there was someone riding in the back of the limousine, Winnie could see a figure through the half-closed curtains; but for all those years, all the transactions were carried out by the chauffeur; she never knew who it was that was eating so much of her produce.

More than anything else, it was the black limousine that gave Jimmy-George hope. Slowly, in the first summer, more and more cars began to pull over, until finally, by the third year of truck farming, Jimmy sold his dairy herd and went into the business full-time, relying primarily on the sales from the farm stand to make do for the whole year. Throughout all those early years, the limousine would pull up; but later, when the business got better, the chauffeur would buy no more than anyone else, and then, finally about 1945, the car failed to show. Late in the 1950s an old man came to the stand whom Winnie's daughter seemed to recognize. It was the chauffeur, grown old now, and half broken by time. He was a changed man; the formality was gone and he began to speak of the years with Mrs. Stoddard and how, when hard times came on "the poor farmers in our valley," she was determined to do something and would make him drive up and down the valley buying out the produce of the poorer working farms. "It was her way, don't you see. It was her way of helping out," he said.

By the 1930s, the full range of the social strata of New England could be found living on the square-mile tract. An energetic, fast-moving farmer named Woolly Wilson had taken over the old Caswell estate from the Peters family and was intending to turn the land into a thriving chicken farm. Wilson had two daughters who are described by the people who remember them as "strange," although what this means is not entirely clear to me, and none of my informants, all of them upright and somewhat formal older people, are willing to elaborate. The two girls would sing arias from famous operas while they helped out with the farm chores, would sometimes walk over to Forge Village to meet boys, and then come back late at night singing at the top of their range, and may or may not have made advances to some of the younger farm boys of Scratch Flat. Ester, the older girl, seems to have burned with a passion that could not be contained by the simple rural life on the tract of land. Early on she left the farm for a European conservatory of music.

Wilson was a man who never moved slowly; everything he did was carried out with a quick, jerky motion and he was forever stumbling over his projects, throwing hammers, or fits, and anything else that was handy. One morning soon after Ester had left for Europe, Wilson's wife heard a shotgun blast in the chicken house and went over to investigate. Woolly Wilson was dead beside the door, the gun still in his hand. With typical politeness, the local people will not be specific. Winnie Starkos and others claim that he was simply rushing to shoot a chicken hawk and shot himself instead, but rumors of suicide spread throughout Scratch Flat.

Shortly thereafter the estate was broken up yet again. The land on the east side of Forge Village Road was sold to a farmer, and the twelve acres around the old Caswell house were sold to a woman named Sanger who moved into the place with her nephew. The old barn behind the house, the site of so many stories and memories, the shelter, perhaps, of the midnight trysts between Eve Caswell and her spirit lover, was torn down. The spare landscape around the house began to change. The foundation of the old barn was cleaned and the ground floor where pigs once rooted in the manure and mud was planted in grass. Ornamental trees, flowering shrubs, beds of flowers, garden paths, reflecting ponds, and the hidden garden spaces of the type that appear in horticultural journals of the 1920s and 1930s began to take shape on the property. From early April through October the place would go into flower, the air around the house would be scented with tea roses, peonies, stocks, and nicotiana, the bright colors of the roses and the beauty bushes dotted the grounds. Sanger had traveled extensively in Alaska and when she came to Scratch Flat she settled down to write a book about her adventures. Her nephew was a concert pianist. He had a porch built off the south side of the old saltbox, and in summer months had his two grand pianos moved out there so that he could be closer to nature while he practiced.

South of the property, at the Case homestead, it was business as usual in the old style of things on Scratch Flat. Mina Case, Levi's wife, had produced a crop of eight children in the small house, all of them birthed in a tiny borning room. The loft of the small barn on the property was fitted with a dormitory and, in addition to the Case children, cousins and friends would come to visit the farm—if you could call it that—during the summer months. The children would all sleep in the barn, scaring each other with stories of the ghost of Enoch Pratt and the hideous Indian, Tom Dublet. Levi kept a white horse, a flock of free-range chickens, a pig or two, and an extensive kitchen garden. Beyond the garden he had a small orchard and on summer afternoons, out in the orchard, whenever the wind was right, he could hear, undoubtedly for the first time in his life, the strains of Mozart and Chopin drifting down from the landscaped estate to the north. The world at large was coming to Scratch Flat.

In 1922 electric wires were strung along the Great Road and the Demogenes farm, and many of the other farms in the area were wired for electricity. The road was paved by 1910, paved again in the twenties; and then in the thirties, with the help of WPA boys and other federal programs, many of the so-called "old" elm trees along the road, the dying ones at least, were cut or trimmed. With the advent of electricity, the old gravity-fed water systems on the Demogenes place and in the Starkos house were replaced and new wells were dug. The chug of honorable old John Deere tractors could be heard on still evenings in Scratch Flat, the putter of automobiles along the Great Road became a steady stream. The old paths and carriage roads that once cut across Scratch Flat from Forge Pond fell into disuse, some of the less productive fields were allowed to grow up to brush, and a mired farm track that cut from the Brown farm over to the Great Road was improved, graded, and then finally in the 1930s paved over. On the shores of Forge Pond people from Boston began constructing summer cottages. Noticing the trend, developers began to buy lots and to advertise in the Boston papers. Summer breezes, swimming, sailing, and good fishing were the main attractions, a rural summer of clean air and rosy cheeks. On the east side of the pond most of the lots were purchased independently; some of them were sizable tracts of twelve and fifteen acres. But on the west side, away from Scratch Flat, one developer laid out a regular summer colony. In order to impress buyers with the wild nature of the place, with marvelous innocence of history, he named the roads after famous Indians—Massasoit, for example, and Metacomet, names that used to make the blood run cold in the veins of the Scratch Flat pioneers. As Toby Caswell pointed out to me, this was not unlike naming streets after Hitler or Goering. The Pawtucket name for Forge Village Pond was never recorded; and since there was very little romance to such an industrial word as forge, the developer invented an Indian name. He called the pond the Lake Matawanakee, which, he said, means "good fishing." Some of the later histories of the area picked up on this and that is now the official name for the pond.

But Chopin and summer people from the city notwithstanding, Scratch Flat was still locked in the old patterns of struggle and survival. Over on the former Brown farm, not far from the plaster-ended house, there were a number of tarpaper shacks, one of which was inhabited by a sometime tenant farmer named Henry Hodgson. Whether Hodgson owned land on Scratch Flat, or whether he was simply tolerated by Brown and later by Sherman, is not clear; Hodgson's name does not appear often in the town records, although he was a well-known figure in the community. In the late-1920s, at the age of fifty or fifty-five Hodgson married a sixteen-year old girl named Naomi Dotson, a woman who was rumored to be part Abenaki Indian. A year later, Naomi began having babies and over the next twenty years produced twelve children, ten of whom survived to adulthood.

The old man was something of a tyrant and a well-known eccentric of the type that appears from time to time in small towns throughout the United States. The family of twelve lived together in a small structure that consisted mainly of one room with several seemingly temporary additions. As the family grew, Henry Hodgson was slowly pushed out until he ended up more or less living in the woodshed, sleeping there even in winter, tumbled among his dogs and dirty blankets. As he grew older, he grew crazier, and for the last twenty years of his life took to wandering the night roads of the community, half-shaven, and decked in a slouch hat decorated with blue jay feathers. He would be seen sometimes as many as ten miles away from his shack, steadily making his way to nowhere, cursing passing motorists, spitting and making obscene gestures to the carloads of teenagers that would sometimes race past him. He would be seen at all hours of the night, his shadowy figure appearing suddenly in the headlights. At dawn he would return and spend the day in a kitchen chair in front of his shack, alternately dozing and waking and only occasionally rising from his station to eat and inspect his domain. He had a few cows, he kept a few acres of beans and squash which he would send into the Haymarket in Boston with Sherman's crops, and he kept a semblance of a kitchen garden, a weedy thing that circled his house like a revolution.

It was mainly his children, under the subcontract of Naomi, who maintained whatever order there was on the piece of property; and it is perhaps a measure of the quality of the soil on Scratch Flat that he and his family managed to live through the Depression, the war, and the postwar period. He wasn't living well; he and his wife and children were on the verge of starvation for decades. Dressed in rags, the children would come to school barefooted as late as the

1950s, and the whole family was of great concern to church welfare groups in the community. But somehow, refusing all aid, the old curmudgeon managed to obey the single most important law of biological life—he stayed alive, and he reproduced himself. The old Hodgson genes, the voyagers through one million years of human evolution, through the vicissitudes of life at the edge of the glaciers in Paleolithic Britain, through Atlantic crossing in the mid-eighteenth century, through the hardships of colonial life, somehow managed to transmit the high, angular cheekbones and narrow chin that were so much a part of the Hodgson physiological makeup.

The Hodgson children now proliferate in the surrounding communities. Some, it must be admitted, are the inhabitants of local jails; some regularly use controlled substances to free themselves from the boring realities of everyday life; and some have either married well or managed, through diligence, to have found regular jobs. One of these is a man of about forty-five named Peewee who works on the town highway crew and who can be seen from time to time along the roads of Scratch Flat, picking up litter, plowing snow, or sweeping up after the winter sanding programs. Like most of the Hodgsons, Peewee has a sharp mind and sense of humor and a healthy mistrust of authority; and, in spite of a pronounced fondness for beer, he manages to make a living, has married, and has two children of his own.

His poor old father died an ignominious death. In his later years, after she had produced all his children, Naomi left the old man and at the age of thirty-six, with one life behind her, went off to Lowell to begin another one with a younger man. Hodgson moved back into the shack and grew older and older there, living in darkness among his dogs and a herd of goats. He was still in surprisingly good shape, and even at age eighty-four or eighty-five was able to take care of himself and tend his crops, although one of his sons would come over and do most of the heavy work. As if to make up for all those nights on the back roads of Scratch Flat, he took to sleeping long hours in his last years, lying on a couch beside the old kerosene heater. One night a passing motorist noticed that the shack was on fire, but by the time the trucks arrived, the place was engulfed in flames; and since it was generally considered to be an eyesore anyway, and was clear that if Hodgson was still in there, he was dead, they let the fire burn out. The remains of the shack can still be seen.

You will not find reference to Henry Hodgson in the official histories of the community. You will not find any references to Corky Trilling either, nor Thomas Fuller, nor Ellie Benson, nor William Patterson, Marcey Landau, Emil Laconte, or Teddy Indian. These men and women were all, at one time, inhabitants of Scratch Flat. Some of them came for a growing season to work the bean fields, some came as state charges who were taken on as foster children for a few years by the farming landholders and then given back to the institutions from which they came because they were too wild for the quiet life on the farm. Some were vagrants who passed through, stayed for a few years, and then moved on, and some were simple-minded, lonely individuals who remained on Scratch Flat for all of their small lives and died there in obscurity, unmourned and unrecorded, except in official lists of marked "deaths." These people live only in the memory of the few families on Scratch Flat who employed them or looked after them for their time; and when these people die, they will drift off and join the untold thousands of undistinguished individuals who have lived and died on Scratch Flat in its fifteen-thousand-year history.

I confess to a pronounced interest in these near-nameless individuals. They are not heroes, nor are they, as you might imagine, the muscle and blood of Scratch Flat, the work force without whose assistance the place could never yield a single bushel of produce. They are not necessarily the salt of the earth; they are not anything but individuals who lived their time and who, in their time, died. But that, it seems to me, is the real story of Scratch Flat, the real history of the world.

Curiously, in spite of farm mechanization and the welfare system, in spite of the increased suburbanization and industrialization of Scratch Flat, some of these obscure individuals can still be found here. There is an old Lithuanian farm worker who lives with his nephew on the north side of Scratch Flat who is stone deaf, who speaks little or no English, and whose sole means of support—other than his nephew's benevolence—is selling berries door-to-door or from a small stand by the side of the road. In the wild tangles behind his nephew's house he grows raspberries, strawberries, and gooseberries; and whatever he does not grow, he picks from the abandoned farmlands to the south of his house. He is an inveterate walker, will walk two or three times a day into town for no particular reason, a

round-trip of three miles. Somewhere along the Forge Village Road
he picks up an old black dog, no relation to anyone he knows, who
will follow exactly four to five yards behind him, his head low and
his tail drooping. I regularly see the two of them pass by on the road,
regularly wave, and sometimes manage to speak to him through sign
language. I tell him the sun is nice, the weather is cold, it is a long
walk, a good day for a walk, and I once tried to ask him to come into
the garden for coffee, but either he didn't understand or he didn't
want to get involved. "Yes," he said, pointing to the town across the
valley, "yes," and then he raised his hand and with a drinking motion indicating that he was going there to have a drink. He went off
laughing to himself.

On another occasion, some five years after I had moved to
Scratch Flat, my car stalled out on a subzero-degree day, the type of
day when the whole world disappears and there is nothing left alive
but the cold snap of bare limbs. As I was walking home, I met a man
so small that, except for his regular features, I would have said he
was a dwarf. Incredibly, in spite of the cold wind, he was anxious to
talk, and not being one to miss a possible story, I stayed there for a
half an hour or so, stamping my feet and beating my arms while he
told me an outline of his life. He had been on Scratch Flat all his
time, had been hired by the Demogenes family in the 1950s, had
worked for them as a general handyman, a mechanic, a chicken
tender, herder of cows, and weeder of weeds. He had watery blue
eyes, a jaunty, happy air, and he was, he said, eternally grateful to
old man Demogenes and his sons. "Wonderful people," he said, mag-
nanimously, "wonderful family. The best there is. The finest people
that ever walked the earth." This was a favorite phrase of his. Everyone he spoke of was the "finest that ever walked the earth." Winnie
Starkos had the most beautiful eyes of "any woman that walked the
earth," or alternately, she was "as fine a woman as ever lived."

He said his name was Orville Porter, but that everyone called
him Captain because for a while he had worked on what was known
as a head boat, a charter fishing boat out of Portsmouth, New Hampshire. He was raised in an orphanage, after his parents died, and was
farmed out to a family when he was a teenager, but was not pleased
with the people and so "went off to seek my fortune." He ended up
somehow in Groton, and was hitchhiking to Boston one June day
when he saw people cutting hay on the Demogenes field beside the

Great Road and joined in. They gave him a meal for his work, then gave him a bed in the former poorhouse cell, and then, after the haying season, hired him as a general handyman. No marriage, no issue, no dreams, no power, nothing but the moment and the cold cycle of the seasons. He keeps to himself; I have only seen him three or four times since that cold day, and each time he appears to be too busy with some unnamed project to talk.

Most of these unassuming inhabitants of Scratch Flat, like the Captain, keep a relatively low profile; but there is one among them whom, partly because he lives in a decidedly conspicuous dwelling, I have come to know somewhat better than others. In 1935 Fred Sherman died and his son, Billy, took over the farm. Billy was not the perfectionist that his father was and he ran the place with an easier hand although, thanks in part to the good soils, the profits never decreased. Before his father died, during one of his trips south to the truck farms in Homestead, Florida, Billy met a number of agricultural workers, and in 1936 invited some of them to come north to work for him. One of these people was a young man named Corky Trilling. Originally from Georgia, and the great-grandson of a slave, Corky came as a young man to Scratch Flat, worked for Sherman during the summers, and would return to Homestead during the winters.

One winter he met a woman named Suzie, married her, and then came north that spring for good. Corky and Suzie Trilling live in a rambling tarpaper shack just off Lawrence Street in the midst of the suburban houses that have sprung up in the strips of land that Billy has sold off along the streets of his holdings and on some of the poorer fields. His house is surrounded in summer by giant marigolds, by dusty dogs sleeping in the sun, old tractors, tractor parts, berry baskets, bushel baskets, horses, washing machines, dead cars, and many of the other accoutrements that make up the landscape of rural America in the poorer sections of this country. Inside the house, Suzie has lined the walls with Indian blankets, fish tanks, dark voodoo masks, statues, and cheap psuedo-African paintings. The room is filled with couches and beds, and dark corners, and inside Suzie spends most of her day in her nightgown and bathrobe smoking cigarettes and listening to music. In the front of the yard there is a picnic table, and there, on Sunday mornings, many of the local black farm workers gather. Corky and Suzie's house is more or less the social center for the floating community of workers who appear on Scratch Flat in spring for planting and then more or less disappear in the winter after the crops are harvested. The other people in the group have temporary or permanent housing in other communities and in some cases in other sections of the country. These people are an anomaly now on Scratch Flat; although black people were once not uncommon here, the surrounding communities and most of the town in which Scratch Flat is located are virtually devoid of Indians, blacks, Chinese, or any race other than white; and it is for this reason, to be frank, that I came to know Corky and Suzie, as anomalies interest me greatly.

Corky Trilling is a man whose life is run by beans and cabbage. He is a hard worker, among other responsibilities, in recent years, he has taken over management of the Sherman place, no small task. But he has a definite hedonistic streak in him. "Got our heads all smoked up last night," is one of his constant complaints. You would say, given his situation, that he should have other, more serious complaints. Billy Sherman's farm is a classic example of the American agricultural sellout, on many levels. Good arable land has been turned into a sterile suburban tract development there; the construction of some of the houses was associated with some unsavory incidents; and Corky and Suzie continue to live in what seems to be abject poverty, while Sherman and his wife live in a substantial townhouse in a fashionable section of the community. But fish as I will for complaints from Corky, patient as I am to press just so much for information and to allow the rest to come out, I cannot get him to complain. "Billy is a good man," Corky says. "I want you to know that Billy is a good boss, a good man to work for." But although he will not complain about his life with Billy Sherman, although he spends his life in apparent contentment, working hard six days a week, getting his head smoked up on Saturday nights and spending easy Sunday mornings at the picnic table discussing the adventures of the previous night, there is in him a darker reality. Once, after I related to him a story of a black family whose new house was firebombed in a nearby community, he snorted cynically and shook his head. "There's no freedom for the black man ever since he was dragged out of Africa," he said. On another occasion, after a discussion of the same incident, he said that you have to make do. There is no freedom, so you have to find a center, a good boss, some land, and make do. "Better than being in Detroit or New York," he said.

Obscure, happy-go-lucky individual though he seems, you can find in him virtually all the fears, all the pain, the fantasies, hopes, and concerns that presumably affected Hannah Barnes, Eve Caswell, Tom Dublet, or any of the other players who have appeared and disappeared in the Scratch Flat history. He is afraid of death; he is acutely conscious of the injustices of the world; he is worried about the loss of farmland in this country; and he has mixed feelings about his marriage to Suzie. None of this would come out in an ordinary conversation with him; you must work at getting him off the subject of green beans and beer and the Saturday nights of his life; and in some instances, in order to read the story, you have to look not at what he says, but at what he does. Of all these larger concerns, it is Corky's view of time that most interests me; not necessarily his view of it, I should say, but his approach to it. And as is often the case, the view is expressed in action rather than words.

Until the mid 1970s, a corporation used to graze thoroughbred horses on the old hayfields between Beaver Brook and Route 495. Corky knew one of the horse trainers, and one year, after some fairly elaborate negotiations, was given a filly who was so seemingly crazy, so totally uncontrollable, that her owners had decided that she would never take a harness and so planned to destroy her. Corky bought the horse for fifteen dollars in 1964 and set out to train her. The local horse world was dubious, from the lowest stable boy to the owners. "No man but the devil could break that thing," the trainer told Corky.

The day after he got the filly, Corky put her in a paddock behind his house, and every evening, after a day in the fields, he would go out and stand there talking to her. After some six or seven weeks, he got a rope around her neck and began walking her around the paddock; and by the end of the first summer, he managed to get her out into the fields on a lead. That much the trainer had accomplished in a few weeks, and as he watched Corky's progress, he mocked him. "You don't understand," Corky said, "I know what you've done with her; I'm just trying to undo all that so I can start again."

The following spring Corky started walking her with a halter, by midsummer he got a harness on her, and by the fall he managed to get a bit in her mouth. And all this time, he was walking. Every evening, every morning before he was off to the fields, he would take her out; and whenever he couldn't take her, he managed to persuade his uncle to lead her, an old white-haired man who, if anything, had twice the patience of Corky. By the second spring he got her to pull a sulky, and throughout most of that summer, they would be seen all around Scratch Flat, a spirited jumpy horse pulling an empty carriage, led by a slow-walking black man with a gold tooth and a gravelly voice. By midsummer he was walking behind her, reins in hand; and by the end of the summer, after three years of soft words and untold miles along country roads, Corky climbed into the sulky, took the reins, and the horse trotted off in total control. For the next few years he and his nephew could be seen on deserted roads in the area, speeding along like an engine gone wild, the horse's legs pumping like pistons and her ears and eyes alert.

I have also, on many occasions, attempted to solicit from Corky his views on place, but his only response has been to tell me that you play the hand that has been dealt you. "You play it as it lays, my man—just play it as it lays." He is, of course, the ultimate disenfranchised individual, the classical uprooted man—dragged out of Africa to an alien continent, dragged out of slavery to landless poverty, and then dragged out of the warm Georgia winters to endure the lonely life of a black man in white New England. He is much less attached to the place that is Scratch Flat than anyone I know, in spite of the fact that he has been here now longer than most of the inhabitants. I asked him once what he would do when Billy Sherman dies, or after all the bean fields are sold off and developed. "Don't know what I'll do, come to think of it," he said. He has a habit of snorting out his breath quickly in a snicker as if to say, "Here comes another bad hand." But in that snicker, in that cynical gravelly voice, there is a profound sense of survival.

One autumn afternoon I stopped at Suzie's picnic table and shared a beer with Corky and another black man who sometimes works for Billy Sherman. Corky told the man that I was collecting stories about the farm, and when I said that I was trying to get together everything I could find out about the people who lived here, the black man asked if I was going to tell any stories about Indians. When I said that I was, he told me that he was part Indian. "My mother was a Choctaw," he said. "Got thrown out on the dung heap with all the other niggers in this world and mated with one of them. Out came me, nine months later."

"Who threw her on the dung heap?" I asked, knowing full well.

"You did," he said, but he was still smiling.

"Well in a way I guess you're right," I said.

"You know I'm right. That's why you're here collecting stories about niggers and Indians."

"Take it easy, Tommy," Corky said. "Just ease up there, he's a good boy."

"He's collecting nigger stories because he never did live, Corky. Where you from anyway?" he asked me.

I told him how I got to Scratch Flat, leaving out, for convenience, the pleasing parts and relating the few hardships that I happened to have endured—most of them by choice.

He saw through the ruse immediately.

"What do you do man? You play nigger in your life, to make up for your slave-owning great-granddaddy? You know what it's like to work? You know what it's like to have some white son of a bitch with squinty eyes tell you not to spill no more peas on the ground, tell you when you can and when you can't piss? Tell you hurry up or slow down, or jump, and he younger than you, and treating you like you was a little boy? You know what that's like? No you don't. Might be that when you were sixteen years old, they spoke to you like that one time. And if you didn't like it, you could go home to your daddy because what the hell, it's only a summer job anyway. You go to college? Yeah, I bet you did, otherwise you wouldn't collect stories about niggers and Indians."

"Don't worry 'bout Tommy," Corky said to me. He was getting noticeably embarrassed by his friend, snorting more and shifting on the bench.

"No, I mean it Corky. Look at this guy. Why's he going to tell our story?"

"Well, why not? What's the hurt?" Corky said.

"Because that story belongs to the black man. What else you got Corky? You got no land, you got no respect, you got no power. All you've got is your own story and now they want to take that away too. It bugs me, Corky, that's all."

This man's anger, although somewhat threatening, was curiously cathartic. He was clearly someone who had been broken a number of times in a number of places, had climbed up to be broken again, and had finally let all the bitterness show. The whites of his eyes were yellowish, and while he delivered his tirade against me, I noticed that he would glance away periodically. It was no more than a split second, but I sensed that he was afraid. In spite of his arrogant delivery, he was hardly the liberated black revolutionary; he wasn't even a black man to me, he was Tom Dublet, and the bear shaman; he was Henry Hodgson, Peter Riley, and all the poor, crippled slaves, black and white alike, who had been broken by diseases, by economic circumstance, and ended up living out their days on the poor farm.

11

TEARING
DOWN TIME

About three weeks after my wife and I moved into the house on Scratch Flat, a small bronzed man emerged from the woods beyond the meadow and began to pick his way through the blackberry brambles. He came forward slowly, almost apologetically, looking down to pick his route, and then looking up with a broad smile to tell me that he was coming, and that he was a friend, and that because of the thorns it would take him a while to get within speaking distance. When he finally extricated himself to the clear meadow, he shook my hand and told me that he was Jimmy-George Starkos and that he owned the farm on the other side of the hill.

Jimmy-George was a veritable potato of a human being, his face browned and creased by sixty years in the sun, his hands stubbed and blunted by groveling in the poor soils of the various farms he had tended in his life, and his legs short and bowed as if to bring him still closer to the earth he loved. He was all nubs and bulges, rounded in some places, squared in others, and although heavyset, not in any part soft. In short, he was very potatolike, a thing of the soils. He immediately began talking in his thick Greek accent about the land onto which I had just moved. "Was good soil here," he said. "Good soil, but they let the place go after the old man died. Was good land. Now too many blackberry, too much poison ivy. What you going to do here anyway? You going to live or you going to farm?"

It was an odd question coming from a man who had spent most of his life farming; and at that point I didn't have any idea what I was going to do, although I had it clearly in mind that one of the prime reasons we had bought the place was the presence of the four acres of overgrown gardens and meadows. I was, when we first came to Scratch Flat, still half in love with wilderness. I was still seeking the emptiness of the black hills that I used to walk through in western Connecticut, still daydreaming of wild landscapes, and roadless places unsullied by human presence; but I was slowly changing. So was the world.

It had come to me about that time that there is really no place that is free from human influence. The discovery of lead in the snows of the Arctic, and the presence of tar balls thousands of miles from land, had undermined my hope of pure escape; and, in any case, I was coming to love more and more the idea of the sort of Jeffersonian landscape with farms and houses interspersed with wood lots. Just before we moved, my wife and I spent some time in the Azores; and there I saw, in a high valley on the island of San Miguel, what seemed to me to be an eternal symbiosis. The Azores are volcanic islands; the soils there are rich, and an almost constant mist or light rain provides plenty of moisture. The islands are frost-free, and except for fuel oil, steel, and a few other commodities, are essentially self-sufficient. The economy is based on export—always a healthy sign, I am told. We spent a week in that valley hiking the ridges above the town during the day, talking to the shepherds on the high meadows, soaking in the warm volcanic streams, and then walking home along the mountain roads in the evening dreaming of an earthly paradise complete with squash and sheep. Here was everything—birds, sky, good food, fish, butter, eggs—who needed the lonely, unproductive mountains of the American West or the North Woods? I came home from the Azores determined to forge a similar economy somewhere in the United States.

I was, of course, not alone in this view. At that period, there were any number of people returning to the land to try to live in a self-sufficient manner in the face of rising oil costs, a dwindling, shoddy economy, small-minded politics, the death of the hopes of a peaceful cultural revolution, and all the other ills that affected the dreamers of the sixties. And so, to find a piece of arable land not twenty-five miles from a civilized city, to find good soil, an honest, if somewhat decrepit house, a good view of the sunrise, a little space for walking, and neighbors consisting mostly of humble husband-men, seemed not all that bad a prospect. In spite of the ominous presence of the highway, we decided to buy. I should have known better. I had done enough homework in land use patterns to know that where there is a highway, no matter how rural the place may seem, there is certain to be development in the future.

In any case, not three weeks after Jimmy-George emerged from the woods behind the house, I began to cut. I had become, at that time, fairly proficient with the scythe, a tool I have come to love and respect; and starting at the rough grasses just behind the back door, I began slowly, patiently to cut down the return of the wild land. In one week, with the aid of friends and a Gravely tractor, I had cleared the tall grasses and cut off most of the blackberries and the poison ivy from a one-acre section behind the house. By the end of summer, I dug in a garden; and in spite of the fact that it was already late August, I put in a few fall crops and an asparagus bed, got some hens, and cleared away Levi Case's fallen barn and a lot of rusting parts of cars, toys, farm machinery and kitchenware that lay hidden in the grasses and in various dumps around the property. That fall I cut off a small section of the woods for fuel wood, and then when spring came, cut some more. I built a back porch to sit on during the languorous summer evenings, and I began to clear more native vege-tation, putting in its place small garden patches. I had learned from the Azores about small-scale agriculture and intensive gardening, and by the end of the second summer there were little plots of corn, peas, potatoes, and other staples spread all over the tract in a some-what haphazard fashion. In the second summer, I brought in an ally in my war on the poison ivy that ran rampant over the land: a young, energetic pig. I would fence him in an area, and then after he had routed out all the vegetation I would move his pen a few yards and plant rye in the freshly turned, freshly manured areas in his wake. I planted flowers, cleared the plum grove of poison ivy vines, mowed more grass, cut more trees, turned over, mostly by hand, more gar-den plots; until finally, some five years later, there was, in the area around the house, a semblance of my ideal—a European monk's garden of herbs and arbors, fruit trees, vegetable plots, and experimental growing areas.

There was great hope in those years. We had fresh greens and asparagus in late spring; we had beets and turnips, peas, and beans by early summer; we had corn and tomatoes by August; beets again and monstrous zucchinis and squashes by the end of summer; and sometimes without effort we would have an accidental crop of apples from Levi Case's trees. We had bread from flour ground fresh from the rye we grew in the wake of the pig, and we would have had fresh pork if a local husky had not killed our willing pig ally one night while we were out to dinner. No matter; we had eggs from our hens; we had cold water from our well; we had wildly beautiful weather fronts sweeping overhead, we had migrations, deep snows, glowing wood fires, and all the other elements of the so-called good life. And yet, there was something missing.

The morning after we moved in the old nature man in me took a short walk around the property. Here amidst the tangles of the grasses were the jeweled webs of yellow garden spiders. Flocks of barn swallows darted over the meadows and the fields across the road, the meadow crickets chimed in the grasses, and during that first night I could hear the dark energies of the insect chorus—the snowy tree crickets, the cone-headed grasshoppers, and other night-singers, hammering out their music. The land was returning to a wild state, creating what is technically known as an oldfield ecosystem, generally recognized by students of the subject as one of the most diverse and interesting habitats that can be found in the New World. It is also, of course, the hardest to manage since by its very nature it is in flux. Fields become scrubby old fields, old fields become young woods of blackberry, rose, birch, and pine, and young woods become climax forests. The deep forest, the Pleistocene ecosystem, is always trying to reassert itself; and European husband-man that I was in those days, like all the other white people who had lived on Scratch Flat since the first English settlements, I had begun to fight it back in spite of my background in ecology.

I was not unaware of the outcome of all the cutting and chopping and digging. I knew what would happen, but I figured—I suppose—that since there were so many old fields around the area, what would it matter that a mere two acres of habitat was altered? But one morning I realized that all the yellow garden spiders were gone. I noticed that the night chorus of the insects, while still throbbing loudly around the property, was more or less quiet in the new garden plots and fields I had cleared. The leopard frogs, the toads, and the small snakes were sadly diminished; and the raucous meadow of wildflowers, the Queen Anne's lace, the hawkweed, the Indian paintbrush, the daisies, and all the other bright eyes of the wild meadow had been evicted and replaced with peas and potatoes. Some of the wild things came back, I should say, once I stopped clearing and had gotten rid of the poison ivy and the brambles and allowed the land to grow up a little more; but the great populations, the rank tangle of wildflowers, never came back with the same vigor.

Five or six years after I moved onto the land, I more or less realized that I could, if I were so inclined, achieve self-sufficiency. I had learned enough about gardening techniques, about soil care, double cropping, green manures, watering schedules, hen care, small-grain raising, and wood lot management to cut myself free from at least some aspects of the economic system. But curiously, no sooner had I realized that it would be possible to achieve this goal than I found myself losing interest in it. I slowly became involved in some of the finer elements of horticulture, the more civilized aspects of the art, beyond mere survival. Year by year I began to plant flowers in sections of the garden where I once grew winter squashes. I cleared more plots of ground, allowed others to grow up to grass. I put in flowering shrubs, began to plant roses all over the place, grew wisteria rather than grapes, and planted row upon row of cutting flowers in the plots where I had lately tended my beans and my carrots. I kept the vegetable garden, to be sure, improved the tomato patches, and continued to plant asparagus beds, but a change had set in. Rather than work in the garden, I found that I was content to sit under the wisteria arbor behind the house, watching the delicate play of the butterflies in the flower garden, listening to Chopin and Mozart, and dreaming of nineteenth-century Europe, of books and poetry, and scented flowers. I still walked, of course, I would rise in the morning and strike out across Scratch Flat before dawn, wandering through the dark pines, swimming in the brook, and poking amidst the old foundations and the stone walls. But I was going about it in a different sort of way now; I was not out there fanatically identifying every species of plant and animal. I wasn't even interested anymore in the details; what I had come to enjoy was the overview, the sweep of the winds in Charlie's fields, the arching blue of the sky, and the bubbling music of the indigo bunting.

"Old age," my wife said. "You're just getting to be one of these old guys. Happens to the best of us."

But all the while I felt younger. I felt a vague liberation from the dictatorship of the garden. In those early years we sometimes would eat food simply because it was in season, which meant of course, living on peas and beans in July, corn and zucchinis and tomatoes in August and September, and beets, turnips, carrots, and other hardy crops in autumn and early winter. One could do worse, of course; but I lost all interest in patiently shelling and freezing peas for the coming winter when the summer sun was still shining. I had become, in short, the hedonistic grasshopper, rather than the practical ant.

It was about this period that I began to become more interested in time and the way it has played itself out on Scratch Flat. And one morning in the plum grove, thinking as usual about history and change and the new interests I had developed, it occurred to me that I was going through an evolution that mirrored almost exactly the things that had happened on the square-mile tract of land on which I was living. It made me understand how inextricably connected to this piece of land I had become.

Scratch Flat was originally what the European mind would term wilderness. It was a place of wild animals and primitive hunter-gatherer tribes. Slowly over the millennia, the hunter-gatherer culture, the true nature people, evolved into agriculturalists, people who would intentionally alter the natural system to subsist. These agricultural experiments became, in the hands of the English farmers, far more refined. Specialized crops were grown to sell rather than for subsistence; and then finally, only very recently, for the first time since the Archaic period, people who were not agriculturalists moved back onto Scratch Flat. They were at first people like Mrs. Sanger and the vacationers in the lake cottages who came to get away from the city; but once Route 495 was constructed people moved onto Scratch Flat because it was a relatively nice place to live and was, because of the highway system, convenient to wherever it was they were working. The final stage in this evolution, and one which has yet to be fully developed, has been the arrival of the small industries.

It is, I am sure, pure coincidence, but this evolution of the place matched my progress from a lover of wild nature, to a subsistence gardener, to a mere inhabitant of the place known as Scratch Flat. But, I think there is a key in this progression of things to an understanding of the changes that have taken place on Scratch Flat and, by extension, in this country. The Archaic and Paleo people had no particular loyalty to a single place. They were constantly on the move, following the game wherever it happened to be most abundant. Myths and legends of Scratch Flat, identification with the place as a place, love of the land only emerged with the coming of the agriculturalists; and ironically, in spite of the mutual animosity of the two cultures, this attitude toward the land, with some variation, crossed cultural lines. Both the late Woodland Indians and the English felt some connection with the place. By contrast, the people who live here now, even the farmers, are more or less camping out here. They could have settled anywhere as long as the environment was reasonably ordered. Scratch Flat offers a little breathing space, a pleasant view here and there, nice farmlands, convenient shopping, convenient transportation, and recreation; a thoroughly convenient somewhat boring life. But if the industrialists move in, if developers alter the place, if the conveniences disappear and the amenities of the landscape change, the people who now live here will get up and move on. And if they can't afford to do that, they will most certainly complain. It is clear that Scratch Flat, the hunting place of the Paleo-Indians, the garden site of the agriculturalists, is going to change. The long and inextricable relationship between the human cultures that have lived here and the natural resources of the place, both wild and domesticated, will come to an end and the place will be taken over by a culture that does not need Scratch Flat to survive. This is, in essence, the greatest change that the region has experienced since the first arrival of the Paleo hunters; and it will, in all likelihood, mark the end of the concept of Scratch Flat.

This is not quite as dramatic as it sounds. In effect, the place is dead already; I have simply reinvented it. There are very few people in the community who have ever heard of such a name, and most of the people who live on Scratch Flat have no idea what they are living on top of. Its abrupt slide into obscurity began toward the middle of the nineteenth century when rail lines were laid into the town, when communications improved and the distinctive quarters of the community became melded into a single town. Scratch Flat was, in those

late years of the nineteenth century, still thought of as an entity
perhaps by the people who lived there, but the concept of the place,
the idea of a flat with a definitive population of neighbors, a tribe so
to speak of agriculturalists, began to slowly erode. The symbolic end
came in 1964 when Route 495 was officially opened.

Scratch Flat's fate was cast in the early 1950s in an upstairs
room at 100 Cambridge Street in Boston. Highway engineers and
planners with white shirts and clean fingernails studied for years
detailed maps of the region and with their plotting instruments drew
lines through hills and orchards, split towns and farms, and then
redrew the lines, prepared alternative routes, and then prepared alternatives to the alternatives. It was all haggling and politics, night
meetings in a hundred town halls along the forecast route for the
new superhighway. It was high finance, a few secret deals, I am told,
and a few trades of land and direction, and then finally, after years of
discussion, the contractors were hired and the bulldozers moved out.

These were in the days before the existence of the Environmental Policy Act. These were the times before the militant highway
fighters of the late 1960s and early 1970s. There were no tools to
study the impact of Route 495 on the regions in its path; and even if
there had been, it is likely that in those innocent years of uncontrolled growth, everyone would have welcomed the highway, even
the landholders in its path. "Good for business," they would have
told you. "Good for the economy." What this path would do to the
sacred land of the Pokawnau, the bear shaman, was not considered.
What it would do to the burial place of Tom Dublet was not discussed. What it would do to history, to the ghost of Enoch Pratt, to
the leopard frogs, the painted turtles of Beaver Brook, the agricultural lands of Jimmy-George Starkos, the home of David Matthews,
Billy Sherman, and all the other farming families that lived in the
one-mile section west of the proposed route was not discussed. It
wouldn't have mattered anyhow; it was the best of times.

It was the worst of times. Fate was cast in the planning boards
at 100 Cambridge Street and executed in the apple and pear orchards
east of Scratch Flat. It was in those years that the men in khaki came
to Ted Demogenes and offered to buy outright the whole of Cobble
Hill. It was in those years that they came with their bulldozers and
tore it down, and it was then that they obliterated forever the last
signs of Tom Dublet—the little cutaway in the hill where he either

lived or stored his corn. It was then that they scraped off the good topsoil from Ted Demogenes's hayfield, soils that took five thousand years to build; and it was not long after the highway was constructed, ten years at most, that Ted Demogenes decided to sell his farm, the former town poor farm, to an industrial developer.

You cannot blame this innocent player. You cannot blame, out of hand, any of the farmers of Scratch Flat who, in their ignorance of history, sell off their heritage. Many of the farmers are old now, they are sitting, in some cases, on as much as one million dollars' worth of real estate, and they are, as farmers, making at the very most twenty-five thousand dollars a year. They have no retirement plans, no health benefits, no secure means of income after they grow too old to work. Billy Sherman has no children. Ted Demogenes's children and the children of Jimmy-George Starkos have gone into other fields, and Charlie Lignos has only young daughters who have not made up their minds what they are going to do. Of all these men, Matty Matthews, stubborn Yankee that he is, is the only one who will not give up the fight, and fortunately he has a son, who not only wants to take over the family farm, but appears to be as efficient a fighter against the forces of change as his father.

And yet, in spite of the seeming inevitability of change, in spite of the fact that the entire force of the economy, is against them, there are still people in the town and on Scratch Flat who fight the tide. The sale of Ted Demogenes's land took place in obscurity. There were no dramatic presentations at the time of the sale; there were no alternative offers from environmentalists or farmland preservation groups—of which there are a few in these parts. The land sale took place without comment. But when the first bulldozers actually appeared, a few of the local residents, mostly the people along Forge Village Road, rose to arms. By then it was perhaps too late; but nonetheless, as required by town ordinances, there were several open planning board meetings; there was a certain amount of heated discussion and there was even a little name calling.

Toby Beckwith was at that meeting and although he already knew it was more or less a lost cause, he asked, very politely, a number of significant questions, and retired peaceably to his seat to hear the inevitable response. I knew, however, that he was brooding on the subject. Toward the end of the meeting he asked to be recognized and when he stood, his entire demeanor had changed. He was no longer the innocent rational questioner; he was rising, I could tell, to one of his prolonged Shakespearian tirades. He began quietly enough, speaking in a low and dramatic voice. "But if I might put the question Mr. Devlin," he said, speaking directly to the developer. "If I might be so crass as to bring forth into this discussion the subject of money. Do you understand what I mean, sir? I am talking about filthy lucre. The thing that makes the very world turn on its axis. You, I think, Mr. Devlin, will make a great deal of money by this development, will you not?"

Devlin nodded without making a commitment one way or the other.

"I don't think this is a question for the planning board, Mr. Beckwith," the moderator pointed out.

"Oh, quite to the contrary, I think," Toby said. *"Radix malorum cupiditas est,* if you take my drift Mr. Devlin."

"Toby, maybe you should sit down," the moderator said.

"Oh no, I am not ready to sit down. I want to make it clear what is going to happen here to Mr. Demogenes's hayfield, if you don't mind. This is very important, Mr. Moderator. This is of the utmost importance. It is the essence of importance, the very core of things, the heart of heart, the heart of darkness, the heart of Mr. Devlin, I might add. We are looking here at the root of all evil. You can see it in this very room if you would but turn your eyes in the proper direction."

"Sit down, Toby."

"Never. I must deliver my message to this man. Who are you, Mr. Devlin? You are a man that burrows into the night in our country. You come out here from the pollution of Belmont. You will bring with you the pollution of your avarice. You will construct on our hayfields a monument to greed, an industrial building, gray and hideously ugly. You will pollute the very waters of our wells with your offal; you will, I might add, ruin one of the better views in this town for the poor inhabitants of the Forge Village Road. You will foul our nest and then go back to your clean suburban home with your clean and manicured lawns and you will count your money, won't you, Mr. Devlin? You will . . ."

Toby's paramour Rosey began tugging on his coat at this point; he looked down, lost his direction for a second, and in the interim the moderator broke in and started talking on another subject, speaking rapidly to keep Toby from interrupting. Toby broke in a couple of times, but the moderator was holding the stage now. Toby remained standing for a long time, half smiling; and then when he had the chance, said that he would like to thank the moderator very much for his "just consideration of my opinions of this subject," and took his seat.

Toby's allusion to the water resources was perhaps the most significant part of his abbreviated attack. In the end, the question of clean water came very close to prohibiting the development altogether.

There is, in the town in which Scratch Flat is located, a singular hero of the environmentalists, a huge, swaggering individual with a foul mouth and a full beard, who was given a job to do, and who then proceeded to carry out his work to the letter of the law, losing sleep, vacation time, and as you will see, other things in the process. The man's name is Bradford Thurston and he is, among other things, the health inspector for the town. His job is to maintain the water quality in the town wells, assure the proper function of septic systems in the community, and deal with related health matters.

The development that was planned on the Demogenes farmland happened to be located near the town wells, which were placed in the floodplain of the Beaver Brook in the early 1960s. As long as there were hayfields in the so-called cone of influence of the well fields, water quality in the wells could fairly well be assured. But if there were, even nearby, industries which would put into their septic systems long-lived chemical substances that are not cleansed by the natural drainage patterns, then theoretically the town could experience the disaster of chemically polluted public wells. Such things had occurred recently in other Massachusetts communities along Route 128 and in the town of Acton, and health officials and environmentalists throughout the state were alerted to the problem. In the end, however, rather than halt the development of the so-called Beaver Brook Industrial Park, as the opponents wished, a compromise was arranged. It was ruled that those industries that had toxic waste water would have to construct self-contained disposal units. Normal wastes, sewage and the like, could go into a regular septic system, but the toxic wastes would have to be controlled separately. The case was closed, the bulldozers moved in, and after six months, the Beaver Brook Industrial Park was constructed. Thurston was not sure the compromise system would work. In effect, he had lost a round. But he was to get another chance.

It was about this same period that Billy Sherman began to sell off lots in his bean fields. He was in the 1960s the largest single landholder on Scratch Flat; he was making enough money from the better fields to live decently enough; but he was, like the other farmers in the tract, facing old age, and dreaming of a sort of retirement, a life without the eternal rounds of beans and cabbage. Slowly, lot by lot, small tract by small tract, he sold off his land, and small developments of moderately expensive houses began to appear on the flat lands below Proctor Hill.

There was, at the time, a growing realization in New England that the agricultural heritage of the Northeast was disappearing at a faster rate than ever before in the region's history, and groups and organizations were forming to help slow or halt the destruction. Never mind that the demise of the farmlands began more than one hundred years ago and that the region may be witnessing the end of an era; there is a certain logic to the move. For one thing, all the new frontiers have been cultivated. There is no new farmland in the United States to speak of; what we have now is all we'll ever have, in spite of the fact that the population of the country is growing. Furthermore, in New England, some 80 percent of the food is imported from the west and midwest, adding the high cost of transportation to the basic cost of produce. What is more, and this is perhaps the most significant aspect of the problem, as any military adviser will tell you, it is very dangerous to draw out your supply lines. One little break, a truck strike, a lack of gas, a snowstorm even, can disrupt the food supply.

As a result, there was a certain amount of concern voiced in the community when it became apparent that Billy Sherman was developing what amounted to some of the best agricultural land in the town. And once again, environmentalists and similarly concerned citizens looked to Thurston as the last hope of salvation. There is no law—so far—against selling off good arable land for development; but whether the new houses could be placed on Sherman's land and still abide by the local environmental regulations was another matter. Billy Sherman's fields are notoriously wet, which is one of the reasons his father was able to grow celery there so successfully. In fact, the area is very well drained; but since the soil base is sandy and the groundwater levels are high, standing water often appears in the fields after heavy rains. The sandy subbase in some sections of the fields meant that the percolation test to determine the suitability for septic systems worked too well; that is, water drained through the soil too fast to cleanse the bacteria from the septage. As a result, true to form, Thurston stated that arrangements would have to be made to improve the septic systems, thereby adding an expense to the developer's dreams. Furthermore, the diligent Thurston found that the groundwater in some sections of Billy Sherman's fields had traces of pesticides, and therefore wells could not be legally dug in the area. Town water would have to be brought in, adding yet another expense to the development. From the developer's point of view it appeared that Thurston was simply nitpicking, attempting to stop development by forcing the contractors to abide by the letter of the law. This was highly unusual the developer argued. In other towns developments with similar problems were able to proceed apace without the petty niggling from narrow-minded bureaucrats. Again and again Thurston had forced developers to follow the regulations closely; had, in fact, halted some ambitious projects and was becoming a recognized enemy of progress.

There is, as Toby Beckwith accurately suggested at the planning board meeting, a lot of money involved in the business of land development and wherever there is money, there are, shall we say, means of applying pressure. And so it was that in the middle decades of the twentieth century, after a period of relative peace, the nasty head of violence loomed over the fields of Scratch Flat.

One night a highly placed town official suggested that Thurston should perhaps be a little more lenient about his regulations and perhaps allow a certain amount of development to take place; otherwise, he said, "there could be trouble." Thurston pressed for details and learned that a group of contractors in the region were "very angry," and were planning to do something about it. A few nights later Thurston got a telephone call from a gruff-sounding individual who seemed to be speaking through a handkerchief to disguise his voice. The message from the caller was very simple. Thurston was informed that he had an eighteen-year-old daughter with a very pretty face and that if he wanted her to continue to have a very pretty face, he should stop hassling developers in his town.

It was, as these things are, the cruelist strategy, an attack upon the weakest point in the battle line, unethical, immoral, without honor, without humor, and without any sense of gamesmanship. Thurston called the local police, told them about the phone call and asked for help. The police, for a variety of reasons, were unable to help; and so there was nothing left to do but call the FBI. The phone call was, in all likelihood, an idle threat, a simple scare tactic that no one intended to follow up on; but there was no sense in taking any chances.

The FBI showed up at Thurston's house shortly thereafter. Two men shadowed his daughter at her college in western Massachusetts; and every night when he came home, Thurston dutifully sprinkled talcum powder over the seam on the hood of his car. "It's just a precaution," the FBI told him. "You look at the powder every morning to see whether anyone has opened the hood. Just a precaution. There could be a bomb."

The first week passed without incident. The diligent Thurston, not one to give up, even in a dirty war, continued to go to work and to apply, as was his wont, the laws of the town. The second week passed and then the third, and the fourth, and slowly, without any more phone calls, without so much as a squint from the developers whom Thurston happened to be working with at the time, the spring season progressed. The trees leafed out on Scratch Flat, the asparagus shoots appeared, and behind the halted housing lots, Corky Trilling planted his beans, just as he had for the last twenty-five years. The opening gambit was over and Thurston had won. The houses were constructed to the letter of the law.

There was one other major development battle that was fought near Scratch Flat in which democracy and the voice of the people via that honorable institution, the New England town meeting, managed to win a small victory. Actually this battle was fought over land that is at the edge of Scratch Flat, just east of the Beaver Brook marshes and no more than three hundred yards or so from the thunder of Route 495. There is a bean field in this small section, and a good pasture where thoroughbred horses used to graze before the piece was sold off to a local developer. One winter it was announced that a major shopping center was to be constructed on the tract, a sort of a regional mall with massive supermarkets and department stores. There is already a shopping center in the town, but it is small, relatively unassuming, and in fact so old now that it has a dowdy air to it. The people who run the supermarket are local, as are most of the employees in the other shops in the mall. The town is small, the supermarket is sufficient, the local hardware store is busy but not crowded, and a five-and-ten, a sewing shop, a liquor store, and a bakery supply most of the other needs for the local people. There is, in other words, no need for any further commercial development to serve the existing community. And yet it was clear to the mall developers that a plaza on Route 495 would draw in a lot of business; all that remained to move forward with the project was to alter an existing bylaw which zoned the land in question for residential use rather than commercial use. And all that was needed to do that was a two-thirds approval at town meeting. It seemed simple.

There is a school down the road from the bean field and there would be, the developers admitted, a certain increase in traffic on the road as a result of the shopping center. There would also be, the developers admitted, a certain amount of runoff into Beaver Brook from the vast parking lots, a little road salt perhaps, and traces of heavy metals from the brake linings of the cars. And because the area is not well-drained, there would be, admittedly, some problems with the disposal of septage. But these, the developers said, were minor considerations. After all, at the behest of the health inspector, there would be no restaurants in the mall, no heavy water use in other words, and furthermore, the developers said they would, in the public interest, donate a part of the property (a wet part) to the town for use as a ball field. Besides, the developers said, the shopping center would bring jobs to the community. It was the best of all possible worlds, jobs to make the money to shop for new things. But for some reason, the women of the community took opposition to the project.

The opposition began, as these things often do, over afternoon coffee in suburban houses. The idea grew, as such ideas often do, until a small ad hoc committee was formed. The planning board hearings concerning the development were publicized by the committee, and at the meetings, a few significant questions concerning water use and the effect of traffic on the local children walking home from school were asked. And the more questions that were asked, the worse the development appeared to be, until finally, the women began to ask the central question: why was this shopping mall necessary?

With the town meeting time approaching, the intensity of the committee meetings began to heat up. Signs began to appear encouraging to people to vote "no" on the zoning change. Informational meetings were held. More hearings were attended, more significant questions were asked, and more pressure was exerted on the developers. In response, the developers began to build their case, consultants were hired, traffic patterns were studied, groundwater flow was analyzed, slide shows were put together, detailed reports assuring the financial benefits of the development to the community were prepared, and then, a week or so before the big meeting, the real estate agent and the local police chief disappeared to Jamaica for a week's vacation.

The town meeting took place on a rainy night in early March. Thanks to the publicity of the ad hoc committee, and in part to the nature of the issue, the turnout was excellent, the highest attendance of a town meeting in some fifteen years it was said. In the hallways of the school one of the women, Jenny Merlin, set up a display that showed a series of photographs of the city of Waltham on Route 128 complete with traffic jams, shopping malls, and sterile, high tech industrial buildings. At the center of the display was the bean field in spring, just sprouting its crops, with the drumlin of Scratch Flat in the background, flowering in dogwood, crab apple, and escaped pear and apple trees. "Our Town, 1990?" the poster asked. Inside the town meeting, the developers would spend the next two hours making their case with slide shows, speeches, and audiovisual displays; but in spite of this, the police demanded that Jenny Merlin remove her poster from the lobby. Jenny is a woman who does not appreciate injustice, and there was a little rattle of verbal gunfire, but in the end, intimidated by the power of authority, she acquiesced.

The meeting was for the most part profoundly boring. In spite of the fact that I was obviously very interested in the outcome, I fell asleep when the authority on traffic patterns attempted to prove that all would go smoothly and little children coming home from school would not be hit by shoppers. I woke up in time for the questions from the floor, woke up even more when it was clear that the developers were going to lose, and woke up to full consciousness of the way things work when, just before the crucial vote, the chief of police interrupted the proceedings to announce that the rain had turned to ice and the roads were slippery and people should perhaps think about going home. The ruse, if it was one, did not work. No one left, and when a hand count vote was carried out, a sea of arms flew up in opposition. By contrast, there was a mere puddle in favor of the development. A resounding defeat for the best-laid plans of those whom Toby Beckwith had termed the mongrels of avarice.

12

FIRE AND ICE

One year during the month of May when the apple trees in Charlie's old orchards were in bloom, when the shoots of grass were shin high in the hayfields and the indigo buntings were chattering at the edges of the woods, and time seemed to stop dead, I got up at dawn and went off into the world to walk. I began with coffee and reflection in the plum grove above my house, and then, inspired by the view of the landscape, and fired up by the coffee, I began to explore. This was in the years before the Demogenes hayfields were developed, before the newer houses appeared in the woods on the southern end of Forge Village Road, when there was, it seemed, more space to roam. It was not all that long ago really, but change has been coming faster and faster now on Scratch Flat, and things seemed different then.

This particular expedition turned out to be a genuine nature walk, filled with the kind of small epiphanies that make exploration of the natural world such a continuing adventure. It was a sultry morning, more like June than May, and it was made all the more splendid by the fact that a two-week period of cold fronts and rain had retarded the migration of songbirds and for the past two days they had been piling in—wood warblers, grosbeaks, thrushes, tana-gers, orioles and finches and buntings filled the air with the kind of full rollicking chorus that can make cacophony out of the nearest woodland. I was not long in the grove. The world was too much with me.

I am not by nature a hiker; I much prefer to poke along, stop-ping for anthills, stopping for birds, wildflowers, or more often, stop-ping simply to listen to the wind and stare into space. I was not even off my property that morning when I heard an unfamiliar warbler song high in the trees. It took me five minutes of searching, but in the end I had identified the bird as a cerulean warbler, a rarity in these parts. Good sign, I thought to myself, a rare day to be out. A few minutes later I heard another call, and after a little more searching, spotted a western tanager. Then in the same tree I saw a parula warbler, and just behind it flitting off to the right, I saw the bird the Cubans call the *candelita,* or little candle, but which we, in our efficient way, call the Blackburnian warbler. It is by any name a spectacular bird, black and flared with brilliant flamelike stripes.

I moved on, passing through the various habitats of Scratch Flat, past deep pine forests where I heard and saw nothing, past uplands of oak and hickory filled with warbler calls and the song of towhees and thrushes, along the marshes of Beaver Brook, through the hayfield of fox tracks and meadowlarks and bobolinks. I lost track of time again that day. I began, I know, sometime around dawn, and spent at least most of the morning there, returning only after the people of Scratch Flat woke up, an event which can be identified primarily by noise—traffic on the Forge Village Road, chain saws, lawn mowers, hammering, and similar petty annoyances.

I have a spot which I often unconsciously migrate to whenever I am out on Scratch Flat, a small rise just above the marshes, the place where Nompenekit and I sat when he told me that the Indian people were still here, and would be here after the white man left. You can get a good view of the stretching marshes from that bluff, and al-though the sun is always in your eyes in the morning, making it difficult to spot the water birds of the area, the sounds and silhou-ettes of the places are enough to remind you of a wilder time and a wilder place. On that particular morning there was a mist filtering over the marshes and the sun was coming in over the grasses and the winding brook with that raking light that can turn even the most prosaic spot into a mystery. The brook is narrow and deep just below the bluff and swings in near the shore, running slowly with its baggage of duckweed, bits of organic matter, and an occasional drifting turtle or black duck. I was staring down into the water when suddenly, not ten yards away, a huge doglike head burst to the surface, all gleaming and dripping with duckweed, grasses, and brook water. It was an immense otter, one of the largest I have ever seen, with a great wide head, blunted nose, and darting, intelligent eyes. It was not aware of my presence and spent a few seconds drifting lazily in the current before it dove again, and then reappeared with a freshwater mussel. It swam to a nearby hummock of grass on the opposite side of the brook, cracked the shell, extricated the meat, and then began to preen, the sunlight flashing off its wet fur. It shook itself a few times, ran its paws over its whiskers like a cat, sniffed the air, and then for some unexplainable reason, stared directly at me and did not move in spite of the fact that otters are notoriously shy. We sat there for a period of time staring one another down. I did not move, and it did not move; we were simply two unrelated creatures caught together in the same habitat for a few seconds.

I have developed an interesting trick whenever I find myself in such encounters. Somehow I learned that if on such occasions you do not act like a normal human animal, you can prolong the meeting between the species. It is a technique that works especially well with woodchucks, rabbits, squirrels, and any other mammal that regularly encounters human beings. I began to play with the otter by scrunching up my face like a rodent, pulling back my lips with a sucking sound to reveal my teeth. The otter ducked slightly when I did this, as if to dive for safety, but then it sat up again and cocked its head. I clicked my teeth hard. It sniffed. So I sniffed. It cocked its head, and so, ever so slightly, not with any gross movements, I cocked my head. Very busily then the otter began to preen again, working hard at what the ethologists call a displacement activity. I sat still, and then quietly made a small animalistic chattering noise. It stopped preening, looked up, and cocked its head again. I called again, half hoping it would chatter back at me. But it continued to preen, alternately checking the strange, nonthreatening creature on the other side of the stream. I began to rock back and forth with a measured rhythm; and then, not staring at the otter, I rose and lumbered along the bank, like an old, tired gorilla. It watched me go, and as I had hoped, became more brazen when it realized it was in no danger from this thing. It bounced along the opposite bank, jumping from hummock to hummock until it caught up with me. I watched it surreptitiously for a few minutes, while I pretended to feed on something in the grass, and then, quite abruptly, our interaction was interrupted. Suddenly, in the midst of that vast landscape of water and grass, I heard a long descending whinny that was somewhat reminiscent of the background noise in a jungle movie of the 1940s. This was yet another surprise of the day, another bird call that was alien to me. I listened carefully, and then, when I saw a small weak flyer rise up out of the grasses about a hundred yards across the marsh, I raised my binoculars to get a glimpse of what I think was a least bittern, another rarity. The otter was gone in a flash; all I heard was a dull plop as it dove. At the same time the bird dropped down into the grasses again, and both my morning discoveries were lost.

I continued south along the bank through the oaks and the morning land birds. There is a narrow trail at this point, kept open at this time of year by fishermen who park on the Great Road and walk in to the brook on land that is owned by the town water company. I was ambling slowly along this trail looking up at the tops of the trees for birds when I heard, just in front of me, a great hiss, as if the air had been released from a giant inner tube. I looked down and saw in the middle of the path the hideous gaping maw of a full-sized snapper.

I confess to a certain love for snapping turtles. Most country people hate them, or at least dislike them, because they purportedly eat more than their share of ducklings, have a nasty bite, and will, so it is rumored, clip off the toes of children in swimming holes, but I find them curiously fascinating. For one thing, most of the rumors about them are untrue. They do indeed eat baby ducks, but then so do foxes, raccoons, and possibly otters, skunks, and possums. Snappers do have a strong bite, I am told by the authorities, but I have yet to meet anyone who has been bitten. Furthermore, even if all the nasty rumors were true, I would still support them. The world, after all, is filled with danger and the presence of monstrous snappers lurking in the obscure depths of some pond makes the place all the more interesting in my view. More to the point, I love snapping turtles because they are to me a symbol of time. They are migrants from the age of the dinosaurs, great lumbering relics of the Cretaceous period that have survived into our era, in spite of drought, in spite of the great crustal upheavals that formed from the American continent, in spite of whatever it was that killed off the dinosaurs, and finally, and not insignificantly, in spite of the exigencies of twentieth-century industrialization. For these reasons, in the early months of summer I often find myself rescuing snapping turtles from small boys and grown men who consider it their duty to rid the world of these modern-day dragons.

The Cretaceous relic in front of me that morning on Scratch Flat was not the largest snapper I have seen; she (it was undoubtedly a female out on an egg-laying mission) measured about two feet across, not overly large as snappers go, and she had fine bright eyes with which she fixed me aggressively. Nonhuman tricks with snappers do not work. The turtles are either too dumb or too smart to play. And so, if I must speak at all, I always speak to them as fellow travelers. I was, as you can imagine, in a good mood that morning, feeling gracious and at one with the world, so I stepped aside. "It is your passage," I said. "Carry on." She didn't move, so I stepped back a little farther, and then a little farther, until slowly she began to lumber forward along the trail.

It was a good day for turtle-watching. Ten minutes later, at the edge of Ted Demogenes's hayfield, I saw a painted turtle digging a nest in the sandy soil. She also halted when she spotted me and, as with the snapper, I circled around and let her continue with her work. Still later, I saw another painted turtle by the edge of Beaver Brook, and finally, when I was on my way home that morning, I found, down by the Forge Village Road bridge over Beaver Brook, five or six baby painted turtles, all of them squashed flat by passing cars. It is not easy to be a turtle in Scratch Flat in the twentieth century.

I had other encounters that morning. I saw more birds that day than I usually see in a week; I found a patch of wood betony on the west side of the drumlin, a flower that I had never seen on Scratch Flat. I saw a phantom crane fly drift past, an insect so like a bit of fluff, and so ephemeral, that until I learned to see them, I always took them for some wind-borne seed. Finally, about mid-walk, just east of Jimmy-George Starkos's beet field, I saw my enemy the fox.

I was in those years a keeper of chickens. In order to save on feed costs, and to improve the health of the hens and the flavor of the eggs, I used to let them free-range around the land so they could pick insects off the garden crops and feed on grubs and wild seeds and greens. I would leave the door to the henhouse open so that the hens could return to the nest boxes to lay eggs and drink water, but I learned early on that if the door was not shut at night, some predator would come and help itself to a chicken. I lost five fat layers in as many weeks the first year, mainly through forgetfulness. Closing the henhouse got to be something of an issue in my family, a prison or chain that kept us tied to the property. If we were off for the afternoon and if perchance we chose to stay on for dinner or for the night, we would have to call the neighbor and have someone walk over after dark and shut the hens in, or more accurately, shut the fox out.

For her part (again my enemy was a female I am sure, a vixen with young), the fox did very well. She had a den under the abandoned house next door and she had a regular route that she would follow each night. The henhouse was on her route, and if she found the door open, it was an easy night's work for her. One night, probably about the time that her young were in the process of weaning, she carried off three hens. I heard the squawling and raced out into the darkness, yowling like a monster just in time to see her making off with the fourth. She was carrying the victim toward her den, holding it high in the air to clear the grasses and the brush. She was determined to keep it, but when she saw that her pursuer was gaining on her, she dropped her prize and made her break for freedom, leaving the hen none the worse as far as I could tell.

After the third or fourth year of this, she became more brazen and would sometimes show up in the early evening when it was still light, tentatively check the yard, and then make for the henhouse or an errant chicken. It was about this time that I got into a philosophical debate with my pragmatic neighbor to the south, whose solution to my problem was very simple. He offered to sit up some night and shoot the offender. That way I could have my free-range hens, his daughter would not have to come over on Saturday nights and lock the door, and I would not have to buy more chickens to replace the lost ones.

It was excellent logic, but I was—still am in fact—operating under a different set of rules. Quite apart from the fact that I am partial to foxes, my argument against his solution was based on time. I reasoned that the fox and her relatives had been eating chickens, or at least birds very like chickens, ever since the oak-hickory habitat had established itself in this region some eight thousand years ago. Evolution had programmed the fox to set up a territory and to nightly check that territory for food for herself and for her young. It was a good system as far as she was concerned; and as long as she could find food and shelter and good water, there would be foxes in the world. She and her mate and the forces of procreation would see to that. If at some point in her history, or the history of her parents or her offspring, a small structure appeared in her territory with edible birds inside, then, I reasoned to my neighbor, it was her right, her duty even, to eat those birds. If I failed to lock the door to the henhouse, then the loss of hens was my fault, not the fox's.

I must have presented my case to my neighbor twenty times in the course of our discussions, but he never could satisfy himself that I was making any sense. "If men were foxes," he said, "you might be right, but men are men and this is a man's world. We're not here to grow foxes." It is, of course, a point worth considering; but I have my views, and he has his, and in the end, I solved the problem by eating the hens myself. Grain had gotten very expensive, and by that time, I was becoming more interested in flowers and scented herbs and the delicacy of Chopin.

My encounter with my enemy on that May morning was all too brief. I had seen her before on several occasions in places other than the night battlefield. I caught sight of her crossing a meadow one dark morning in December, her gray fur blending with the browns of the dead grasses. I saw her sitting at the edge of Charlie's fields one evening in late summer, smiling broadly and panting, as if she were daring me to give chase. And I saw her once running through the woods on a definite mission, so busy that I am not sure she even knew I was there. On this particular morning, she was in the woods again, sitting on top of a rise about thirty yards back from Jimmy-George Starkos's open land. I stopped when I spotted her, crouched over and began to sway in order to trick her, but she would not fall for the ruse and within a second or two, trotted off. This was one of those high-energy days for me, the type of morning when anything seemed possible, and it occurred to me that I might be able to catch up with her. Before I analyzed the failure inherent in such an act, I was off and running. I gained the rise where she had been sitting and saw her on an old stone wall to the left. I turned and charged toward it. She crouched for a second, then jumped off the wall and made a direct line for a tangle of shrubs near the open fields. I was after her with renewed vigor; I circled the island of shrubbery and caught up with her on her way out, still far ahead of me, but thinking seriously about running harder now. She crossed another wall, broke out of the woods, and began running along the edge of the field, circling around in other words. I cut toward her at an angle, tripped on a fallen branch, stumbled, and kept running. Just as I got into the open, I saw her cut across the end of the field about fifty yards ahead and dash into the obscurity of a thick tangle of slash and blueberry in a section of land that Jimmy-George Starkos had had timbered a few years before. It was her best choice; passage through the crisscrossed fallen branches and the dense blueberries is difficult even for a walker, and all but impossible for a runner. I gave up the chase and sat down on the wall in the woods to rest. Five minutes later she reappeared from the slash and sat upright at the edge of the field, panting and smiling in the doglike way of foxes. I don't believe in anthropomorphism, but in her fox mind, from my point of view, I would say that she was shouting out, "Catch me if you can, you blundering fool."

"Hey," I shouted out loud. "You like to play me in a fair race. My mind against yours. None of this physical stuff."

She was gone before I finished the sentence.

I didn't realize it at the time, but the walk that morning was, in a characteristically small and personal way, something of a historic event. That summer things began to change in Scratch Flat, and they have been changing ever since. First to go was the hayfield where the painted turtle laid her eggs. Not three weeks after I saw her digging the nest hole, bulldozers moved into Ted Demogenes's fields, scraped off the topsoil, and dug the foundations for the buildings in the Beaver Brook Industrial Park, effectively putting to an end some eight thousand years of turtle nesting in the sandy soil left by the glacier. By the end of summer, the developer had located a septic drainage field in the same general area in which the turtle had nested, and about a year later, even though the company that finally occupied the building vowed that it would not be using industrial chemicals, trichlorolethylene was found in the septic system. As a result, the town required that specialized receiving tanks be installed, thereby tearing up even more of the remaining hayfield. Not that it mattered much; most of the field was occupied by parking lots or buildings by then.

That same summer one of Charlie Lignos's heifers died in the pasture land below my house; he removed the others and that year did not cut hay on his Scratch Flat fields. Two new houses went up on the end of Forge Village Road, constructed by the same developer who was building the industrial park. On the north end of Scratch Flat, not far from the point of land where Tonupasqua had held her visionary dance, one of the longtime landholders sold off a large section of pine forest, and in subsequent years a fashionable and expensive housing development was built. All the houses were carefully designed and the natural features of the woodlands were maintained; but land, and trees, and good nesting space were destroyed nonetheless. The whippoorwills have not called in the area since; and although I used to commonly see grouse in that part of Scratch Flat, I have yet to see any since the houses went in.

The New England Electric Company, which had cut through the northern section of Scratch Flat a few years before, planned about that time to widen the swathe of power lines. This meant that one of Matty Matthews's good hayfields would be lost; and since Matty Matthews is, among all the people of Scratch Flat, the most stalwart fighter for the rights of the beleaguered farmers, this incurred a protracted battle with the electric company and a number of hearings on the matter, some of which I attended. Matty went straight to the top, as he often does, called the Massachusetts Commissioner of Agriculture to come out to Scratch Flat and walk the land and meet with the company officials. The commissioner agreed and the great encounter was held on a cold Thanksgiving weekend in a back room at Matty's house. Although the commissioner listened with concern, and although he was a staunch supporter of the farmers of the state, there was not much he could do. In the end the electric company took the land by eminent domain, and yet another hayfield was torn up for the greater good.

Matty was getting cynical by that time. He is the son of a Yankee farmer whose family has been making a living from the New England soils for nearly two hundred years. He took over the Scratch Flat farm in 1953 and has been expanding ever since. The soils were good and although it was, as always, hard times for New

England dairy farmers, Matty made a go of it by mixing Jersey cows in his herd of Holsteins and feeding them a lot of hay, thereby keeping his costs down. But with the hayfields going over to power lines, and with grain costs rising, Matty began to find himself in the position of many of the farmers of Scratch Flat and the rest of New England.

"I'm going to go into trucking," he told me after his loss. "I'm going to get a rig and start hauling goods. Leave the land and stay on the road with Alice for the rest of my life. Can't beat 'em, join 'em, right?"

"Don't know," I shrugged.

He was only joking, of course. Matty is fifty-eight years old, has been a dairy farmer all his life, and is not prepared at this point, even if he were able, to take up a new career. In any case, it may not be necessary in his lifetime. He has established a reputation for himself and the town and the local developers will not touch him. About three years after the electric company takeover, the town began looking for a new dump site. One of the alternatives on the list of possible spots was a wooded section of Matty's land; and since the place was away from surface and groundwater and yet within easy access of a major road, the site came under serious consideration until someone on the dump committee pointed out that Matty Matthews was the owner. "Well, that settles that," the head of the committee is reported to have said. "That site's a no go."

Matty's dairy operation is now the last full-working farm on Scratch Flat. Elsewhere things were not going well. Billy Sherman's mind began to slip. He started forgetting things, could not keep track of what was planted where or when, and finally more or less retired to his townhouse and let Corky run the place. One by one, sections of what was once considered the best truck farming land in the town were sold off for house lots; and with each sale, it seemed, Sherman got a little more senile, until finally he began waking up in the middle of the night calling out for Corky and ranting about beans and cabbage.

"No good," Corky said to me one afternoon.

"Hard times coming."

Shortly after this pronouncement, I saw Jimmy-George Starkos helping out at the voting tables at a local election. He looked pale and had an expression of insecurity or fear, something I had never seen before in him. About three weeks later, in spite of the fact that he had by then admitted to Winnie that he was having pains in his chest and had been walking around with a strange feeling inside him, he went out to harrow one of his beet fields. Winnie was nervous and kept walking around to the back of the house to see how he was doing; but since she could hear the tractor she assumed that he was all right. Finally, when he didn't come back, she went over the rise to the beet field and saw that the tractor had run off the field. Although it was still throbbing and smoking, it was not moving. She didn't dare investigate. Jimmy's younger brother, Elias, went out and found his brother slumped over the wheel of the tractor with one hand caught in the buttons of his shirt. The tractor was butted against a stone wall and was stubbornly churning away as if it had a life of its own. By contrast, Jimmy was pronounced dead of a massive coronary.

And all the while I watched. I watched while the industrial park was planned, protested, and constructed. I watched while the new houses went up at the end of Forge Village Road, while the heifers were removed and the good hayfields began to grow up to chokecherry and birch. I watched while the pine forest near Tonupasqua's dancing ground evolved into a fashionable suburban tract, watched while my wife and other women of the town mobilized to stop the shopping center. From time to time I would sally forth, write a letter to the local press, and serve on some ad hoc committee or other. But all the while I was the observer rather than the player, the aloof journalist watching the world play itself out on the stage of time. Tonupasqua and Nompenekit had taught me by then that the world is very long and that the games that the recent white tribesmen play in it are very short. I was saddened by the destruction of good farmland and good habitat for birds and foxes; but nevertheless, I waited and watched while they took apart Scratch Flat.

Then one November evening about four years ago I came home and smelled wood smoke in the air. That is not an uncommon odor on Scratch Flat—many of the residents heat their houses with wood —but this smoke had a different smell to it, somewhat punky and vegetal. I learned the next morning that Charlie Lignos's large chicken barn, where he kept the hay for his heifers, had burned the night before and that, although the fire department had arrived on the scene, the firemen had allowed the place to burn down. The barn was in ill repair, the firemen said later, and the fire was pretty well along by the time they got there.

After that, we did not see much of Charlie Lignos on Scratch Flat. The land grew up a little more and that March a late snowstorm caved in the roof of the other barn on the land. On Halloween night the following autumn I looked out of the kitchen window on the north side of my house and saw an immense tower of flame rising out of the cedars that surrounded the abandoned Barnes house next door. I had never seen a fire so close to home. In spite of the fact that the house lies on the other side of an open meadow some sixty or seventy yards from my house, the flames had a terrible aspect. A huge tubular column of fire shot up into the black sky and from time to time would sweep across the tops of the cedars like the tongue of an invisible dragon. And all the while a great roaring hiss filled the air, punctuated with unexplained snaps and cracks. The scene was one of violence, an uncontrollable chemical process totally indifferent to history, property, or human life.

Within half an hour the firemen had halted the flames, and I went home to spend a sleepless night. The eerie blue lights of police cars and fire trucks were pulsing across the garden in the back of the house, and about four in the morning more trucks arrived with a great deal of clanging and chugging. There was more noise about seven in the morning, so I got up and went over to see what had happened in the night. Firemen were there drinking coffee and making jokes about hot dog roasts; the violence of the occasion did not seem to affect them at all. As it turned out, either the fire had resprouted in the depths of the structure, or vandals had returned to finish the job. It made me very uncomfortable to think that renegades with firebombs were cruising the roads near where little children were sleeping, and I walked around Scratch Flat for the next week or so feeling that I was living in the wrong place, that there must be a spot on the earth—someplace like the Azores—where there was peace, and sanity, and good gardens.

Early that following spring I was on my way to town on a Sunday morning when I saw another column of smoke rising from a field just east of Scratch Flat. Around the turn of the century the field was the site of a relatively well known trotting park and because of its history, the stable for the park, I was later informed, might have been a candidate for the national historic register. Although it had not been used for a year or so, the stable was in good shape, had once housed the governor's horse guard, and had murals of prancing stallions painted along the interior walls.

Earlier that winter a proclamation had gone out from the town decreeing that all the dilapidated houses and barns in the community were to be taken down or fixed up, or the town would have them destroyed or removed at the owner's expense. The horse barn was one of the first victims of the decree and since the vigilant fire department needed practice, it was decided that the barn would be destroyed by fire. I went over to watch the destruction and fell into conversation with a man in a Tyrolean hat. He said that the barn really was in bad shape, and that there were many such barns in the community, and that all these run-down buildings were hurting real estate values in the town. "There's a really bad one over on Forge Village Road," he told me. "That barn with the caved-in roof. Real eyesore. They ought to do something about it." It was, of course, Charlie Lignos's last barn, and as it turned out, "they" had already been doing something about it.

On several occasions, I was told later, Charlie had been summoned to court by the town and asked to fix up or tear down the barn on Forge Village Road. Charlie is a busy dairyman and, he says, has little time for petty bureaucrats from other communities telling him what to do. He never responded to the various summonses that were sent to him. On a bright May morning about six weeks after the stable was burned, a dump truck and bulldozer pulled up in front of Charlie's barn and a work crew began tearing off siding and loading it into the truck. I went out on the front porch and for about twenty seconds watched in awe. Then finally, after having watched the slow destruction of history and not doing anything about it, after watching the demise of good agricultural land on Scratch Flat, something changed quite abruptly in me, and I walked determinedly up to the town crew and asked what the hell they were doing.

"Tearing down this fucking thing," the crew chief said. "Order of the selectmen."

"How about Charlie? Does he know about this?"

"Charlie's an asshole," I was informed. As it turned out, the crew chief was, for some reason, the sworn enemy of Charlie Lignos.

I went back in the house and called Charlie to tell him they were taking his barn apart. Then I went back to the crew and asked if it would not be possible to wait until Charlie arrived. A certain Officer Day had arrived on the scene by that time, and before I could even finish my explanation, I was informed in no uncertain terms that this was none of my business, and that unless I wanted to face arrest, I was to clear out and get back on my property. I stared at him for a few seconds—I was wondering what the charges would be since I was standing on a public way—but I could see an intense and somewhat inexplicable rage building in Officer Day. His eyes narrowed menacingly, and he pointed a shaky finger at my house and, unconsciously I am sure, rested his free hand on the handle of his weapon. I retreated without further comment.

Instead of going home, I went down to the town hall and explained to the selectmen's assistant that I had told Charlie about the act and he had no knowledge of what was going on; and since it was, after all, his barn, it seemed to me that the town was operating in a questionable legal area. When I got back to the barn, Charlie had arrived, and there was, to put it mildly, an altercation in process. Charlie was shouting at his enemy the crew chief in a loud voice and the crew chief was shouting back and flipping a hammer in his hand. The whole thing might have ended violently if the chief of police had not shown up at that point and called off the operation for the day. Charlie would be issued an official notice, the chief said, and the work could resume the next day.

That afternoon, I was poking around the foundation of the old barn, feeling nostalgic about time and the destruction of the New England landscape, when I saw a small brown bird fly out of the barn. I went inside and found a nest of eggs, and then went home and wrote a letter to the selectmen informing them that I had discovered a federally protected bird nesting in the building and that to destroy the nest would be a federal offense. I suggested that the work be called off until the young had fledged. Never mind that the bird was a phoebe and that phoebes are not an uncommon species in these parts; they are indeed protected under the Migratory Bird Act. As a result, there was a period of grace; Charlie got his respite and during the next few months removed, piece by piece, the better timbers in the seventy-five-year-old structure. After that, the work crews came back, hauled the rest of the building to the dump, and bulldozed the finely crafted granite foundation. That summer mullein and jimsonweed grew in the heap of soil that had been the barn, and the swallows that used to nest in the hayloft disappeared from the wires along Forge Village Road.

That was not my last sally into the world of politics. That winter I happened to see a small item in the local press announcing the fact that a historic building owned by the town was to be burned by the fire department to rid the town of the expense of upkeep. Among other things, the piece noted that although the plans had been proceeding for months, at the request of the selectmen the press had withheld the news. The building was to be burned on Sunday, the story said, three days away. Once again I was jarred.

Part of my concern was caused by the fact that although it had been privately owned since the 1900s, the building was once the town hall, the place where Uncle Peter Hazzard had broken the orderly contra dance lines into frenzy, where a number of important figures had lectured at the lyceum, and where for a number of decades during the nineteenth century, the affairs of the town were carried out. The building was abandoned, but it was structurally sound, and was a handsome federalist design with some interesting architectural details. Not the least of my anger was caused by the fact that the press had complied with the selectmen and had withheld the news from the public, thereby preventing any alternative solutions.

I wrote to the paper and said as much, and the next day I spent the morning on the phone with various state-level officials attempting to get a cease and desist order. Staff people from the state historical commission came out from Boston and photographed the building, identified its value as a historic structure worth salvaging, and then attempted, through the attorney general's office, to get the town to halt the operation. Local officials had covered all the legal ground, however, having burned buildings before, and there was nothing that could be done in so short a period. Fortunately, however, the weather managed a respite. The weekend of the proposed conflagration was bitterly cold and the operation was called off.

By that time I had lined up a number of people I knew of around New England who expressed an interest in salvaging the building and reconstructing it in another place. On a Tuesday night of the following week, I went before the selectmen and pleaded for an extension. They were very polite, but stated that they had been troubled with this particular structure ever since the town had purchased it in 1968 and that the only apparent solution was to burn it. The fire department needed the practice anyway, I was told.

"Well, will you give me two weeks to find someone to take it away?" I asked.

"No," they said.

"Will you give me two days?"

"Mister," one of them said, "we won't give you two minutes."

I went to the Boston *Globe* then and called several other local newspapers to tell them that the town was about to destroy a historic building on the next weekend and there might be an interesting story in the act since the state historical commission had tried to halt the destruction. On Saturday, the day of the fire, the reporters showed up and began asking a lot of questions. Fire trucks from the surrounding communities arrived. Brush was laid around the building like faggots around a martyr; there was a lot of joking and noise, and clanging of fire trucks; and then a thin wisp of white smoke rose from somewhere deep within the building. The fire began slowly enough, but by the time it caught, destruction was assured. One by one, flames leaped out of the old twelve-over-twelve windows; after half an hour, the roof broke through and the great dragon tongue of fire, something I was becoming more and more familiar with, began to lick around the central chimney. Another tongue broke through the roof, and then another, and then the three tongues joined in a great shaft that billowed high above the trees. The firemen began to spray the building to keep the fire under control and a light rain of mist and bitter ash began to fall on the crowd that had gathered for the event. At one point a wind sprang up and it looked as if the shaft of flame was going to get out of hand. Great fisted gusts began to batter down the flame so that it swirled toward the nearby houses. More firemen moved in, sprayed the nearby buildings to keep them from catching, and began pouring streams of white steamy water into the center of the fire. The tower of flame subsided; they let it rise again; beat it down again; until slowly, almost majestically, the fine old structure gave up and caved in on itself.

I went home long before the end and spent the afternoon drinking sherry and talking to friends about time and Peter Hazzard. It wasn't defeat I felt; it was inevitability.

Development and change have moved forward in fits and starts on Scratch Flat since that time, controlled for the most part by the state of the national economy. There has been a certain hiatus over the past few years and the farmlands, in spite of their precarious state, are still holding on. Matty Matthews has a son who has just completed agricultural school and who is determined to take over the family farm. He has recently taken up with a woman who loves cows and turkeys and who slops around town in high rubber boots caked with manure. I sometimes see her and Jackie Matthews necking and wrestling in the cow yard. Together they have taken on some battles of their own with the town officials over their rights to keep animals on their property, which is located in a developed area that is zoned residential.

Jimmy-George Starkos has a twenty-two-year-old granddaughter who, like Jackie Matthews, intends to take over his farm. She keeps a few sheep on the land now, has put in more strawberry beds, and she says she will reopen the farm stand throughout the growing season when she gets far enough ahead to hire the help she needs to plant market crops once more. Winnie continues to live in the old house, giving her all the support that she can, and Jimmy's brother, Elias, always the backbone of the Starkos experiment in the later years, lives there with them. Sometimes on Sundays the granddaughters, Elias, and Winnie, and whoever else in the family happens to be around, gather in the living room and speak of the better days on Scratch Flat, when there were a lot of good Greeks around, when Sherman was still the Cauliflower King, and when nights in summer were redolent with cabbage and celery. On spring evenings when the wind is in the right quarter, I can still hear the lowing of Matty's cows. And whenever the air is moist and warm, I sometimes catch the faint, not unpleasant odor of the cow manure that Matty spreads on his fields.

But nearby working farms notwithstanding, Scratch Flat is not the place I first came to. For one thing, something has happened to the great chorale of songbirds that I used to hear when I moved here. There are still bird calls to be sure, but now they sound out individually—a robin here, a blue jay or an oriole there. In May the piercing calls of the warblers still break from the treetops, and I can hear thrushes and flycatchers. But the unified chorus has ended, I am told, because the plots of forest have been intruded upon by human beings and there is simply not enough land to support the full population of birds that once thrived here.

Things are changing. On spring and summer mornings after Scratch Flat wakes up, the world of humankind is very much in evidence. In a former hayfield in the town of Westford on the other side of Beaver Brook, a sort of model airplane flying club has established itself, and on Saturdays now you can hear the high whine of tiny airplanes, as if giant mosquitoes had emerged from the Devonian swamps and were working over the marshes of Beaver Brook. As hunting on the open lands of the town has been cut back because of increased development, people have been using the sportsmen's club more often. Hunters, pistol fanatics, skeet shooters, and gunners of one sort or another periodically drive down the small road through the woods and fill the air with the noise of war. Lawn mowers fire up and roar along for a while on the neighbors' lawns to the south, and one of the signs of autumn is the whine and growl of surrounding chain saws as people get in firewood for the coming winter. The increase in development in the pine woods has increased the traffic on Forge Village Road, and every morning between eight and nine, people who do not live on Scratch Flat arrive at the industrial park and spend the next eight hours there under roofs and artificial light, laboring for companies that have headquarters in London, Chicago, New York, and Boston. Unlike the human beings who have gained a living in the area in one way or another over the past fifteen thousand years, they do not need Scratch Flat to survive.

13

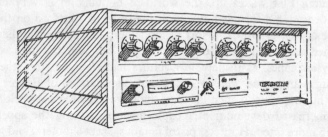

THE AUTUMN
OF TIME

One day early in the autumn several years ago, I telephoned Tonu-pasqua, ostensibly to catch up on a few folktales, and was informed by a recorded message that the number had been disconnected. A day or two later I called Nompenekit to see what had happened.

"She's gone," he said. "Got married and went to Rhode Island to live. Married a white man, I heard."

He went on to say that he was leaving too.

"Too crowded around here. I'm going up to Canada with my people. Me and my brother. We're going to get some land back in the forest. I got some money saved up, and there's no future for the Indian people around here."

"How do you mean that?" I asked him.

"I mean it's the same thing for the Indian as it is for the white man. You go to work, get money, come home, drink some beer, go to a few weekend ceremonies maybe. But what's the difference? We might as well be white people only with a different religion. We're not Indian people as long as we're living around here. No ties to the forest. Nothing. You know what I mean? Me and my brother got a place. We're going to take our families up there and start living. I'm ready to retire, see. Got some money, so I'm going to cut out early. This is something I've been thinking about for a long time."

Losing Tonupasqua and my source of Indian lore and legend, not to mention the friendship that I thought we had developed, was something of a shock to me. And the thought that Nompenekit would be leaving too and that the few Indian people that I had come to know over the past years would be gone began to change my thinking about Scratch Flat. Up until that autumn, I had half believed that Nompenekit and Tonupasqua were right and that as long as there were trees and birds, there would be Indians; and that the recent white invasion was possibly a short-lived thousand-year experiment, after which the hunter-gatherers would return and things would go on as they had for most of human prehistory. After their departure, I started thinking less and less about the past in Scratch Flat, and more and more about the present and the future. But nostalgia for what had been lost in the area kept invading, forcing out any positive thoughts I might summon up on what was to come.

From the perspective of the old nature man in me, things did seem fairly bleak. Only a few years after they were built, some of the new industrial buildings in the Beaver Brook Park began to age prematurely: the aluminum siding and the gutters stripped away in some places; yellow water stains began to drip down the white sides of some of the outer walls of the buildings; a lighted sign slipped and lost its face and no one bothered to repair it; and although the well-manicured landscaping of shrubs began to grow up and fill in nicely, the wild nature of the place, the rough edges of the old hayfields and the woods were gone, as were the habitats of the turtles and the meadowlarks. In winter, from a window of my house, I could see the cold light of one of the buildings gleaming through the woods. Traffic had increased on Forge Village Road and the Great Road, and the place was filled with the noise of twentieth-century life.

On the other hand, the old isolated corners of Scratch Flat—the marshes of Beaver Brook, Charlie Lignos's old fields, the hemlock grove, and the extensive forest of pine, oak, and hickory—were still untouched, and so that autumn, I simply became more specific in my wanderings, selecting those areas which I knew had not yet been invaded. There was indeed still space enough to walk; even with the increase in development, it was possible to spend a full morning wandering over the square-mile tract of land without meeting any other person or running up against new buildings.

I woke up early one rainy morning in September of that year and wandered out through the dripping woods for a walk. Unconsciously almost, I found myself working toward the corner of stone walls on the old Caswell estate where the Indians—whoever they were—were supposed to be buried. It was a dank, very dark morning, but the woods were filled with that rank, old-season odor of mushrooms and life, not an unpleasant sensation in my view. I poked around in the general area of the purported graveyard for a while, sat down to think, poked around some more, and then sat down again. Tonupasqua and Nompenekit were very much on my mind, as were the Indians who were lying somewhere below me. I was struggling again with the paradox of time, the fact that some known event, such as a burial or the construction of a stone wall, occurred in this very place at some point in the past, but that because of the nature of time as we measure it, the event is all but unknowable. I felt that I was more cut off from the past than ever, and my frustration was made all the worse by the fact that my nonwestern guides had deserted me and that without them, all my exploration through the experience of ceremonial time was at an end.

I began to wonder, as I often do, what was the point of all this hard labor of life, the thirty, forty, or even fifty years spent by the individuals of Scratch Flat getting a living out of the soils, or, as with the Native Americans, out of the streams and marshes and woods. It was easy enough for me to tell myself that there was only the journey, the pure biology of the trip from cradle to grave, and that the universe, as Tonupasqua once said, was neither kind nor cruel, simply indifferent. Nevertheless there was something very unsatisfying in such a simple dismissal of human history; and in any case, up until that autumn, the question of what happens to a place when all the elements of its past are obliterated seemed of paramount importance to me. I was walking around Scratch Flat that fall wondering what was going to happen to Tom Dublet after Beaver Brook was buried in a culvert or channelized. What would happen to the ghost of Enoch Pratt when Charlie's fields were turned into a suburban housing tract or an industrial parking lot?

When I was younger, I used to think that as long as people remembered an event or a person, then that event or person was still alive, existing in a sort of non-Christian afterlife. Thought or remembrance were creation. But that fall I began wondering whether the present and the future need the past to exist. It occurred to me, perhaps for the first time, that it is indeed possible to live out a life in a place and not know anything about it, and that knowledge of the huge spans of time that make up the history of every place in the world, full knowledge, that is, is simply a palliative to change. Knowing that it has all gone on before, and that indeed there is nothing new under the sun, and that the past is prologue, and that all the other homilies about time are true, simply makes a life easier to get through. In comparison to the recent handiwork of the glacier, for example, a new parking lot on Scratch Flat, even if it does disrupt the turtle's nest, is a relatively benign change. If industrialization doesn't kill off the painted turtles of this part of the world, the next glacier will.

I was leaning against a tree in the Indian burial ground that morning, reviewing all this, when for some unexplained reason, I felt again the old presence of some being or entity, the thing that I used to feel when I first began my exploration of Scratch Flat. Goaded by whatever it was, I got up and began to wander through the rainy woods. I walked down toward the lake, crossed the crackling power lines and the bare strip of soil, and headed south-southeast toward home. The thing, whatever it was, was on my trail again and the ambience seemed ripe for some kind of meeting. Heavy ground mists and fogs alternated with brief, strong showers, and except for the eternal dripping of the trees and the occasional roar of a downpour, the world was silent beyond imagining. Inadvertently I think, I walked toward the hemlock grove where the last bear in the area had been killed, and in time, soaked from the rain, I came to the place and went in.

I say went in because the grove is very different from the surrounding woodlands. For one thing, there is no underbrush beneath the trees, and for another, the branches crisscross overhead in a thick mesh, effectively keeping out light. On this day, it was especially dark and I felt that I was moving backward from the morning into some peculiar night. The place had the feeling of a large dark room; I would say that it was cathedrallike except that the branches are lower, and the feeling is closed and intimate. I sat down against the largest tree in the grove, the same tree, I think, in which the bear was hiding when it was shot, and I waited for whatever it was that was stalking me to catch up. I knew the pattern, knew that if I turned around and looked for it, it would disappear, and I knew that probably I would never see it, and that the thing was not real at all, but simply my imagination.

I felt a definite sense of comfort sitting there against the tree with its baggage of legend and history. I was ready to meet the spirit bear if that is what it was. I was ready, I think, for Enoch Pratt in full regalia, ready at that point for any sort of epiphany. The thought of a break with reality as we know it was not at all frightening to me; I think I had learned something by then about ecstatic experiences from my Native American friends. And in time, sitting there, the stalker finally revealed itself.

Typically, the thing came not as a spiritual, out-of-body experience, not as a break, but in an entirely rational manner. It came as a mere thought, a realization, and all it was was a full appreciation of mortality. The thing that had stalked me in the woods of Scratch Flat for all those years was nothing more than death. But it came to me very clearly that morning that it was not simply my own death that walked a few steps behind me; it was the full realization that my own cohort will die, that everyone whom I now know, whom I have known, and whom I will know, is going to die; and that, in spite of this horrifying fact, the world, huge and momentous and indifferent, will carry on. There is no escaping this devastating reality. The mysticism of Tonupasqua and the supposed endurance of Pokawnau, the bear shaman, will not alter it. The solid foundations and heavy timbers of the seventeenth-century English structures on Scratch Flat could not alter it, and for that matter, neither will an account of fifteen thousand years of history on a square mile of land. No matter where I looked, in the running walls that line the woodlands, in the folktales of the American Indians, or in the town records or verbal accounts of the area, I realized I was reading the obituary of my era. History sends out its message in any form you choose: we are the future of the past, and the past of the future.

I began to think differently about Scratch Flat after that morning. For one thing, I stopped worrying about the fact that the place was, as I had phrased it, going downhill, or in the process of destruction. It became clear to me that it was simply going through yet another change and that although the place would be very different some fifty years from now, and although in time it would in all probability disappear from the earth as a place, it would not matter. Time has obliterated and will obliterate all the places and all the living individuals of this earth in its course, and we are living in a little match snap of light and life in a dark and dead universe and there is not much that can be done about it in the end. I found the thought curiously comforting, and armed with this new perspective, began purposefully walking around the parking lot edges of the industrial area, and after a while, began talking to some of the people who worked in the local industries. It was in this way that I met Peter Sarkesian.

Not long after the Beaver Brook Industrial Park was built, a man who represents the old order of things on Scratch Flat, Corky Trilling, used to see a man who represents the new order jog past his bean fields. The blacks of the Sherman farm used to refer to the man as "Mr. Marathon" and after a few months, after it was clear that he was becoming something of a regular on Scratch Flat, they would toast him with a beer can as he swept past the picnic tables in front of Corky's shack.

"All right brother," they would shout. "You gonna make it. Keep on working."

I would often see the runner, too. He was a well-built sort, about thirty-five years old, without a trace of fat, and with a shock of black hair that fell down in front of his eyes whenever it was not held back by a bright bandanna headband. I too got in the habit of greeting this runner whenever he would go by, but without half the jesting that the blacks gave him. I would simply raise my head in a friendly nod, and he would always return the greeting in the same way. His was a pleasant gesture; it said somehow, I'm working hard, and I know it seems ridiculous, but believe me, it feels good.

There are at present eight different industries located in the Beaver Brook Park, and in contrast to the fifteen thousand years of human labor on Scratch Flat, not one of them has anything to do with food gathering or the production of food; virtually all of them are involved in one way or another with the exchange of information. There is, for an example, a warehouse in the industrial park that stores books for Harvard University Press. There is a medical publishing company; there is a small company that markets computerized change makers; a company that produces a machine which aids with the interpretation of psychological tests; a company that produces computerized models to help with planning; and then finally, and perhaps the most advanced of all, a company that produces a synthesizer that refines radio waves coming in from outer space, either from satellites or from stars.

I had a lot of trouble when I first began to explore the industries on Scratch Flat. There was a curious sense of suspicion or warfare that seemed to lurk just beneath the surface of the receptionists and managers whom I talked to. I had to explain my mission very carefully to one company official before he would tell me what his company did, and another official, the man involved with the money changers, was downright paranoid. "You could be an industrial spy for all I know. I'm not going to spend my valuable time exchanging my valuable information so that you can spread this information around." He wasn't abrupt with me, he spent quite a bit of time making his case, but I was never able to get real information about his company.

The receptionist at the company that produces the synthesizers was quite the opposite from these others. "I'll let you talk to Peter," she said. "He's the only one who can explain."

I went into an empty conference room decorated with pleasing, high-resolution photographs of Swiss mountains and Hawaiian beaches and sat down at a long table to wait. In time the door at the end of the room opened and out came the runner, talking in his marathon style, before he even sat down.

"Sure I can tell you about this company," he began. "It is a good group, I've been here since they started. We make direct-frequency synthesizers, dynamite machine, ceramic ICs, metal can transistors, spurious outputs—very low, you see what I'm saying, fast-switching, low-phase noise, wide resolution; I like it here, plug-in design, too. . . ."

Fifty to seventy-five percent of what he explained that day was lost on me, and in any case I became more interested in the man than the product. It was clear that Peter Sarkesian represented a new sort of personality on Scratch Flat, the sort of man who did not measure time by generations, or growing seasons, or even years, but in microseconds and wave frequencies. Unlike many of the local people on Scratch Flat, most of whom lived either in the past or in their own

personal futures (mostly what they would do after they left Scratch
Flat), Peter lived in the present. He was born in Watertown of Arme-
nian parents. His father had worked as an engineer with the Army
Corps of Engineers and the family moved upward from Watertown,
to Arlington, to Concord, and then, upon retirement, to Florida—
not an atypical migration for people in these parts. Peter early on
developed an interest in electronic toys, had a ham radio when he
was eleven, and describes himself in those years as an "MIT fink,"
the type of young man who, he says, could be found in every high
school in the nation—complete with pencil holsters, slide rules (before the age of the computer), clean clothes, and excellent grades—
especially in math.

"I didn't know anything about anything except math, electronics, computers, and sports cars. Had to get married to learn about
life. She was a good Jewish girl from Arlington, an English major at
Wheaton, a graduate student at Radcliffe, and a totally screwed-up
woman at twenty-eight. We were married when she was twenty-four,
had Josh when she was twenty-six, and when she was thirty she came
home from her women's group one night and said she wanted to
walk. 'Is it another man?' I asked. 'Yeah,' she said. 'Her name is
Nancy and she's the Queen of Night.' Blew my mind. I didn't know
a thing, a thirty-one-year-old twelve-year-old. But I was beginning to
learn."

After the divorce, Peter got joint custody. He takes his son,
Joshua, four days a week, and his former wife has him the rest of the
time. They alternate holidays, and when things don't work out, Peter
brings the boy to work. He has a special place in his work cubicle
where he keeps toys and remnants of synthesizer parts for Joshua to
play with. At lunch, if the weather is right, they walk out behind the
building into the woods of Scratch Flat.

When Josh is not with him, Peter runs at his lunch hour. "I
don't sweat a lot," he said, "and no one around here cares what you
smell like anyway, as long as sales are up, and the synthesizers work.
You got to keep the body in shape. Got to keep pumping those
endorphins through your blood. Otherwise you start feeling low. It's
all physical. Really. In a job like this, you've got to move.

Shortly after the breakup with his wife, Peter started attending
what he called empowerment workshops. There he learned that he
was too much the intellect and not enough the forceful, "integrated"

self. He started working on self-improvement at this time, began running, and lost the fat that he said he had been accumulating since high school. Fat seemed to be something of a metaphor for Peter, as if to have even an extra ounce or two was the sign of a lost human being, an individual who had never come to terms with himself and was living the unexamined life.

On weekends when Peter is not with Josh, he often attends workshops on empowerment, or self-improvement. He has spent a week at the Omega Institute for Holistic Studies, plays a fierce game of tennis, he says, and does not pass through a single day without growth.

"It's like a long spiral, like one of those jack-in-the-boxes or caterpillars that comes out when you open the lid. Only it comes out in slow motion, and if I play it right, will keep coming out until the day I die. Continuous growth."

"What's the end result?" I asked him once.

"Integration," he said without flinching. "Total integration. Mind, body, spirit. Union with the self, co-union with the other selves you share this space with. No barriers."

"And then what?" I asked him.

"What do you mean, then what?"

"I mean what happens after the barriers are down?"

"Total communication."

"I know, but what then?"

"Then that's it. That's it man. You've got it."

I met Peter Sarkesian in the spring, and during the course of that summer and early fall got in the habit of meeting him on his lunch hour (or hours—regular work schedules had little meaning for him) and we would often spend the entire afternoon together. From time to time we would walk along the trail beside Beaver Brook, or, on occasion, wander at will to some of my special places on Scratch Flat. During these walks he would often hold forth at length on the future of telecommunications, on empowerment, the integrated self, Armenians, Turks, or any of his other favorite subjects. Not long after I met him I realized that, in his own curious way, he could serve as a sort of replacement in reverse for Tonupasqua and Nompenekit. Unlike my Native American mentors, he was a man who was almost totally free from tradition. In fact, every aspect of traditional behavior, from political affairs to human interrelationships, had been examined and either accepted or rejected by him as a path to the integrated personality. Except for the fact that he was almost too enthusiastic, he made an excellent sounding board. He would not listen for very long to anything that I might have to say; and in the beginning at least, I found it hard to direct the conversation—he would jump off and then charge ahead with a monologue on empowerment or some related subject. I finally learned that I could adjust the conversation by being equally forceful on my own favorite subjects and would sometimes interrupt him and carry on as long as I could about some event or personality associated with Scratch Flat. Toward the end of the summer, I think he got the idea that I had interests of my own, and that although I was not the new-age personality that he believed I was, he had found in me a fellow traveler who in essence shared his goals, but happened to be seeking them by a different route. On one particular day in late summer, after a prolonged discussion on my part about land and the sense of place, I managed to ask him if he thought that a human being needed a place or land to achieve this communication goal that he held so dear.

"Got to have land," he said in his trip-hammer, high-speed way. "Got to have space for birds, for other forms of life. Otherwise you're dead. Alone. You've got other spirits moving around here and they have to be considered too. It's the environment, okay? Human spirit lives in a body that needs air and exercise. Running here is very different than running along the Charles River in Boston. Less exhaust here. I run over by the bean fields there, smell the soil and the rain. You've got to have that to be complete. If I had a company— which someday I might—I'd locate it in a nice place like this—farms around, woods, streams. It would be a different organization than this place I work at. Functional on a human, humane, nonsexist level. Daily encounters on the manager/worker interface. Exercise at lunch hours, like the Japanese firms, flextime, bring your kids in to work, your husband, your wife. Work at home for that matter. You don't need to go out. Okay? Computers will cover it all. We're all worked up in this country about transportation lines. You can see it right here in this town. You got Route 495 there and Route 2 and the planners think that's going to make this place into something because the trucks can get here. But the fact is, the stuff you got to sell in the future doesn't come in trucks, it comes in from the mind, on lasers, fiber optics, comes in on microwaves and radio waves. The telecommunication infrastructure is the new transportation system. We're not moving beans around any more, not moving textiles and heavy machinery. We're moving the news, okay? It isn't the highways that count, it's the high-tech telephone switchboards, satellite antennas, and the data transmission cables. Got to get those lines clear, get the companies out in places like this where the microwave radio traffic isn't all clogged up. Cities are all clogged up—crime, traffic, radio waves. A place like this you're free from all that. So far at least. Clear signals here and I mean that mentally, too. I think better out here. You know these guys I know in Waltham on Route 128, they go over to Kenny's or someplace every day at lunch and get juiced up. They're selling, so they say that it doesn't matter maybe, but what kind of way is that to think straight? To communicate with another human being? All clouded up. I get drunk too sometimes, you got to release those bad energies that can build up inside you that keep you from integrating yourself. Getting drunk, getting stoned, a line of coke now and then, something like that never hurts you. Freddy Brazil, my counselor in psychosynthesis, told me that too. 'Blow it out,' he says. It's the ecstatic release, cleans out the noncommunicative poisons that build up in you. But you can't count on it. Blow it out and move on. But these guys in Waltham, every day they want the ecstasy. Now they can't talk without it. Sick, right? I'd rather run, rather play with Josh. Sit on the floor there and play with Josh. I come home sometimes from here, even a good place like this, and I'm stuck, you know? I'm still in that work space, high-energy, move forward, get it done. I can't relate to him. He's showing me some truck, really trying to get through to me on his level. He's integrated you see, I'm off, can't connect. Now I know what to do. I say 'Josh, let's go for a run.' He gets his bike and we go down to the schoolyard and lope around the track there until I'm ready to drop. I can feel it come in, everything smooths out, and there he is, my own son. I'm down at his level and we can go home and play. Okay? You've got to have the space, got to have trees like this so you can breathe. So you can get to your kids. Otherwise, what's the point. You're not talking. You're dead.''

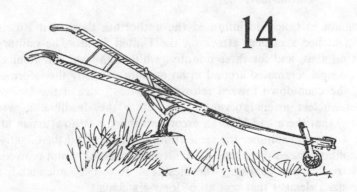

14

NOMPENEKIT'S
NEW WORLD

I had some difficulties when I first began to think about a future for Scratch Flat. It was easy for me, given the abundant evidence of past cultures, to summon up visions of historical or even prehistorical events. And on some levels at least, the present was, and is, easy enough to comprehend since I go around living in it most of the time. But the future has no footprints, and perhaps partly because of the overwhelming sense of time past in Scratch Flat, I found that I could not bring it to mind as easily as some event that may have taken place three thousand years ago. It was through the persistent edging of Peter Sarkesian that I learned to think of Scratch Flat as an independent entity, free-floating in time and unbound by tradition. With his help, I was able to draw some conclusions about things to come, and after sorting through a number of possibilities and testing them on my guide to the new age, it seemed to me that Scratch Flat was faced with three possible futures.

The first of these possible futures is the least pleasant and, I hope, the least probable. A few years ago there was a frightening little incident which, unfortunately, was never very well publicized. A computer in the military command center beneath Cheyenne

Mountain in Colorado informed the authorities there that Russia had launched a nuclear attack on the United States. The military went on alert, and for three minutes, while high-level communications people scrambled around in an attempt to verify the information, the countdown toward release of at least part of the United States nuclear arsenal began. Long before the deadline, it was learned that there had been an error and there was no Russian attack. Later that summer the same thing happened, and then finally, the military traced the cause to a faulty computer chip and replaced the part that was confusing the messages. It was, I understand, a dime-sized element that cost all of forty-six cents.

Faulty electronic equipment notwithstanding, it is also possible, given the thinking in certain political arenas, that there could be a genuine, declared nuclear war. With this in mind, I began to consider what a nuclear attack would do to the Scratch Flat environment. There was a study published a few years ago in *Scientific American* which described in lurid detail the effect of a direct hit of a nuclear warhead on the city of Boston, not an unlikely event if there were an accidental or declared nuclear attack. Boston is more or less a prime target since a great many defense-related industries are located along Route 128 surrounding the city. I need not describe here in detail the great seared crater that would replace Boston in the event of a direct hit, nor the effect of the blast between Route 128 and Route 495. What is important in this case is the fact that the world immediately beyond 495, including Scratch Flat, would be cleared of trees and buildings and would be buried in a layer of radioactive dust and ash.

This is clearly the most precipitous change that could affect Scratch Flat in all its history. And yet it does not necessarily mean that life would end on the tract of land. After all, shortly after the blast at Hiroshima, flowers whose seeds required heat to sprout bloomed from the ashes of the destroyed city. Depending on the extent of the nuclear exchange, a similar phenomenon might take place on Scratch Flat. In other words, barring the advent of some unforeseen astronomical disaster which would destroy the earth prematurely, it seems clear that Scratch Flat has a future. It may be a nonhuman future; it may even be nonmammalian; but the place will be here in one form or another. In fact, it is probable that the devastation caused by a nuclear exchange would not be as total as the changes wrought by the late great glacier—a mere 20,000 years ago, for example, Scratch Flat lay under a mantle of ice one mile thick.

Given the Hiroshima model—the only data we have to work with—it is possible that even after a total nuclear war, heat-released seeds such as the seeds of pitch pine or jack pine, which may have lain dormant in Scratch Flat soils for decades or even centuries, would sprout. Burrowing mammals and insects that would normally be underground when the blast occurred might thrive, lacking predators, and Scratch Flat might then become an underground nation of moles, earthworms, and mole crickets. And if by chance the exchange occurred in winter when many of the small mammals were hibernating, the effect might be even less devastating. Woodchucks, chipmunks, woodland and meadow jumping mice, the little brown bat, and other local hibernators would emerge to feed on the fire-released plants of the new world and the cockroaches and other pests which we are told will undubitably survive. It is possible that the heat of a total nuclear exchange would be so great that the ozone layer would be destroyed, allowing harmful ultraviolet rays to enter the earth's atmosphere. If this were the case, according to some biologists who have studied the subject, all diurnal mammals and birds would be blinded, leaving the world and Scratch Flat to subterranean mammals and insects and the creatures of the night such as bats, owls, whippoorwills, possums, skunks, raccoons, and any of the other local nocturnal animals that happened to survive the firestorms. And since there would be time enough, it is certain that from these small, nocturnal and subterranean beginnings, the world would be reborn.

All of this presumes that the world would not experience the dreaded nuclear winter which scientists from both Russia and the United States believe could occur after a total nuclear exchange. Clouds of radioactive dust, combined with the smoke from the millions of uncontrolled fires that would result from even a few nuclear blasts would block out the sun for months, it has been theorized. Sub-zero temperatures would occur in the northern hemisphere even during the summer, and the world might be so darkened that photosynthesis could cease and plant life could die off. Faced with a malignant and alien environment, it is believed that many species of higher animals, including *Homo sapiens*, would become extinct.

Even though I may be wrong, I prefer to believe that somehow, somewhere, enough disparate groups or colonies of human beings would survive to perpetuate the species.

There are approximately two and a half billion human beings on the earth, most of them infused with a strong desire to procreate; and given time, and the presence of even a small band of these lonely postholocaust individuals, the world could be repopulated. Since Scratch Flat lies so close to the epicenters of the many strikes that would undoubtedly occur in even a limited nuclear exchange, it is not likely that there would be any people living in the immediate area after the wars are ended and the world is burned. But again, I am thinking in the long term now; the human animal itself is only one or two million years old and astronomers believe there will be some five billion years before the star we call Sun swells and expires. After ten thousand years, it is possible that some primitive peoples of the high valleys of New Guinea who happened to have survived the war might learn the art of seafaring, push eastward through the Pacific Islands and across the sea to the American continent. They would form tribes and new tribes; they would look east and north and, because they are human, they will wonder what is there and move. The younger ones would go first perhaps, carrying with them yams and potatoes, and hunting whenever they could. They would push through the forests, or deserts, or whatever the ecology of the postnuclear environment would be, until they come again to the seacoast. They would turn northward and southward, reproducing, settling, and reproducing again, creating more explorers, more adventurers. They would begin to move in a reverse migration of the American Indians, north through Central America, and they would fan out across the continent, leaving villages and perhaps by then, cities, in their wake. At some point, in the very distant future, they would cross the Hudson River, cross the Connecticut, cross the Nashua River, and pass the Big Hill, the Wassachusetts of the American Indians. They would wander east toward the sun until finally, after who knows how many thousands of years, human consciousness would again arrive in the place that was Scratch Flat and human history would begin again there. Nuclear war is without question the greatest ecological disaster that could be wreaked by the human hand, but it might not be the end.

It sounds paradoxical to say so, but as far as the natural history of Scratch Flat is concerned, there could theoretically be a similarly dark future for the area even without a bomb. There is not a single individual on the planning board or among the selectmen of the town who will admit it, but unplanned, uncontrolled growth will probably be an important part of the future of the town in which Scratch Flat is located. All the officials involved with the place, that is, the planning board people, the developers, the real estate salesmen and the selectmen, will tell you that the town has a great future and that although there will be "growth and change" as they put it, because of the existing laws, and the presence of new bylaws which will be enacted, the important ecological systems that are now working well on Scratch Flat will endure forever. The waters of the Beaver Brook will be forever clean, the marshes will provide nesting space for marsh wrens, bitterns, ducks, and herons, and although the woodlands of the drumlin may have houses in them, there will be room for birds and raccoons and foxes. There will be clean water to drink, fresh air to breathe, and the people of the town will pass their lives as good citizens in a good environment.

All this is perhaps possible. But Scratch Flat happens to be located in a state in which industry and the economy are not suffering some of the changes that other sections of the United States have experienced in the latter part of the twentieth century. Transportation lines, as Peter Sarkesian suggests, may not be as important as the past planners believed. But on Scratch Flat, as Peter Sarkesian also makes clear, the microwave clogging is not so bad; and since the exchange of information through electronics seems to be a major part of the future of business, and since there are already a lot of computer and communication companies in the general area, and even a few on Scratch Flat itself, it seems likely that more will be developed here as the real estate values on the existing farmlands climb ever higher and the owners are forced to sell. At that time, since at least half of the farmland and a good deal of the woodlands on Scratch Flat are presently zoned for industry, it seems likely that new industrial parks will appear in the area. One of the selectmen admitted at one of the many hearings concerning the controversial shopping mall near Scratch Flat that because of the existing highway crossroads, the town seems to be in the process of becoming a place in which people work, rather than a place in which people live. And even if the industries do not appear, given the growth in population in the region, new houses will. The town has more than doubled its population in the last fifteen years.

If the recent past is any indication of future trends, then it is likely that, in spite of what the planning board people and the selectmen say, this inevitable development will be relatively uncontrolled and fairly similar to that which has taken place in the communities east of Scratch Flat: suburban tracts, small communications industries interspersed with tragically small and unconnected "conservation areas." Increasingly, ecological studies of these protected areas indicate that in effect, they don't work. The trees and other plants can survive there, as can insects such as katydids, snowy tree crickets, and, of course, mosquitoes. But the larger species, the songbirds and the higher mammals, need more territory to breed, raise their young, and disperse their progeny. All the little pockets of open space have to be linked up with extensive greenbelts, it seems, if the existing ecological systems in these habitats are to survive.

In any case, it does not seem likely that one of these conservation areas will ever appear on Scratch Flat. Except for the tracts in the Beaver Brook watershed where wellfield land is already protected, land in Scratch Flat is simply too valuable to give over to birds and mammals, even if the pocket park system did work. Furthermore, preservation in the town seems to be something of a thing of the past. Large tracts were preserved during the late sixties and early seventies; and although the selectmen and the town will speak generously of the need for open space, economic realities preclude action. Scratch Flat, in effect, could become a small city like Waltham, Massachusetts; Levittown, New York; Euclid, Ohio; Eugene, Oregon; or Stockton, California.

If this happens, if the hayfields are paved for parking lots and industrial buildings and the woodlands are developed for house lots, it is likely that my old enemy the vixen will have to live out her life somewhere else. And since foxes do not accept other foxes in their territory, even if there is space enough elsewhere for her to live, it is doubtful if she will survive for long. The birdsong of the spring mornings will become further diminished, since nesting space will be destroyed. Small mammals such as squirrels, rabbits, possums, and perhaps a few raccoons may be able to adapt to the new environment: such species are sighted in the small cities of America, and in fact seem to thrive well enough provided there are old trees for nesting and garbage cans for raiding. But the deer that I spot from time to time will disappear. Recreational use of Beaver Brook will undoubtedly increase with the growing human population, and so it is also likely that the American bittern and the otter—both of whom cherish solitude—will disappear. The snappers and the painted turtles will probably get by as long as there is clean water and as long as they can find a few sandy pockets in which to lay their eggs. But the rare or endangered species such as the least bittern, the sora rail, or the blue-spotted salamander will no longer breed. And if the human population continues to grow, as more and more land is developed, slowly the few creatures that manage to survive in the small open spaces of the American city will disappear and the life at Scratch Flat, so diverse and multifarious for the fifteen-thousand-year post-glacial period, will be given over to those few species such as starlings, rats, and pigeons which can survive well in the highly developed human community.

But even this scenario is not so bleak. I am speaking here of the short term of five hundred years and this is nothing in terms of geological time. I have no vision of what Scratch Flat will be like when and if, for reasons unknown, the human population of this part of the world disperses or dies and the small cities and towns are deserted; but Toby Beckwith—imaginative thinker that he is—has given me a view from time to time, and I present it here for what it is worth. He believes very much in the persistence of the vine. "There's something about vines," he says. "They work their way into things, burrow into the night until they get a foothold and then, when they have the chance, they take over." He sees deserted cities in his visions, long empty canyons of streets, flowering vines cascading down the walls of the buildings of Scratch Flat, peregrine falcons feeding on the remnant populations of pigeons and rats, nighthawks nesting on the flat roofs of the industrial buildings and calling in the summer skies. Nightly, flocks of bats will emerge from the broken windows of the houses, the "new age caves," he calls them. The scavenging coyote will return, slinking through the deserted streets, snatching remnants of offal from the deer kills the mountain lions have left lying at the corners. Barn swallows, phoebes, and cliff swallows will nest inside the houses; the floors, he said, will be "beshitted with the dung of birds, bats, raccoons, and other mammals. The human presence will be diminished, the vines will return, and the world will begin again at Scratch Flat."

As it turned out, this was not the only view of the future that Toby Beckwith had entertained himself with. Like many who have an interest in archeology and the distant past, he is a man who takes the long view of history and is therefore acutely conscious of the temporal nature of human endeavor. Although he plays very well the role of the existential absurdist, although he prances his phony Shakespearian theater before the world, it seems that, at the base, he is profoundly optimistic and has even crafted for himself a new world vision. He presented this scenario to me one evening and during its delivery, for the first time since I have known him, he grew serious.

Toby, Rosey, and I had enjoyed an excellent dinner in the large dining area of his reworked barn. It was one of those bitterly cold winter nights when the wind was up and the stars above Scratch Flat were brittle and glasslike; the world beyond the warmth of Toby's wood stove seemed inhumane and heartless. We were all feeling the isolation, I think, and the conversation, generally so witty and animated, had a definite nostalgic cast to it. I was feeling unusually close to this eccentric couple; they were easily the most interesting and enigmatic people that I had encountered on Scratch Flat, and over the course of the past few years, we had become good friends.

I think it was the wind that kept us quiet. With every blast Toby would drop whatever he was holding forth about and cock an ear. He was clearly distracted; something was brewing inside him. At one point the conversation fell off altogether and we sat there sipping Rosey's good coffee and listening to the lonely growl of the wind.

"Tell me about that medicine woman again," Toby said suddenly. "She said something about all the Indians coming back, did she?"

"It was Nompenekit," I answered. "He said the Indians of Scratch Flat are still here, and will be here as long as there are trees or squirrels. Something like that."

"You believe it?"

"I don't know," I said. "Maybe. Maybe not. Where do the Indians go after they turn Scratch Flat into Waltham?"

"Maybe they won't do that," Toby said. "I know what will

happen in all probability after the mongrels take over. But that doesn't mean there isn't an alternative."

"Yes, but in all practicality, you have to compromise with your so-called mongrels of avarice. You have to sell out a little bit, don't you?"

"No, you don't have to do that. You could have an independent nation here on Scratch Flat. You could cut yourself free from America and all that it stands for, and I mean the worst of America, the greed, and the avarice, not the best."

He grew silent again, slouched in his chair, his neck against the cane back. I noticed that the subtle smirk he usually carried had disappeared and his mouth was relaxed and serious.

"All Scratch Flat needs from America are three or four things —all of them negatives. Population control, clean groundwaters, no nuclear meltdowns at Seabrook, and no nuclear wars. Not much to ask, is it?"

"Then what?"

"Then we can remake the world here."

He stopped talking again for a while and then suddenly with an arching motion swung his arm over and slapped the table with the flat of his hand, rattling the coffee cups and waking Rosey from her reveries. Back in character, but still serious, he began to describe to me the framework for his remade world; and as he explained later, although he was thinking of Scratch Flat as the model, the system could function, given certain conditions, almost anywhere in the world.

He had calculated that nearly half of the square mile that makes up Scratch Flat is still arable. The other half is made up of the marshes of Beaver Brook, several bogs, swamps, and small ponds, and the extensive woodlands of oak, hickory, and white pine. The human dwellings are located for the most part in the woods along the Great Road, Forge Village Road, and the interlacing roads of the summer houses and the new development near Forge Pond. The pond itself is relatively unpolluted and contains a number of edible species of fish; the Beaver Brook runs slowly but steadily and also has an abundance of wild food resources; and the industries are all clustered together at the southeast end of the tract and are within walking distance of any of the dwellings on Scratch Flat.

Toby explained that the homesteading literature produced during the hard years of the 1930s suggested that a family of four or five individuals could subsist rather well, given proper management, on four acres of land. There are, he said, approximately 640 acres in Scratch Flat, 300 or 400 acres of which are already cleared and ready to plant. There are also approximately 150 people living on the square-mile tract, which means that, again with the proper management, the place could easily support those who live there. History has proved as much. In its small way, Scratch Flat was something of a breadbasket, feeding even with the somewhat limited nineteenth-century farming technologies, many more than 150 people. In fact, it would be difficult to estimate exactly how many people the tract supported in any given year during the height of its agricultural career. Toby said that if hard times were to come again, and the residents were willing to regroup and work together in a communal system on the existing farmlands, clearly there would be food enough for all, plus some for export—how much would depend on what was grown and, to some extent, how it was grown.

This retrenchment would not necessarily mean that the residents would have to give up all the amenities that they have—in these flush times—become used to. A few years ago on a nearby estate, Toby found a caved-in greenhouse which was on its way to the dump. He managed to salvage the cypress framework and enough of the lights or glass to reconstruct a small attached solar greenhouse on the south side of his barn. For a few years—until he lost interest—he was able to maintain subtropical plants in the greenhouse throughout the New England winter, which meant that he did not have to go beyond Scratch Flat to get fresh greens.

Toby said he had thought at length about the abundance of local natural resources and explained that he would like very much to reorganize Scratch Flat to function along the lines of a small version of the Chinese commune. He wanted the people in the tract of land to put in a few hours a week working on one of the farms. It would be a healthful, not to say meaningful, experience for someone who spends forty hours a week in an air-conditioned or heated office to turn soil, to shovel manure, to weed a row of beets or two, or spend a hot summer afternoon picking beans. Furthermore, he said that with modern mechanization, a farmer would not necessarily need 150 hands to work the farms of Scratch Flat, so you could rid Scratch Flat of farm mechanization altogether and start doing things by hand and with the aid of animal power. He said that many of the farms in Scratch Flat still had horse-drawn plows and harrows lying about. Most of these machines could be restored, so it would not be necessary to leave the commune to get the machinery to work the soil. If one of the farmers of the area would agree to sell one of his tractors, enough horses and oxen could be purchased with the money to work the entire tract of land and to buy enough livestock in the form of cows, pigs, goats, chickens, and sheep to feed the Scratch Flat people the high quota of meat, milk, butter, eggs, and cheese that they have become used to.

He claimed that in the many small ponds of Scratch Flat, and with a little reworking in some of the deeper spots of Beaver Brook itself, it would not be difficult to raise native and imported edible fish. One would not necessarily need the ponds to raise fish, he said. One year, when he was living in Arizona, he said, he maintained a miniature aquatic ecosystem in a rain barrel complete with algae, higher plants, aquatic insects, and a catfish. He said that the catfish is the pig of the self-sufficient homestead. "You keep them in rain barrels, feed them organic garbage all summer; and then in the fall—" and here he raised his hand and kissed the tips of his fingers "—delicious. Ask Rosey. Delicious."

"What about the winter?" I asked him. "How will your commune keep warm without the international oil cartels?"

"You ought to know the answer to that," he said.

"Why?"

"Look at history. People did live on Scratch Flat in the icy years following the retreat of the glacier, adapted quite well I think you told me," Toby said. "My friend Scott regularly spends the winter with the Cree moose hunters of Mistassini in northern Quebec. He says that in spite of the fact that the temperatures are often twenty to thirty below zero, he is more comfortable there during the winter than he is in his house in Concord." The Cree, Toby explained, live pretty much in the same way that the Pawtucket and the other Scratch Flat Indians lived. Two or three extended families share a wickiup or a longhouse during the winter—a simple framework covered with evergreen boughs or animal skins and warmed by a small central fire which is used both for cooking and space heating.

Scratch Flat is located in a part of the country in which there is a lot of forestland; many of the people who live here have already turned off, or turned down, their central heating systems and have installed wood stoves in their houses. Toby said this is a resource that can be exploited further. Wood is now cheaper than oil if it is used efficiently, and it provides a warmer, more centralized heat. Furthermore, properly managed, about four acres of hardwood forest per household can provide an indefinite source of fuel. You cull the deadwood, use selective cutting practices, replant the hardwoods, if necessary, or allow them to reseed themselves, and by the time the first cutting is used up, the second growth will be ready for harvest.

This is one of those areas in which I had carried out a little research of my own. I happen to be very lazy about cutting and splitting wood, but from my limited experience I believe that if I religiously managed the two acres of woodland that I own, I could easily heat my house on less than four acres. In any case, Toby said that there are more than four acres of woodland per household on Scratch Flat, so that even with improper management, it would be possible to heat the houses of the tract perpetually using wood as fuel. The labor required would not be a problem, he said. The wood heaters of Scratch Flat, most of whom have regular jobs, already glean their firewood on their own, during weekends, or belong to firewood cooperatives. As a part of his reorganization, meetings would be regularly held to decide which sections of the forest to cut and which trees to glean, and the existing work force would be mobilized to harvest fuel from Scratch Flat on a cooperative basis.

Toby says that the residents of Scratch Flat already have all the modern skills required to survive in the twentieth century. There are several people with advanced secretarial skills, there are a number of computer programmers and several systems analysts, there is an architect, a business manager, a salesman, a barber, a teacher, a part-time policeman, a psychologist, several farmers, a number of day laborers and agricultural workers, an aquatic biologist, and the manager of the local electric company. There are also a number of retired people who, although advanced in years, are still able-bodied and are also wise in the ways of making do, having survived in this general area, some of them, for more than seventy years. Most of these people have skills in other fields as well—carpentry, electronics, gardening, sewing, food preservation, and other practical arts.

Coupled with this potential work force, there are the eight industrial buildings on Scratch Flat. Toby believes the Scratch Flat commune should buy or otherwise take over the existing industries on the tract, and using their skills as managers, salesmen, electronic workers, secretaries, and the like, run the businesses cooperatively. It might be necessary to bring in a labor force from the town, he said, and set up a system of trade and communication with the outside; but in effect, given the human resources, the existing buildings, the telecommunications infrastructure, the electronic equipment, and the tools, he believes he and his Scratch Flat people could found a sort of independent nation, complete with its own natural resources, trade goods, and population. Slowly, over a period of decades, as the supply of nonrenewable resources in the world beyond Scratch Flat began to dwindle, as the food lines or gas lines grew, as the prices of goods and services rose, the agricultural-technologists of Scratch Flat would use their technological and practical skills to alter the existing industries (which they now would own cooperatively) to the production of tools for the creation of a constant energy supply for the needs of the commune. Photovoltaic solar arrays would be manufactured and either retrofitted to existing structures or arranged in some centralized site on the tract such as the south side of the drumlin. The silicon and other raw material needed to construct the arrays would be purchased or bartered with the excess food supplies which the Scratch Flat people would produce, since by this time, he says, each household would have become self-sufficient, leaving the larger spreads of arable land for food production intended for trade or sale. On a percentage of these arable lands, quick-growing crops would be produced, mixed with organic garbage and the human waste of the Scratch Flat people, and fed into methane generators to produce cooking and heating gas. Wind generators, again purchased or bartered with Scratch Flat's food products, would augment the electricity supplied by the photovoltaic arrays or pump water.

Toby's point was that the physical needs of the commune would be no problem. But critical to the success of his experiment, he said, would be a new attitude among the people who live on the tract of land. The concept of material gain, of the acquisition of goods as a way of life, would have to give way to a smaller, more focused understanding of the essential needs and the essential pleasures that make up a well-lived life. The understanding that less is in fact more would be of paramount importance, he said, and the people would have to understand at a deep level that the essence of civilization is not the multiplication of wants, but the elimination of needs.

Toby admitted that given the existing attitudes of the culture that now inhabits Scratch Flat, it is not likely that such a radical change in thinking would come about abruptly. But he said that the seeds of the new worldview are already here, buried in the skills of the older residents and to some extent in the minds of the younger people. And since the future nation of Scratch Flat would not have closed borders, inevitably there would be an immigration of people of a like mind so that, in time, the chances for the success of the experiment would increase.

"You of all people, should understand this new world," Toby said to me.

"What I am getting at is the creation of a postindustrial tribe. A group of people, bound together by a common belief, existing in a common territory with enough natural resources to supply themselves with food and fuel and shelter. You may say it is an idealistic vision, that it is clearly fraught with complications, but I say it is not impractical in a physical sense. The only problems are the human interactions. To get by that problem I want a new-age shaman here to arrange encounters to work out the inevitable human conflicts. I want a sagamore, an eloquent individual, man or woman, versed in the art of oratory, who would be able to direct or redirect the general will of the group. You understand this would be a person without power; all decisions of the Scratch Flat tribe would be made communally, everyone would have a voice. I would have another sagamore to see to the business of trade and negotiations with the world beyond the tribe, a warrior chief, but this man would deal not with war, but with business matters. Same thing, right? And I want a genuine shaman to attend to the spiritual needs of the people in the tribe. In time we would consolidate living quarters. The existing houses on Scratch Flat would be taken down and rebuilt in a centralized location, clustered around a common, like the traditional New England village which we all know is the offspring of the cathedral city which we also know is the offspring of the Paleolithic village. Full circle. There would be perhaps a great central hall, a town meetinghouse, or, if you prefer, a mead hall, and the tribe would gather on a regular basis for business or for pleasure. And in this great hall there would inevitably be communal dancing, line dances like the contra dance of the New England forefathers, which we all know has its roots in Paleolithic fertility dances. Full circle again. Time moves forward. Time moves backward. Past and future, no different."

He got up from the table, walked in a circle a few times, came back and poured some brandy in his coffee, and pushed the bottle over toward Rosey.

"What do we know anyway?" he said. "We only live here sixty or seventy years. What do we know? You want to see something?"

He got up again and went up to his loft where he kept all his artifacts. He had an Archaic projectile point with him when he came back.

"Hold this," he said, handing it to me. "You know how old that thing is? Eight thousand years maybe. The last man to hold that spearhead lived maybe six to eight thousand years ago. And you know what he thought? He thought he and his people were forever. Well, didn't happen did it?"

He sat down again. Drained off his coffee and brandy and poured another one.

"Didn't happen. So why do we worry about a few shopping centers. You know what I don't like? I don't like these complacent mongrels who stand up there at these town meetings and talk about things as if they knew what life and the human voyage are all about. Listen. There are certain nights here, you know what I mean? There are winter nights very like this one when I feel that the real world is not the everyday world and that really, unless there is a bomb, unless we blow ourselves into the stars, it's all going to be all right. I believe in your Indians. Tell me again what that guy said about coming back."

"He said they are coming back. They are waiting in the trees, but they are coming back."

"They are coming back. How? Coming back in feathers and headbands?"

"No, I asked him that. Not like hunters."

"Well then how?"

"Well, if I remember it, he said that they will not be coming back as wild Indians; they will come back as an idea."

He leaned forward, the old smile working across his face. "You understand, don't you?" he said, nodding enthusiastically. "You get

it? We can remake the world. The model was created eight thousand
years ago, right here on Scratch Flat."

In spite of the cold, I walked home that night, crossing the flat
fields of Sherman's farm, the rolling fields of Jimmy-George Starkos,
and the wooded ridge of the drumlin. Toby's vision was on my mind,
but perhaps because of the cold, I was thinking not so much of
communes and resources, but of the glacier. It seemed to me that all
was interlude, the two-thousand-year reign of the Paleo-Indians, the
long span of the Archaic peoples, the period of the Woodland Indians, and the brief flash of the Western civilization. I was thinking
that there will come a day on Scratch Flat when people will remember that somehow the winters were once warmer and the summers
were longer and hotter. Future history will look back on itself and
report that the natural habitat of the region is changing, and that
northern species such as the spruce and the fir are more common.
The winters will continue to grow longer and longer, the growing
seasons shorter and shorter, until finally there will be nothing but
winter. Life on Scratch Flat will become intolerable, the members of
Toby's erstwhile tribe will migrate south, following the general drift
of other tribes or nations. To the north the snows will pile up, year
after year, century after century, until, compressed by its own
weight, and with nowhere else to go, the great ice pack will begin to
move south and the place that was Scratch Flat will disappear for
another sixty thousand years.

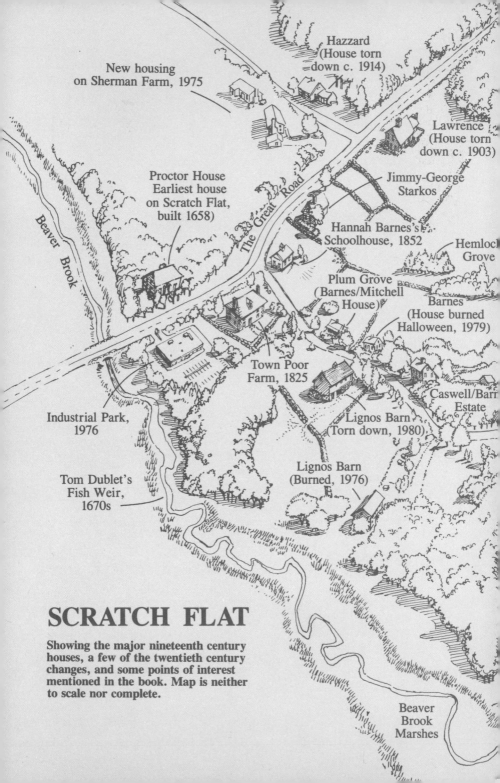

Hazzard
(House torn
down c. 1914)

New housing
on Sherman Farm, 1975

Lawrence
(House torn
down c. 1903)

Jimmy-George
Starkos

Proctor House
Earliest house
on Scratch Flat,
built 1658)

The Great Road

Beaver Brook

Hannah Barnes's
Schoolhouse, 1852

Hemlock
Grove

Plum Grove
(Barnes/Mitchell
House)

Barnes
(House burned
Halloween, 1979)

Town Poor
Farm, 1825

Industrial Park,
1976

Caswell/Barr
Estate

Lignos Barn
(Torn down, 1980)

Tom Dublet's
Fish Weir,
1670s

Lignos Barn
(Burned, 1976)

SCRATCH FLAT

**Showing the major nineteenth century
houses, a few of the twentieth century
changes, and some points of interest
mentioned in the book. Map is neither
to scale nor complete.**

Beaver
Brook
Marshes